# MERV

## the FULL STORY

# MERV
## the FULL STORY

BY PATRICK KEANE, IN ASSOCIATION WITH MERV HUGHES

HarperSports

An imprint of HarperCollinsPublishers

**FRONT COVER PHOTOGRAPHS**
Left: Australian Picture Library/AllSport — Joe Mann
Right: Sporting Pix — Tony Feder
**BACK COVER PHOTOGRAPHS**
Top: Sport. The Library. — Ian Kenins
Left: Sport. The Library. — Jason Childs
Right: Sporting Pix — Tony Feder


**Harper*Sports***
An imprint of HarperCollins*Publishers*


First published in Australia in 1997
by HarperCollins*Publishers* Pty Limited
ACN 009 913 517
A member of HarperCollins*Publishers* (Australia) Pty Limited Group

**HarperCollins*Publishers***
25 Ryde Road, Pymble, Sydney NSW 2073, Australia
31 View Road, Glenfield, Auckland 10, New Zealand
77–85 Fulham Palace Road, London W6 8JB, United Kingdom
Hazelton Lanes, 55 Avenue Road, Suite 2900, Toronto, Ontario M5R 3L2
*and* 1995 Markham Road, Scarborough, Ontario M1B 5M8, Canada
10 East 53rd Street, New York NY 10032, USA

National Library of Australia Cataloguing-in-Publication data:

Hughes, Merv.
Merv: the full story.

Includes index.
ISBN 07322 58227.
1. Hughes, Merv. 2. Cricket players - Australia -
Biography. I. Keane, Patrick, 1967-. II. Title.
796.358092.
Printed in Singapore by Tien Wah Press on 115gsm Arctic Matt Art.

5 4 3 2 1        97 98 99 00 01

To Ian Chappell, Dennis Lillee and Rod Marsh.
For their service to their country and the inspiration they provided for
me to be able to achieve my goal of playing for Australia.

This book is also dedicated to Murray Leahy for his courage
and determination.

— Merv Hughes

## ·· A C K N O W L E D G M E N T S ··

I would like to thank my immediate family — parents Ian and Freda, sister Peta and brother Gary — for their support throughout my cricket career and my entire life. I am deeply indebted to Sue and Madeline for their patience during the hardships I have put them through while I have pursued cricket, work and the production of this book. I thank them. I also thank Joan and Liz for their support.

I will always treasure the valued assistance over many years of Puma Australia, particularly John Forbes and the staff at Moorabbin; Chris and Col at West Point Ford; Hugh McDonald and all the staff at Tubemakers and Tubemakers Metal Land; Steve, Sandy and Sandra at Oakley Sunglasses; Craig and Katrina at Word of Mouth and, of course, Peter Thompson and David Emerson at Edge Sports Management, and their families, for the direction they have sent me in over my life.

To Ron and Bette — the many hours on the bench kept me going for the past 10 years of my career.

I would like to thank Geoff, Ali, Mel and Graeme at Harper*Sports* for the fantastic arrangement of the book.

Finally, I must thank Patrick Keane, a bloke who I've admired and respected over a lot of years. I first approached Patrick three years ago to write this book and I was pleased he said yes, even though other opportunities were offered to him. He put his life on hold for nine months, as did his family, to do this project and that is greatly appreciated.

**Merv Hughes**


**Patrick Keane** would like to thank Vanessa for her understanding over the course of this book and Michael for being himself; the Australian Cricket Board; Geoff Armstrong and Ali Orman at Harper*Sports* for their tremendous behind-the-scenes work; and all those in cricket — both in Australia and overseas — who so willingly agreed to be interviewed on the subject of Merv Hughes' life.

Merv, Patrick and Harper*Sports* are grateful to Charlie Wat for compiling the statistics section, and Ian Russell for checking the manuscript.

# CONTENTS

Foreword by Tony Dodemaide . . . . . . . .   viii

1. No-one came near him . . . . . . . . . .    1
2. A country upbringing . . . . . . . . . . .    9
3. You're a bowler now . . . . . . . . . . .   17
4. The cherished baggy green . . . . . . . .   37
5. He thinks he's a fast bowler . . . . . . .   61
6. Merv mania! . . . . . . . . . . . . . . . .   81
7. Sledging . . . . . . . . . . . . . . . . . .  113
8. A mountain of a man . . . . . . . . . . .  125
9. That's the way he lived . . . . . . . . .  153
10. Play until you drop . . . . . . . . . . . .  173
11. The closing curtain . . . . . . . . . . . .  205
12. Anything but friendly . . . . . . . . . . .  217
13. Burnt out? . . . . . . . . . . . . . . . . .  241
14. A quieter summer . . . . . . . . . . . .  257
15. It's not personal, it's business . . . . . .  273
16. What's the use of the friendship? . . .  283
17. The Merv Hughes way . . . . . . . . . .  305
18. One of the best . . . . . . . . . . . . . .  313

Postscript . . . . . . . . . . . . . . . . . . . .  323

Appendix One — The best of the best . . . .  326

Appendix Two — Merv: the statistics  . . . .  338

Bibliography . . . . . . . . . . . . . . . . . . .  353

Index . . . . . . . . . . . . . . . . . . . . . .  354

# FOREWORD

**A**nother wicket falls. The players gather mid-pitch to congratulate the successful bowler. The rookie is keener than most to be involved, and finds himself in the centre of the group. In fact, he thinks it strange that the others appear a little distracted, with hands in pockets or turned half-away from the circle.

He soon finds out why. A quick flash of hands, and the previously concealed ball thuds into his lower abdomen. Not hard enough to injure — just enough to ensure the intended shock is delivered. A familiar raucous laugh, and arms pump the air.

'Yes, got 'im! Another one to the big fella,' the culprit screams in high-pitched semi-Bill Lawry imitation. The other players chuckle and swap knowing smiles. 'He'll learn. You just don't leave yourself open like that when Mervyn Gregory Hughes is about!'

It is typical of the man that this scene is just as likely to occur at a Lord's Test Match as it is at a district game at the Whitten Oval in Footscray. In his eyes, Shane Warne or Steve Waugh is just as susceptible as the newest Footscray recruit. Wherever he is, his first and only instinct is to enjoy himself and to take everyone with him along for the ride.

We arrived at Footscray at roughly the same time, me a self-conscious 15-year-old, Merv a loud and extremely annoying 17. I did not know him well for the first few years, as he was always a grade or two in front of me. In fact, he thought so highly of me initially that I was not on the guest list at his 21st — a fact I still bring up occasionally whenever he has the upper hand in an argument! Our friendship was sealed finally when we crossed paths 12,000 miles away at Chelmsford, Essex, in 1983. Merv was finishing a scholarship stint with the County, and I was part of an Australian Youth tour. Relishing the fact that another Footscray boy was so far from home, he sat me down at the local to share many a drink and joke (too many, as I recall).

Whilst roughly following the same cricketing road since then, we have been through many highs and lows together, often needing each other's support and guidance along the way. One of the great things about cricket is that the game often lays bare your insecurities and weaknesses as well as talents and, as such, you get to know your team-mates much better than in most other workplaces. You need good friends, true friends, and they don't come any better than Merv. I can never recall a time when he hasn't been there for a friend, often with a phone call from the other end of the world. And always that laugh or practical joke! After 17 years or so, my 'sixth sense' to a Merv prank is fairly sharp — although he still gets me on occasions!

In the time I have known him he has been a clown, a confidant, an inspiration and an infuriating frustration. He has been a training partner, team-mate, workmate, best man, and father to my beautiful god-daughter, Madeline. Both myself and my wife Danielle value his and his family's friendship enormously, and hope to have been good mates in return. Merv Hughes has deserved every success attained throughout a stellar career, and will continue to be loved by all for doing what he does best — being himself.

TONY DODEMAIDE
June 1997

# CHAPTER ONE

# NO-ONE CAME NEAR HIM

English crowds are rarely rivalled in their status as the fairest in the cricketing world. While the Poms can celebrate a Test victory as deliriously as any nation, especially when it's a recent and rare one against Australia, English cricket fans are unfailingly appreciative of performances above and beyond the call, no matter which country a player should represent.

On the stroke of 5 p.m. August 22, 1993, Australia had dismissed England for the 11th occasion out of a possible 12 times in that Ashes series. Of the 120 wickets that could have been secured at the start of the northern summer, Australia had collected 116, denied only the last four when England had managed to bat well enough to declare at six-down in the second innings of the drawn third Test.

Allan Border's side needed 391 on a fast Oval wicket in just under seven hours for a 5–0 whitewash and, as is the custom, the Australian top-order batsmen waited politely while last pair Mark Ramprakash and Devon Malcolm headed from the field, before dashing up the steps to change.

As it so happened, bowlers Paul Reiffel (mid off), Tim May (mid on) and Shane Warne (square leg) had all been fielding in the furthest positions from the players' entrance when Merv Hughes had finally dismissed Ramprakash to end the innings.

The trio dawdled from the field, waiting for Hughes to collect his jumper from umpire Barrie Meyer, departing as a group of four well after the other nine combatants had exited the arena.

*Opposite: Merv Hughes at The Oval, sixth Ashes Test, 1993.*

*The Australian bowlers on the '93 Ashes tour:*
*(from left) Wayne Holdsworth, Shane Warne, Brendon Julian,*
*Merv Hughes, Tim May and Paul Reiffel.*

The Oval crowd, no more than half-full late on the fourth day of the last match of a one-sided series, rose as one to salute the weary quartet.

Hughes, Warne, May and Reiffel had bowled Australia to its defence of the Ashes and those at the ground knew enough about the game to realise how spectacular their efforts had been.

Spearhead Craig McDermott had been expected to lead the attack, but had not taken a wicket for the entire series, returning home early after succumbing to a major bowel problem during the second Test. Young all-rounder Brendon Julian had shown glimpses of his huge potential in two Tests but, in the end, had managed just three wickets before also falling to injury. Meanwhile, the unpredictable Wayne Holdsworth had been unable to adjust to English conditions at all and was never seriously in the running for a Test position.

Warne and May had carried an awesome load of bowling for captain Allan Border, with Warne's 2646 deliveries the most-ever by an individual in one series in the 120-year history of Ashes cricket. Warne's 34 wickets had been the revelation of the series, but he and May owed much to the pace bowlers for the consistent early wickets achieved with the new ball.

Reiffel did not appear in the side until the fourth Test, requiring Hughes to carry the pace attack for much of the summer. He had responded to Border's requests in magnificent fashion.

Hughes had bowled almost 300 overs to snare 31 wickets at 27.25, becoming only the seventh Australian bowler to reach 200 Test wickets during the course of the tour. His haul of 31 scalps in an Ashes series in England had been bettered by only three other Australians: Terry Alderman (twice with 42 and 41 wickets respectively), Dennis Lillee (39 wickets) and his team-mate Warne.

The public image of Hughes on that Ashes tour was 'Sumo': the big fast bowler charging in with the new ball to torment England's batsmen one more time.

Built on big lines, Hughes could be a very intimidating prospect from the other end of a cricket pitch. Height, size, appearance, intentions and commitment gelled in this fast bowler who very much fitted the traditional image of speed merchants — dangerous angry men teetering on the borders of mayhem.

Tall at 193 cm (6'4" in the old scale), he seemed much more imposing than other fast bowlers of that height, because of his build, ranging from a fit 93 kg at the start of his international career, to something closer to 105 kg in his final years. In his bowling stride, Hughes dominated the crease and

In 1993, Hughes played the 'Sumo' image for all it was worth.

few batsmen could avoid automatically rocking to the back foot, somehow driven back by the presence at the other end.

While the superb West Indian, Michael Holding, earned the moniker 'Whispering Death' for his rhythmically smooth run to the wicket, there was little finesse in the Hughes approach. A long angled run, begun with several short mincing steps, thundered to a crescendo at the crease with much grunting and heaving as the ball was delivered, leaving the umpire and the two batsmen in no doubt as to the effort involved.

Once Hughes was established in the Australian Test side, his face alone probably secured its share of wickets. His hair was invariably short, contrasted wildly by a huge bushy moustache, and a stubble growth dating from the start of the Test match concerned. Sweating profusely, his eyes would lock on a batsman and dare him to look away after a close call or a particularly good shot.

Whatever bounce in the wicket would be closely gauged through a spell, with a batsman left in no doubt that to survive would require a searching test of physical courage. If the batsman intended still to be at the wicket in 80 or 90 minutes when Hughes was relieved, spells far longer than the vast majority of other international bowlers, then that batsman would have to deal with a large number of deliveries directed into the ribs and the heart, and at the head.

Last of all, should a player be struggling with the enormity of the task in front of him, he would certainly not be left to suffer in silence. Theatrically anguished appeals, cutting one-liners and straight-out abuse were also very much a part of the Hughes package. You weren't wanted out here in the middle and you would be told so. If that approach upset you and forced you into a rash stroke, mission accomplished. After all, this is a man's game.

The Hughes on-field approach certainly won him his fair share of critics and landed him in hot water on a number of occasions. However, while even his team-mates blanched occasionally at some of the things he said and did on the field of battle, there were no lasting enemies among his opponents. At the end of the day, Hughes was always the first to shake the hand of a victorious opponent or console a defeated foe.

Certainly there was opportunity for humour in the game, when a naturally gregarious personality would bubble to the surface. It was only

Merv Hughes who could walk up to Test umpire Robin Bailhache during a Sheffield Shield game and state that Victoria had declared the bowling because they couldn't get a wicket. At the height of the South African rebel tour controversy in the mid–1980s, he asked another umpire for a 10-year ban so that he didn't have to continue bowling on a particularly flat Adelaide Oval pitch.

However, it was never the time for fun when the ball was in his hand at the top of his run-up. If the captain wanted something done, Hughes was always ready to put up his hand and take the ball. No bowler ever got a wicket standing in the outfield.

*Hughes, bruised, battered but still belligerent, confronts England's Alec Stewart at The Oval.*

The on-field Hughes was well-known to all cricket followers, even if the vast majority never got to meet him. Australian Test players receive saturation media exposure during their tenure in the national side and their faces become recognisable nation-wide. While Victorian AFL legend Tony Lockett can wander through Sydney with only an occasional second glance and former Queensland and Australian rugby league captain Wally Lewis can hide from prying eyes in Adelaide, Merv Hughes was public property from Perth to Brisbane. It is the off-field Merv Hughes that few knew.

At the start of each Test-match day on the 1993 Ashes tour, Hughes would pop two digesic painkillers into his mouth to dull the throbbing, chronic pain in his left knee. He would then take the new ball for captain Allan Border. Midway through the lunch break, he would take another two and they would last him through until tea, when a further two of the now-banned painkillers would be required. Upon stumps, Hughes would be last to drag his body into the Australian dressing-room and would

*Hughes, with Australian physio Errol Alcott (left) and captain Allan Border, after breaking down during the third Test of the 1993 Ashes series.*

collapse in front of his gear, placing ice-packs on both knees, his right shoulder, his groin and occasionally his back.

Come the morning, or the next game, he would do it all again, simply because it was the chance to represent Australia. If he had not put up his hand to take the ball, there would have been no-one else of his calibre to take the fight to England.

The pain tolerance of men like Allan Border and David Boon is renowned within Australian cricket. Border never missed a Test match through injury in 16 years of international cricket, despite two broken thumbs (which made gripping the bat intensely painful) and numerous broken fingers during his 156-Test career. Boon never flinched, either at the crease or in the danger-zone at bat–pad, and confirmed his legendary status for toughness during a Test match in Jamaica in 1991, having stitches inserted in his chin without an anaesthetic so that he did not have to retire hurt and expose the tailenders to a rampant pace attack.

Australian team physiotherapist Errol Alcott has been responsible for getting and keeping Australia's Test cricketers on the field since early 1984 and he rates Hughes ahead of both of these men.

'There's only one person, in my 14 years with Australian cricket, with a heart as big as Phar Lap who would keep going and going and that was Merv Hughes,' Alcott says. 'There is no other person who would keep going with injury like him. He's a long way ahead of Boon and Border when it comes to playing with pain. In bowling terms, it's much harder to do what he did. A batsman could play with a broken finger and, while it was still painful, it wasn't like being a bowler with a sore knee. On a weight-bearing knee, to be able to bowl like he did, no-one came near him. No-one at all.'

Alcott marvelled at Hughes' constitution, as did his team-mates, but the fast bowler would pay a heavy price for his efforts on that 1993 tour. At the conclusion of that epic Ashes performance, Hughes went in to have surgery on his knee to clean up the joint and prepare for the 1993–94 season back at home. What the surgeon found was a chunk of dead bone around the size of a 50-cent piece. For the last few months of the tour, the chronic pain Hughes had felt was actually the grinding of bone on bone, with no cartilage whatsoever for shock absorption.

The heavy workload had seen part of the bone within his knee die off, meaning it had to be cut out and time allowed for new bone to grow in its place. He would miss some six months, including a crucial pre-season fitness campaign, and would never again be able to win his career-long battle with his weight. And, while Merv Hughes would return briefly to the Australian side, he would never again be the same force in international cricket. By bowling Australia to its defence of the Ashes, Merv Hughes had prematurely bowled himself into retirement.

This is the story of Merv Hughes' time at the top for Australia and Victoria . . .

# CHAPTER TWO

# A COUNTRY UPBRINGING

O n December 13, 1985, the small Victorian country town of Euroa was admitted to a select club. Located just 50 kilometres from Glenrowan, where Ned Kelly had made his final stand just over a century beforehand, Euroa could now take its place alongside a range of Australian locales — from big cities like Melbourne to tiny outposts such as Exton in Tasmania — as the birthplace of an Australian Test cricketer.

Merv Hughes had become the 332nd cricketer to wear the baggy green cap for Australia, coming into an Australian side that was searching for stability in the wake of defections to South Africa. Just 20 days into his 25th year, Hughes had been chosen for the first Test against India at the Adelaide Oval on the strength of his raw pace, undoubted aggression and impressive stamina.

Previously, Euroa's cricket community had been able to boast that former Australian fast bowler Harry Alexander had lived in the town for part of his life. Alexander, who played one Test in the infamous 'Bodyline' series of 1932–33, was born in Melbourne but gave the young cricketers of the area a tangible link to the national side. While Alexander's one Test brought him the solitary wicket of tailender Hedley Verity at a cost of 154 runs, he had been an impressive performer in Shield cricket for Victoria over eight seasons and none would scoff at the fact he had represented his country.

Five days after Merv Hughes had made his debut, he would joke that at least he was able to emulate 'Bull' Alexander's feat of reaching the highest level, even if he couldn't do any better. Merv Hughes finished with 1–123

*Opposite: Hughes at Trent Bridge, Nottingham, third Ashes Test, 1993.*

from his 38 overs, made a five-ball duck and was summarily dropped. If it wasn't for his determination to fight back and win a second cap, that would have been the summation of his international career.

Mervyn Gregory Hughes was born at Euroa Hospital on November 23, 1961, some 11 months after his sister, Peta. Weighing in at a hefty nine pounds, one and a half ounces on the old scale, he arrived, appropriately (as later events would prove), at lunchtime.

The young boy's start to life would not be without its dramas though, surviving a severe attack of meningitis that left him in intensive care as a 10-month-old. Their baby had not looked well when Freda Hughes had put him to bed one evening, and she asked her husband, Ian, to check on him before he retired for the night. He found Merv rigid, whimpering softly, and a panicked call to the local hospital had him to a doctor within the half hour. But for his parents' sixth sense about their child, it could have been much worse than a stay of several days in the hospital until the danger had passed.

Ian and Freda met in 1954 and were married in Euroa in early 1960, but were not living there at the time of Merv's birth. Instead, the young couple and their two small children were resident at nearby Baddaginnie, some 30 kilometres up the main highway, towards Wangaratta.

Ian Hughes was a primary school teacher with the Department of Education and the family would regularly re-locate around country Victoria as he took each new posting. After marrying in Euroa, and then welcoming Peta and Mervyn while at Baddaginnie between 1961 and 1963, the Hughes clan would have stints in Apollo Bay (1964–66), Euroa (1967–68), Werribee (1969–71), Violet Town (1972), Werribee again (1973–75) and Myrtleford (1976–77) during Merv's formative years. As a consequence, Peta and Merv are both exceptionally close to their parents, along with younger brother Gary, who arrived 17 years afer Merv.

Ian Hughes earned a considerable reputation as a country cricketer and footballer, retiring only in 1989 when his own knees finally gave way, while Freda played netball and is still to retire her tennis racquet. At each new posting, once the couple had settled, there would soon be a knock at the Hughes' door inquiring if the new man in town played sport at all. Yes he did, would be the overwhelming answer, and Hughes senior would slot into the firsts at both cricket and football. Basketball was also played socially by Hughes senior and his young son would be tagging along from the time he was able to walk.

Young Merv started kindergarten while at Apollo Bay, and his first year at school came when the family was back at Euroa. Organised sport began in grade 3 at Werribee and the Hughes boy, tall for his age, always seemed to be playing with older children. He pestered his father relentlessly to be allowed to join the grade 5s at Werribee at footy practice and was able to hold his own, despite the fact that he was one of the smallest players when out of his age group.

Young Merv's enthusiasm for sport was now unquenchable.

'He was pretty good at his sport and the fact he always seemed to be playing with older kids helped him along a bit,' his father remembers. 'Sport wasn't compulsory and it wasn't organised in any way, but all the kids played it most days of the week. It would be the usual schoolyard stuff where two kids would pick teams and off they would go, be it footy or cricket.'

Hughes wasn't a brilliant scholar but neither was he a child who found his lessons all too hard. While his personality may have bubbled over regularly in later life, he was well-behaved while at primary school and rarely found trouble. After all, it was impossible to be the class clown when your father was standing at the front of the classroom.

At secondary school, the focus definitely tended to slip more towards the sporting fields and away from the classroom. His parents impressed upon him the need to work hard, but the foremost qualities Merv's father wanted to see in his son were loyalty and respect. If someone was your friend, you were always to be his in return. If there was a problem, your parents would always be there to stand behind you.

'Dad's always been very important for me because he was sport-oriented. If I have a bad patch, I go and sit at his kitchen table and we talk. He's seen me come through and he's always been helpful with me.' Hughes says now.

'Obviously I've changed a lot over the years but I hope the crucial areas of my personality haven't changed. I hope I still treat people at face value, which I think has a lot to do with a country upbringing. I was always encouraged to play sport by dad, and the friendships I've formed [through sport] are lasting.'

The Hughes family: (from left) brother Gary, Merv, father Ian, mother Freda and sister Peta.

The longest of all his friendships has been with Gavin Whiting. 'Snapper' was seated next to a young Merv in grade 3 and the pair are still tight now, reciprocating as best men for each other. Gavin and Merv would later trek through northern Australia together and made a yearly pilgrimage to Adelaide for each Test Hughes would play in the City of Churches. While Merv was enthusiastic about all sports as a child and teenager, he wasn't the boy prodigy you would expect of someone who would eventually reach international level.

Whiting says of Hughes, 'He didn't really stand out with his skills as a kid. He was just a big log who wanted to play everything and had enormous energy when he was young. The time he really kicked on was in the two years the family had at Myrtleford. He just shot up, came back a lot taller and slimmer, and the two years he had spent playing against men were really good for him. He had been all right in the juniors but when he began to play against the men, that was when all of us noticed a big difference in him.'

Merv attended form 3 and form 4 at Myrtleford as a 15- and 16-year-old. During the summer he and his father would play in the same cricket team but in the winter the younger Hughes preferred to remain in the Under–16s football side.

Now at his full height and starring as a centre-half back and occasional full back, most thought it would actually be football where he could progress further. His bowling would be treated harshly at times by the men of the local area, whereas on the football field his height gave him an advantage over most, and the strength that would come later in his teenage years would see him continue to improve.

At the end of his second year of football, a nervous Hughes was drafted into the Under–18s to play in an elimination final. He performed solidly, even though he was playing outside his age group. When questioned as to why he had spent the year starring in the Under–16s when he could actually have held his own an age group higher, the young Hughes began to recognise his potential:

'Being up at Myrtleford taught me a lot of valuable lessons by playing senior cricket at a young age. It was the end of the second footy season, and I hadn't thought I was good enough to play in the Under–18s until I played for them in a losing final side. A few blokes asked me why I hadn't played for them all year and it taught me early that I should believe in myself and push myself to the next level. Every chance I've had since then, I have always tried to grab the next level, rather than being content with where I was.'

In 1978, the Hughes family would again be transferred back to Werribee for a third time. This year also saw the arrival of the third Hughes child, Gary. Merv was now in form 5 (which would be his last year at school), with sport the major focus of his life.

Without a driver's licence, Merv relied on Snapper to drive him wherever he wanted to go. Football or cricket training on Tuesdays and Thursdays, plus a weekend match, was complemented by basketball, indoor cricket and the occasional round of very-low-standard golf. (Even today, when playing rounds across the world, Merv Hughes still falls back on a local rule he first implemented at Royal Werribee Golf Course. If a player can replace their ball and complete another swing within 10 seconds of his original Mulligan, that is perfectly legal under the Royal and Ancient Hughes' rules.)

Back at Werribee again, but keeping in touch with the friends he had made in Myrtleford, it was time for Merv Hughes to decide what to do about his sport. Up to the age of 16, sport for Merv was fun, a way to fill in a weekend and the best way to keep in touch with your mates. At 17, it was time to wonder if there was the prospect of going any further with it, and perhaps even making some money.

In Werribee, the natural thing to do was join the local football side in winter, and then the cricket team once summer rolled around. Werribee Football Club were playing in the second division of the VFA (Victorian Football Association), which was then a strong competition immediately below the premier VFL (Victorian Football League). The VFA provided the grounding for many young players hoping to crack a game with a VFL club and was also home to the ageing VFL stars who were earning lucrative money as player-coaches in their final years on the field.

Unlike the VFL though, the VFA was a much more rough and tumble competition with an old-fashioned stoush as much a part of Sunday games as kicks, marks and goals. Werribee boasted the services of former Richmond hard man Ricky McLean, who had terrorised VFL backmen in the early 1970s as part of a lethal forward set-up that tagged him with Neil Balme. McLean was assisting senior coach Kevin Morris, and also kept an eye on the club's reserves side. Hughes' size, coupled with his ability to take a mark, saw him fast-tracked from the Under–19s through to the senior side midway through the season. At 17, Hughes was holding down a key defence post, though McLean would ride him as hard as any coach when he felt Merv had stumbled.

'Why don't you just give this up and go and play something else if you're going to play like that,' McLean would berate Hughes when he stepped out of line.

Years later, when Werribee would hold a reunion at the height of Merv's Test career, McLean would approach his former charge and congratulate him on finally taking his advice and choosing another sport.

For the summer, Hughes joined Werribee in the sub-district cricket competition which, like Werribee in the VFA, was immediately below the best standard of cricket across Melbourne. A number of grade scouts had sighted the raw fast bowler in country week tournaments and Hughes senior and junior had decided to spend a summer with Werribee to assess the best options for Merv.

Footscray, Prahran and South Melbourne had all made invitations. The pair decided they would follow the grade scores of each club's seconds and thirds extremely closely to decide which club was short of bowlers. The young Hughes certainly did not expect to walk into a district firsts side at 17 and the weakest seconds team of the trio would give him the best opportunity of making an initial impression.

As happens with the best of plans though, fate intervened and the move to a district club was made much earlier than anticipated . . .

Merv's boisterousness became more apparent as he got older and a prank, no matter how childish or silly, was always good value. At Werribee Cricket Club, the first-grade captain was fastidious about his dressing to the extent that he would throw a tantrum should any of his younger team-mates mess with his laundered and ironed clothes to wear after the day's play. In Merv's eyes, if someone was going to be that precious about life, the only thing to do was hide one of his socks and make him walk through the social club barefoot, after his shower, to look for them. It sounds pretty innocuous but it was the kind of foolish stunt that fills in 10 minutes after a game.

Expecting their skipper to be a little peeved, Merv and Snapper were taken aback to be fiercely berated in front of most of their team-mates and told, in no uncertain terms, that their attitude was a primary reason why the side hadn't won too many games. Their failings, both as people and cricketers, were then recorded at length.

Over a sock, it hardly seemed worth the trouble. If that's your attitude, you can stick your club. I'm leaving.

Ian Hughes told his son he had to complete the second day of the two-day game the following Saturday, because he wouldn't allow him to let down his team-mates, but agreed it was time to find a new cricketing home.

Hughes senior felt that Footscray would offer Merv a decent chance in the seconds, and maybe the firsts in a year or two if he continued to improve. Added to that, it was the closest club to home and Merv might appreciate a little bit less travel.

He walked through the door at Footscray in time to play on Melbourne Cup Day, 1978.

# CHAPTER THREE

# YOU'RE A
# BOWLER NOW

For a relatively young club in district cricket terms Footscray had much to offer Merv Hughes when he arrived, unannounced, in the summer of 1978–79. Though the club could not boast the proud and lengthy history of opponents such as Melbourne and Carlton, it had done well in the primary task of producing players for higher honours. In the years up to 1978–79, five players — Ron Gaunt, Ken Eastwood, Les Joslin, Alan Hurst and Ray Bright — had gone on to represent Australia.

Australian cricket has prided itself for more than a century on the belief that young players will be adequately schooled in the game by the older, harder heads, discovering as much in the hour or two after stumps as they did on the field during play. When Hughes first arrived at the Western Oval, Eastwood was captaining Footscray's seconds while Gaunt was the club's bowling coach.

Eastwood will probably be forever remembered as the unfortunate opener who was pitchforked into the Australian side for the decisive seventh Test against England in 1970–71, sensationally replacing dumped skipper Bill Lawry. Picked at the age of 35, he made just 5 and 0 in his two innings and then disappeared from the international scene, much in the same way that another Victorian opener, Wayne Phillips, was burnt just over two decades later.

While his Test career was unspectacular, Eastwood built a strong record for Victoria over a dozen seasons, scoring nearly 3000 runs at an average better than 40, and was a dominant figure in Melbourne grade cricket.

*Opposite: Hughes bowls Sri Lankan captain Duleep Mendis at the MCG, Victoria v Sri Lanka One-dayer, February 1983.*

Gaunt's disjointed three-Test career between 1958 and 1964 never progressed because he was stuck behind three legends — Alan Davidson, Ray Lindwall and Graham McKenzie — but he was a star at domestic level, securing 266 wickets at 26.65.

For a young cricketer at Footscray, there were plenty of good role models about. Eastwood kept an eye on the batsmen at the club while Gaunt looked after the development of the bowlers.

When Merv Hughes arrived at training, he introduced himself to Gaunt, and was asked what he did.

Merv replied, 'I'm a bit of an all-rounder. I bat a bit and I bowl a bit.' Hughes had been batting in the middle-order for Werribee, even if his early first-class batting would make that seem hard to believe.

'Who have you been playing for?' Gaunt asked.

'I've been playing for Werribee in sub-district cricket and last season I was playing up at Myrtleford in the seniors.'

'The nets are a bit full at the moment. Let's have a look at your bowling now and we'll have a look at your batting later.'

Hughes marked out a ridiculously long run-up (which would not be shortened until the winter of 1988), and bowled a few deliveries in a bid to impress Gaunt.

Hughes remembers the day clearly: 'Ron Gaunt just looked at me for a couple of minutes and said, "Right son, you're a bowler now". After that, all I did at practice was either bowl or have fielding practice. The batting got totally left behind but I think the lack of work on my batting probably made me as a bowler. I didn't have to worry about anything else.'

Merv Hughes would not bat at practice for the next two and a half seasons, bowling sometimes up to two and a half hours a night on both Tuesdays and Thursdays. When he played for Footscray, rising through the ranks to the firsts, he was sent down to number 11 in the batting order and rarely batted on a weekend. It was no wonder his batting was deplorable when it is realised he did virtually no work on it for some 30 months!

His debut in Footscray colours was against Essendon; a young Merv Hughes was put into the thirds to see what he could do. He hadn't met his captain and only a couple of his team-mates' faces (from practice during the week) were familiar.

Footscray batted first and the early part of the day hardly went well as they were fired out for 68. At number 11, Hughes failed to contribute a run, being dismissed for a duck. With virtually no target to defend, the only hope was to get at least a couple of early Essendon wickets before defeat inevitably arrived, and secure a few measly bonus points. The captain tossed Hughes the new ball.

'You're the fast bowler who's supposed to be reasonably quick, aren't you?' he asked.

'That's right,' replied Hughes.

'Well, I haven't seen you bowl but you've got the new ball. Let's set a field and see if we can get a few wickets.'

Essendon could manage just 65 all out, crashing to a sensational defeat by 3 runs. Hughes would be the destroyer, securing 8–35 in his only match for the club's thirds. Next game, he would be into the seconds and playing under Ken Eastwood.

Footscray's seconds had won the flag the previous year and had mounted a reasonably impressive defence of their title. With four matches to go, Footscray vied with Melbourne for second spot, trailing minor premiers Carlton and just ahead of fourth-placed Prahran. Less than one game separated the four sides and Hughes made a workmanlike start to his time in the seconds, securing six wickets in his first three matches.

In the final round, Footscray were due to meet Melbourne, having now secured second spot behind Carlton and the right to a home semi-final. Footscray would play third-placed Melbourne again the following week and the final match offered the chance to build a psychological advantage over their opponents.

Melbourne, however, racked up 9–316 to cruise to victory and were feeling confident indeed for the semi-final a week later. Whatever hope Footscray had of building an advantage over the traditionally powerful Melbourne side had been wrecked by an afternoon of wayward bowling.

If Footscray were to make the final and defend their title, Eastwood reasoned that the only hope of success would be to bat first and make a significant total and hope Melbourne folded under the pressure of a run chase. If Footscray were to bowl, there was every chance the chastened attack would not be able to apply enough pressure to restrict their opponents.

*Hughes in the days before Australian coach Bob Simpson insisted he work on his batting — comprehensively bowled after an unsuccessful late-innings slog against WA's Terry Alderman.*

In the semi-final, the former Test opener fought hard to top-score with 41 but his charges could not resist the medium-pace of a young bowler named Steve McCooke (who, more than a dozen years later, played as an off-spinner with Victoria). McCooke snared 7–31 as Footscray tumbled out for 163.

Eastwood introduced himself into the attack early and was buoyed to make the initial breakthrough with his left-arm spin. The choice now was what to do with his 17-year-old fast bowler, who had not opened the bowling. Hughes had been decidedly wayward at times in his four games for the seconds, but he did have genuine pace. By not giving him the new ball, Eastwood was hoping Hughes would not waste the shine but would instead be able to control an older ball.

Just over an hour later, Melbourne was all out for 74 and Footscray were toasting their fast bowling discovery and the prospect of another flag. As he had risen to the occasion in his debut for the thirds, Hughes had stunningly bettered that performance for the seconds, taking an incredible 9–25. But for the fact that Eastwood had taken the first wicket, Hughes probably would have snared all 10.

Minor premier Carlton would offer a stern challenge but Footscray had won their only meeting with Carlton during the season and the final would be on neutral territory at University Oval. The Carlton side would contain a young batsman, who was also just 17, by the name of Dean Jones.

Footscray batted first, again, and had the minor premiers under enormous pressure by reaching 310. A brilliant 150 by Gary Anderton in just under six hours left Carlton with an uphill task for victory. Jones would fight it out for almost four hours for 43 but Carlton would be bowled out for 243, giving Footscray the second-grade premiership. Again Hughes was the star, taking 6–57 from 20 overs.

Working off a ridiculous 45-pace run-up at the time, Hughes would usually take six minutes (and often as many as eight) to bowl an over, yet he never flagged in his pace over the day-and-a-bit that Footscray would be in the field.

The effort made an impression on Jones, as did the batsman on the bowler. Their careers would now run side by side for some 15 years.

'The Carlton boys had heard about Merv because he had taken nine-for in the semi-final against Melbourne,' Jones remembers. 'I faced him in the seconds' final and all I can remember was this guy pushing off the sightscreen and just bouncing the crap out of me. He was young and quick and he just stuck it up me all day. He could bowl an outswinger at that stage too, but he bounced me a hell of a lot and got me out in the end.'

The young Jones' cockiness at the crease had both annoyed and impressed the Footscray side. Everyone at Footscray knew Dean was the son of district legend Barney Jones, who had played the game hard over almost 20 years with Carlton. Even as defeat loomed, Jones couldn't be convinced that he was going to be beaten and swaggered about the crease until his departure.

Hughes, meanwhile, kept charging in, bowling fast and impressing upon the Carlton side that this fast bowler wouldn't stop until every last batsman was gone. While later in his career Jones would torment struggling bowlers verbally (as well as with his actions), just as Hughes would engage in some sledging of his own when established as a first-class cricketer, neither had a word to say on this day. As the junior members of their sides, any 'chatter' was carried out by the senior players and the youngsters were there to concentrate.

Jones recalls: 'I don't remember him sledging or really saying anything at all to me. I didn't sledge him either. We were both quiet kids going about our games. We were too busy trying to impress to worry about how you could get an advantage over someone else.'

While neither Jones nor Hughes would yet delve into the mind games of cricket, it was certainly something both were being taught. Hughes is extremely thankful for the education he got at Footscray, both on and off the ground. The verbal side of the game, as well as the nuts and bolts of bowling, were equally as important in his grounding as a cricketer, in his opinion.

'We had good leadership and guidance. The on-field leadership was very strict and we had the coaching of Ron Gaunt off the ground. I couldn't have picked a better club to go to. When I first started, Ken Eastwood said what needed to be said. At that young age, I think you begin to speak through frustration at the batsman doing well, rather than [using] aggression to upset a batsman. I wasn't an experienced sledger. As you get more experienced, you know what to say and when to say it and, most importantly, who to say it to,' Hughes says.

The transfer from Werribee had been an overwhelming success, bringing a premiership in the seconds. He had backed himself to succeed at a higher level and had been rewarded. For the 1979 football season, Hughes would start in the seniors at Werribee but there was the thought as to where he could take his cricket the following summer.

'When I came to Footscray, my goal was to play and be competitive. When I was playing in the seconds, my focus was more on winning a premiership than getting in the senior side but after taking nine-for and six-for in the two finals, I thought over the winter that I might be a chance to play in the seniors.

'But at that age, I was pushing more to be a footballer than a cricketer and was hoping to get picked up by Geelong.'

As it turned out, he was a certainty for a first XI place under Lindsay James in 1979–80. After another winter in the first XVIII at Werribee, the young Hughes stepped into first-grade cricket as Footscray chased their maiden top-level premiership.

Rising another grade, Hughes would manage regular hauls of two and three wickets without threatening to tear through a side at any stage. His pace was impressive but his control would often let him down, particularly as the day progressed.

The run-up, which stretched to some 40 metres, earned him plenty of notoriety as Footscray marched impressively towards the finals. However, for an 18-year-old mad on his sport, there could be no better life than competition on the weekends, training through the week and catching up with mates in between.

*Hughes in the summer of 1981–82, sans moustache.*

A full-time job wasn't a high priority and it's fair to say Merv Hughes wasn't hugely committed to his tasks at a clothing factory. Over Christmas, the young paceman was asked if he would be a net bowler for the Australian team who were preparing for the Boxing Day Test and he jumped at the opportunity to show his wares.

Hughes' request for three days unpaid leave was refused so he resigned. This opportunity was too good to pass up and work could be worried about later. While the enthusiasm was admirable, it was a big risk for a teenager in his first grade season and not yet even in the Victorian State squad.

Close friend Clint Prisnall, who had known Hughes since his days in Myrtleford, was one who counselled his mate to think long and hard about what he was doing. Hughes and Prisnall had opened the bowling together in Country Week games as 15-year-olds and Prisnall had headed to the city to pursue his dream of a VFL career with North Melbourne. He progressed as far as the reserves before a knee injury brought him to the realisation he would not break into what was then one of the finest teams in the league, and settled into a nine-to-five job. Watching his close mate take the same risks for sport worried him deeply, but at least he was eventually able to offer Hughes a job, as a storeroom packer, after Merv had spent more than a year on the dole.

'For a long time, I thought he would just play a bit of Shield cricket and that would be it,' Prisnall says. 'That was sensational — to get that high in the ranks — but I was asking him what would he do with the rest of his life? To his credit, he believed in his own ability and just kept going and going.'

Footscray finished the minor round in fourth position, behind minor premiers, the Collingwood Magpies, a powerful Melbourne side and St Kilda. Drawn to meet Collingwood, Footscray were not expected to trouble a side containing former Victorian batsman Bob Baldry and regular State representative Trevor Laughlin.

Footscray crashed to a meagre 105 with no batsman reaching 20. However, the score was a parlous 9–80 at one stage before Hughes belied his previous efforts with the bat to contribute an unbeaten 9 at No. 11, sharing a valuable partnership with his captain James.

Collingwood moved smoothly to 1–37 in reply and then 4–68, needing a further 38 for a place in the final, before Hughes struck. Just as he had done in the seconds' semi-final and final the previous season, the young fast bowler lifted for the big occasion and sparked a stunning collapse.

Laughlin edged a catch to the wicket-keeper, as did partner John Miller, as the Magpies lost a stunning 6–6, being bowled out for 74. Hughes took 3–1 in 20 balls to finish with figures of 5–32.

In the other semi-final, St Kilda upset a Melbourne side containing former Test star Paul Sheahan. Footscray would be boosted for the final by the return of Test spinner Ray Bright from the Australian team's tour of Pakistan.

Batting first again, Footscray reached a respectable 221 and blitzed St Kilda for 121 to win by exactly 100 runs. While Hughes would take just one wicket in the final, it was the opening scalp of high-scoring opener David Robinson and his pace and enthusiasm throughout that had impressed every observer.

On August 21, 1980, a letter from the Victorian Cricket Association (VCA) arrived at the family home.

'I am pleased to extend an invitation to you to be a member of the Victorian Sheffield Shield squad for the coming season,' the letter from VCA acting secretary Ken Jacobs read.

Victoria had won the past two Shield titles back-to-back. The 18-year-old would be part of a 37-man squad, nominally as cover for a pace-bowling attack that had been spearheaded by the ageing Max Walker (32) and Alan Hurst (30), and the injury-plagued Ian Callen.

However, over the next 18 months, the Victorian cricket scene was to change dramatically. Fresh from consecutive Shield titles in 1978–79 and 1979–80, Victoria plunged to the bottom of the ladder for the 1980–81 season. A poor start to the 1981–82 season followed, including three successive outright defeats before Christmas. In less than 18 months, a powerful side had disintegrated completely and heads were on the block.

Veteran John Scholes, who had been recalled in 1981–82 to captain the ailing Victorians in place of Graham Yallop, had been impressed by Hughes, who was now a few weeks past his 20th birthday.

'It didn't come as a surprise that he would kick on because he wasn't a quitter and wouldn't give up at anything he did. He had those qualities that good players in the past had had and that suggested he may go a fair way, given the opportunity,' Scholes remembers.

As Victoria reeled towards disaster through the 1981–82 season, the axe fell with a vengeance and few heads were spared. For a one-day McDonald's Cup match in Adelaide over the New Year, regulars Richie Robinson, Paul Hibbert and Rod McCurdy were all axed while Max Walker had retired the previous week, perhaps sensing the bloodshed to come.

*Hughes in the nets, 1982.*

Among the five new players to come into a squad of 13 were Hughes and another 20-year-old, Dean Jones. Jones had already scored 398 district runs at 66.50 that season, to win his place in the line-up, while Hughes would join Len Balcam in a decidedly raw pace attack.

Meanwhile, Hughes' football form with Werribee during 1981 had been so impressive that he had been invited to pre-season training with Geelong. However, with his State selection, cricket suddenly shot to the head of his sporting priorities. The turmoil among the senior players in the Victorian Shield team was going on well above his head and he was happy just to get a game.

'I didn't notice any dramas when I started, but that was probably because I just wanted to play,' Merv remembers. 'I was lucky that the Victorian team was in a rebuilding stage and the younger blokes had a bit more leeway. The selectors obviously had a look around at a few blokes and said, "Right, we're going to stick with him".'

However, Hughes may never have made his debut at all if it wasn't for a chance meeting with an old friend just after Christmas 1981.

During the district cricket break for Yuletide celebrations, he headed down to Ocean Grove, two hours drive south-west from Melbourne, with his Werribee football mates, well away from newspapers and television news reports. Walking down the street, he ran into a football colleague, Geoff Billman, and his wife, who congratulated him on being chosen for Victoria.

Bemused as to what they were talking about, he bought a paper and discovered he was indeed in the Victorian side. Also, he was due at training that night and had better get straight on the highway if he was going to make practice. It begs the question as to how long his debut would have been delayed if he had not made it to his first practice session as a State player.

The young fast bowler would take two wickets in his first two overs before coming in for some harsh treatment from flamboyant South Australian captain David Hookes. In fact, Hookes' early pastings of Hughes would be a major stumbling block for the fast bowler. Not until after he had made his debut for Australia would Hughes be able to face Hookes confidently, and only late in the batsman's career would he finally square the ledger for the punishment he copped in his early seasons.

As a novice amid fellow fast-bowling babes, Hughes settled easily into the Victorian side. The same could not be said for Jones however, who felt abandoned by his senior team-mates. As a young batsman amid much more senior players, Jones did not feel he received the support a youngster deserved.

'The environment was bad when we first started,' Jones declares.

'That's not a reflection on John Scholes but on the selection policies of the time. There were sackings going on and some of the guys still in the side got the shits because they lost a few of their good mates. Ray Bright was upset because he was from the old school. I got 30-odd in my first game on a tough deck but I worked my backside off after getting dropped on nought. I was [batting] on a pitch that was bouncing and swinging, coming off Melbourne where it never bounced above shin-high.

'I thought I had done a good job and Brighty walked into the rooms and took his cap off while I sat down thinking, "Thank God that's over".

'He opened a beer and proposed a toast to the worst batsman he'd ever seen put on a Victorian cap. That wrecked me for two years, that one statement.'

In contrast to Jones, the biggest problem for Hughes to confront was his team-mates taking the mickey out of him. As the youngest member of the side, he invariably seemed to be on the end of a number of practical jokes. At this stage in his career, the young Hughes was still in his shell; he had adopted the old philosophy of keeping his mouth closed for the greater portion of time and trying to learn as much as possible.

For the young quick's first one-day appearance, against South Australia in Adelaide, Scholes felt Hughes would be able to settle more easily if he was brought down a rung or two. Aware that the youngster had told all of his family to watch the telecast of his maiden game, his plan was swung into action.

'For his first game, Merv was young and as keen as mustard,' Scholes says. 'I felt like [playing] a prank and I just told the scoreboard attendants we had this new kid in the side called Merv Hill. All the guys were listening when the announcer started reading the side out and came to the last name, "And making his debut is . . . Merv Hill".

'Merv was shattered because he was telling us his mum was going to be watching on TV but now she would tune out because she wouldn't think he was playing. Nicknames come and go but guys who played in that era still call him Hilly.'

Over his first five games of his maiden season, Hughes snared 18 wickets at 31.50, including a haul of 4–69 on a flat wicket against Queensland. Hughes' willingness to bowl for long periods won him immediate respect from Scholes and marked him as a player of the future.

While the sudden departure of a number of senior players provided the opportunity to play at an early age, Scholes felt that Hughes would not develop as quickly due to the absence of a mentor. In later years, Hughes was able to look back and agree. The presence of Walker or Hurst would have been invaluable, and when Rodney Hogg returned to the Victorian squad in later years (after the rebel tours of South Africa in 1985–86 and 1986–87), all the bowlers in the squad flocked to him as

When the South Australia—Victoria McDonald's Cup match in Adelaide on New Year's Day 1982 began, the scoreboard operators, acting on the advice of Victorian captain John Scholes, had the name of the Vics' new fast bowler as 'Hill'. By the end of the home team's innings, it had been corrected to 'Hughes'.

someone who had done the business at international level. Hogg had left Melbourne for Adelaide in the mid–1970s, and gone on to play 38 Tests and take 123 wickets between 1978 and 1984.

The promotion to State level ended any thoughts of joining a VFL club to do a serious pre-season, convincing Hughes to remain with Werribee for the 1982 VFA season. Cricket would have his full attention for 1982–83. Barring any disasters, cricket would be where he was to make his name.

While Hughes may have had grand plans on making himself noticed at a higher level, fate would turn a blind eye to him for his second season. In the very first trial match of the pre-season period, Hughes badly tore a left hamstring, ruling himself out for eight weeks until mid-November. In his return to district ranks, he tore an intercostal muscle in his ribcage, the bane of all fast bowlers. A tear in the intercostal muscle makes even running impossible and Hughes now found himself on the sidelines until Christmas, with less than three full district games for the entire summer so far under his belt. He would not return to the Victorian side until early February and played only four first-class games for the season, returning a meagre 11 wickets at 54 apiece.

At the end of such a depressing summer, football loomed once again as an attractive alternative to days spent slogging it out in the sun for cricket. As Hughes sat down to weigh up his career options, there was the real thought that perhaps he should go hard at football and let cricket play the support role for a while. As he considered his decision, fate stepped in again to ensure he would remain a cricketer . . .

On the eve of Werribee's first game of the year in mid-March, Hughes received a letter from the Australian Cricket Board (ACB), announcing that the Test selectors had nominated him for an Esso scholarship to England. It was a total bolt from the blue. The Esso scholarships were introduced in 1981 to foster young talent and involved allocating a rising player to an English county side for 12 weeks.

South Australian batsman Mike Haysman and Queenslander Rob Kerr had been assigned to Leicester and Notts respectively and their selection came as no surprise to pundits across the nation. Both were tipped for much higher honours with batting places expected to open up in the Australian team within the next two years. A young New South Wales all-rounder by the name of Greg Matthews had also been chosen and would be sent to Worcester. Matthews saw himself as an off-spinner but already his gritty batting had made a much more lasting impression in his debut year of 1982–83. Buttressing the Blues' middle-order, Matthews had averaged 49 in his maiden season but struggled to take only 12 wickets from seven games at more than 40 apiece.

Hughes was the outsider and his selection seemed incongruous when so many fast bowlers were present across the country. While Dennis Lillee and Jeff Thomson were certainly in the twilight of glittering careers, New South Wales' Geoff Lawson was at the peak of his powers and the likes of Carl Rackemann, Terry Alderman, Rodney Hogg, Mike Whitney, Rod McCurdy, Len Pascoe and John Maguire were scattered across the States. The selection of a 21-year-old from a State that had won consecutive Sheffield Shield wooden spoons seemed strange indeed.

If Hughes' selection could be debated, he was blessed a second time with the county side chosen for him by his Esso benefactors. Hughes would be assigned to Essex for 1983. Traditionally one of the weakest county clubs, Essex had begun to build a formidable side in the late 1970s and by 1983 were the dominant outfit in English county cricket.

Hughes would find himself alongside bowlers such as former left-handed paceman John Lever and future Test quick Neil Foster and being able to bowl in the nets to class batsmen, including Test batsmen Keith Fletcher and Graham Gooch. In county Second XI cricket, under the leadership of another past England skipper Mike Denness, he would do as much bowling as he would in two full summers at home, but he would learn more than he had in his career to that point.

'Merv came over to Essex and we didn't really know what to expect from him at all,' says Graham Gooch. 'We found out very early that he just kept going whenever you asked him to bowl. That was a theme throughout his career. We'd got this young, raw bowler who wanted to go all day. At the end of the season, we gave him one firsts game against New Zealand and he took six wickets. When you look back, he should have played first-class cricket for us for a fair part of the summer.'

On the personal side, Hughes would also form a lasting friendship in 1983 with a young Victorian all-rounder by the name of Tony Dodemaide.

Dodemaide, who also played for Footscray, was touring England with the Australian Under–19 squad and their final match on tour was played at Essex's home in Chelmsford.

The 18-year-old had joined Footscray in the same year as Hughes, over the summer of 1978–79, but a huge night out together in Chelmsford cemented the bonds that remain in place today.

'I had met Merv a few times but we were by no means mates because he was a bit ahead of me in the grades, being a couple of years older. After our last game [of the tour], he grabbed me at the local pub and said I was with him because I was from Footscray, just like him.

'We got to know each other from there and that's my first memory of us starting to get along. Once we both got back, I spent a lot more time with him because I was taken from the Under–19s straight into the State squad and we became very good mates from then,' Dodemaide recalls.

Word of Hughes' efforts soon filtered back to Melbourne and he was expected to make a significant step forward for the summer of 1983–84. Unfortunately, though, he would manage less than half a season, feeling he had slipped further back into the queue. During the year, Hughes was diagnosed with stress fractures in his lower back and would play just four games, managing only five wickets at more than 81 apiece.

In those four games, he crossed paths for the first time with a young red-headed fast bowler from Queensland by the name of Craig McDermott, who had made a stunning impact as a 17-year-old. The pair would share the new ball for Australia some eight years down the track.

In December 1983, against Victoria, McDermott prepared to bowl his first ball to Hughes and told the umpire he would like the second new ball, just to ensure that the lowly-rated tailender didn't cause too many problems.

'That's the biggest waste of 50 bucks this season,' Hughes called up the wicket.

Hughes then duly nicked the first ball to 'keeper Ray Phillips.

To top it off, the umpires refused Hughes' request to be allowed to use the same ball for the start of the Queensland innings. He knew the ball had swung so why not ask if he could use it?

Cricket was Hughes' priority but a return to Werribee for some football in the winter of 1984 would not hurt. Or so he felt. Spending another season in defence, Hughes lifted his senior games tally to 95 in the VFA. Football offers many things and for Merv Hughes it offered companionship, enjoyment and a way to break up the monotony of a pre-season training for cricket. However, the constant pounding was doing his long-term future little good and, at the start of the 1984–85 summer, there was further despair. A season of football had not allowed the stress fractures in his back to heal and he would not be able to bowl until well into the season.

If he was to make it in cricket, football would have to go. To manage just five games of cricket in 1984–85 and a total of 18 in all over four seasons, when he could have played as many as 40 for the Vics, was devastating.

As so often happened in the developmental stages of his cricket career, fate smiled on Hughes yet again when things seemed to be at their lowest. He realised he would not know his capabilities on the cricket field until he applied every energy to success there but, even then, he was unsure if he could ever cut it as a potential Australian player.

In early 1985, news broke about the formation of the rebel Australian side to tour South Africa. Those who went on the tour were being threatened with bans, ranging anywhere from a year or two to a lifetime, from the Australian scene.

Hughes was certainly never on the shopping list of Dr Ali Bacher, the former South African captain-turned-administrator who put together tours by rebel teams. However, the names that were removed from the pool of Australian first-class cricketers suddenly opened up considerable opportunities for those left to battle for places within the Aussie Test side. Rodney Hogg, Rod McCurdy, Carl Rackemann, John Maguire and Terry Alderman had all signed for two seasons in the Republic. All five pace bowlers had played either Test or One-day matches for Australia within the last 18 months and were now all out of the picture.

Geoff Lawson remained the undoubted spearhead of the Australian Test attack after a brilliant summer against the West Indies, and McDermott had made a big impression but, beyond that, the selectors would have to return to ageing stars such as Thomson or gamble with untried young bowlers. Thomson was chosen as a stopgap measure for the 1985 England tour, however Australia's selectors have always looked to youth in times of trouble and there was no doubt places would be up for grabs in 1985–86.

Hughes had to give himself every chance and so football was definitely off his agenda. He would train during the winter to prepare himself for the cricket opportunity ahead, but the question of what he would do for the rest of his time was unresolved.

In April, 'Snapper' Whiting knocked on Hughes' door in Werribee to tell his best mate that the doctor had told him his hernia operation needed a full 12 months rest. Working as a roof-tiler, he could do himself a permanent injury unless he had a break, so he was stopping in to tell Merv that he was going to get on the road for a while, head north, maybe to Queensland, and catch up with a few of the boys up there. Danny Burns, another mate from Werribee footy club, was playing at Southport on the Gold Coast. There was an offer to stay with him for a while and then perhaps head further north and over to Darwin to have a look around. Just stopping in to say goodbye and I'll see you when I see you.

It took a few minutes thinking for Hughes to announce he didn't have anything to keep him in Melbourne, so he would come too. Snapper organised a service on the car and they left the next day. The pair drove out of Melbourne in early April with the only plan being that Hughes would be back in time for the start of Victorian training in mid-September.

Heading up the eastern coast of Australia towards the Gold Coast, the pair would pull into a caravan park at night and sleep on a mattress in the back. If either one managed to find a bit of work or they liked a place, they would stay a bit longer. Otherwise, the Federal Government helped out with money as they passed from place to place.

Once settled at Danny Burns' flat, the pair stayed for five weeks. Hughes joined the local football team's training each day to keep up his fitness work. Living so close to the beach, he could go for a run on the sand in the morning and then train with the club in the afternoon.

After more than a month on the road, he was a sight to behold. His hair was now well past his shoulders, while a full beard made any sign of his mouth hard to find. Merv Hughes had always been able to grow a luxuriant moustache within a few days and six weeks without a razor saw him looking like the biker out of the 'Village People'.

*'Looking like the biker out of the Village People'...*
*Hughes in 1985.*

Heading out of Southport, Snapper and Hughes trekked up through Mackay and Townsville on the way to Cairns, timing their movements with the concert schedule of 'Mental as Anything'.

From there, it was across to Darwin for a month or so and then down to Alice Springs. In the Red Centre, Hughes would spend a part of each day at an indoor cricket centre, bowling for an hour or more until he tired. Management didn't mind and he and Snapper could always hang around in the evening in the hope of picking up a game if a team was short.

On the one evening the pair did play, Snapper had to tell the wicket-keeper it would be safer not to keep to Hughes. He was quite quick you see.

Having led the team to victory with two lightning overs, and also winning a slab for hitting a tiny rectangular sign behind the bowler's arm, Hughes had to come clean and admit to the bemused locals that he had been playing first-class cricket for the past four years. More than a dozen years down the track, he still catches up with his Alice Springs' acquaintances every 12 months or so.

As well as indoor cricket, Hughes again trained with a local football club to work on his fitness but, this time, could not resist the temptation of playing a game. Given a permit for one week, he played for Rovers against Pioneers and lined up at centre half-forward.

According to the myth Hughes has propagated at Sportman's Nights for a decade, he lined up on a 5'8" player (172 cm) who proceeded to spend the day standing on Hughes' head for regular 'speccies' and making him look stupid. His opponent was named best on ground and finally convinced Hughes that retirement from football was his best option.

According to Snapper, the truth was considerably different.

'Merv played centre half-forward and kicked five or six goals. He stood out because he was 6'4" (193 cm) and could take a mark. He won the glass, in which you had the right to tap anyone on the shoulder for the night and they had to buy you a beer. He was asleep by about seven o'clock and wouldn't give me the pot to use.'

Merv Hughes arrived back in Melbourne hoping to push for an Australian place. At the same time, New Zealand's great fast bowler, Richard Hadlee, was part of a squad chasing their first series victory in an Australia–New Zealand Test series.

# CHAPTER FOUR

# THE CHERISHED BAGGY GREEN

For the summer of 1985–86, Australia was due to play New Zealand in a three-Test series which would be completed before the end of the first week of December — prior to hosting Kapil Dev's Indian side for a second three-Test rubber. The series against India was set to be completed by the first week of January, stressing the need for Merv Hughes to make a good start to the season. If he started slowly, the Test matches would be gone before he knew it and another summer would have passed him by.

It was no surprise to Hughes that he was not in the running for the early Tests against New Zealand, played in Brisbane and Sydney. Even though Australia had lost the Ashes 3–1 during 1985, the fast bowlers from that tour had the inside running for the early Tests on home soil.

Craig McDermott, who had taken 30 wickets in England in his first full series, shared the new ball duties with senior bowler Geoff Lawson, while New South Wales' Dave Gilbert was there as back-up for the opening Test at the Gabba.

However, the scene would change dramatically in the space of a few weeks. The trio of Lawson, McDermott and Gilbert would take just four wickets between them against the Kiwis in Brisbane, as Australia was humiliated by a massive innings and 41 runs. New Zealand's first Test win on Australian soil was spearheaded by a peerless bowling performance from Richard Hadlee (9–52 and 6–71) and a chanceless 188 from batting star Martin Crowe.

*Opposite: Hughes at the Adelaide Oval, third Ashes Test, 1986–87.*

Defeat was a heavy blow for captain Allan Border, but he was heartened by victory in Sydney in the second Test, despite the absence of Lawson and McDermott through injury. The pair returned for the series decider in Perth, where Australia was beaten by six wickets. While it would be unfair to diminish Hadlee's incredible performance to take 33 wickets at 12.15 apiece during the three Tests, it was clear that Australian cricket standards had slipped a long way indeed.

In the Victorian side, Merv Hughes had begun his campaign well. Bowling with pace, as always, and better control, he secured his maiden five-wicket bag against New South Wales in Newcastle by taking 5–74 in the first week of November.

Further impressive performances against Tasmania and Western Australia caught the eye of the national selection panel. Hughes' efforts in Victoria's game against India, in the week before the opening Test of that series in Adelaide, would be seen as a pointer to the future. If Hughes could do well against the Indians, he would be the bowler first in the queue if anything happened to the frontliners: Lawson, McDermott and Gilbert.

Greg Chappell, then a Test selector, said Hughes was being looked at in 1985–86 as a prospect for the next summer's home Ashes series against England. With just one five-wicket bag under his belt, the panel wanted to see a bit more consistency but were hopeful the Victorian could develop into something for the future.

Chappell recalls, 'Merv was a big, strong bloke who could bowl quick in short spells in those days. Basically, he didn't look to be the sort of bloke who could bowl long spells but he looked aggressive. He looked intimidating and perhaps could put pressure on the batsmen, provided he maintained a good line. What he needed to do was improve his control and his fitness, and that would come as he got older.'

Yet again, the circumstances for Hughes would change suddenly and dramatically. While he was involved in the match against India in Melbourne, Lawson had withdrawn from the New South Wales side to meet Western Australia in the concurrent match at the Sydney Cricket Ground due to a back problem.

Lawson's injury was to be diagnosed as the fast bowler's curse — stress fractures of the lower back — and he would not return to the Australian side for more than 12 months. (When he did return, it would be for one Test only and he would not be a regular member of the Test team again until the 1989 Ashes series.)

Gilbert was battling a heel problem and, with Australia's sudden injury worries, Hughes was being talked of as a candidate, ahead of schedule, for the Adelaide Test match.

Sure enough, he was named in the Australian XII for the Test starting on December 13, along with another debutant, Western Australian batsman Geoff Marsh, and a third, Bruce Reid, who was on stand by for Gilbert, should he fail a fitness test.

Chairman of selectors Lawrie Sawle recalls that the panel plumped for Hughes on the basis that he could genuinely bowl fast. While further control was needed, that could be developed and the fact that he started with pace on his side was a major plus.

'Since the retirement of Dennis Lillee a few years before, we were looking for a fiery strike bowler. Merv was in our sights for that role. He had

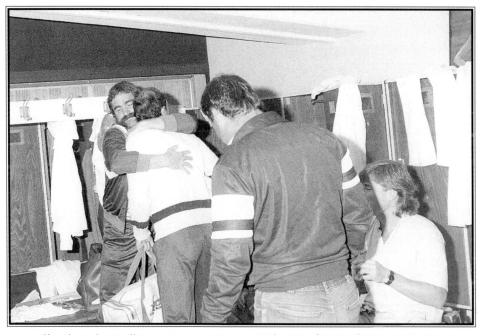

Hughes hugs Victorian captain, and now Australian team-mate, Ray Bright, after hearing of their selection in the national side for the first Test against India, 1985–86.

*Australian captain Allan Border (left) with coach Bob Simpson in 1986.*

been considered for about 12 months before we picked him. He had that kind of approach in him that we, as national selectors, wanted,' says Sawle.

While Hughes had heard the media talk of his possible Australian selection, he hadn't paid a lot of attention, not really considering himself to be seriously in the running for a Test spot. When he heard his name read out over the radio, he sat — stunned — in his car for some minutes.

Hughes drove to the Australian Cricket Board offices in Jolimont to pick up his gear. To collect his first Australian cap was an almost religious experience. For the boys in Werribee, celebrations were the order of the day and Hughes, Snapper, Clint Prisnall and Danny Burns, now returned from Southport, settled in for a long night.

By late that night, with the effects of a considerable amount of beer playing on Hughes' reactions, there was little he could do when his three best mates began posing in his newly-acquired Australian gear. Before he had even worn his first Test cap, a helmet, two jumpers and his cherished baggy green were being modelled around the house in Werribee by three 'tired and emotional' friends.

When Hughes joined the Australian squad, his only Victorian team-mate was Ray Bright but he knew most of his new team-mates from one or two meetings in Shield cricket. While he claims to have settled quietly into the line-up, because he was in awe of Allan Border, that memory is not shared by his colleagues.

Border, who knew only vaguely of Hughes, recalls him imposing his personality on the national side immediately.

'I had played against him a few times in his pre-moustache days but hadn't formally met him at all. When Merv first started for Victoria, a lot of the big names were still around and he was a long way back in the reckoning. The only reason he stood out to me was because he had this enormous, great run-up and I couldn't believe he ran that far. He was a good, fiery young bloke but you can never tell who's going to come out of the pack,' Border says.

'When he got picked, I had heard he was a livewire but he was a character straight away and he was just a pest in the dressing-rooms. His behaviour in the dressing-rooms, even in those early days, was great for the team. He was very loud and infectious.'

On match-eve, Hughes was struck by nerves as it dawned on him that he would represent his country on the 'morrow. His parents had come across from Melbourne, as had nearly all of his close friends, along with the guys he had met in Darwin over the winter.

What if he just wasn't up to it and embarrassed himself? How would he look in front of all of those people who meant something to him, let alone the thousands more at the game and all those who would be watching on television?

Unable to rest, he headed down to Charlie's Bar on the ground floor of the team's hotel, the Hilton, to join Border and Marsh. Test selector Greg Chappell and ACB media manager Ian McDonald were also in the bar, along with most of the national touring cricket media.

Hughes drank soda water for several hours and headed to bed around 1 a.m. However, while he was in Charlie's Bar, he was very loud and the centre of attention, perhaps trying to cover his nerves. For those who didn't know his boisterous personality, he seemed to be behaving like someone who'd drunk too much alcohol.

Come match day, with Australia batting after Border had won the toss, media reports were carrying stories that Hughes had been drunk in a bar the night before his Test debut. Unused to such public scrutiny — and a factually incorrect story — Hughes was devastated as he waited through a rain-affected first day for his turn at the crease.

'The big myth from my debut was that I was seen in Charlie's the night before the game drinking heavily. I have no idea where it started. I was certainly in the bar but I drank soda water until after midnight so that I didn't go crazy by myself in the room. I got nailed the next day and I couldn't understand why.'

The Hughes personality was a new one for the press corps and his embryonic career could have been destroyed in that moment but, thankfully, both Chappell and McDonald had been present, as part of Hughes' circle, and saw that he had not been drunk.

When questions were asked on the opening day of the Test, both were able to dismiss the reports out of hand as a furphy. Chappell, though, did take the bowler aside late on the first day of the Test to tell him how perception would be every bit as important as reality now that he was representing Australia.

Chappell says of the incident: 'He was just being Merv and making a lot of noise. He certainly wasn't rolling drunk, because people didn't realise how loud he could get at that stage. The thing that came out of it though, was that there was a bit of speculation that he had been drinking. I had a bit of a chat with him and told him not to put himself in a position where he could be criticised.'

Before he had even bowled for Australia, Merv Hughes had learnt a salutary lesson. Australia finished the first day on 4–248, celebrating David Boon's maiden Test century, and Hughes could now prepare for his first opportunity to bowl at a powerful Indian line-up.

Kapil Dev closed out the Australian innings at 381 on the second afternoon with a spell of 5–4 in 21 balls, leaving India just under 100 minutes to negotiate to stumps on a second rain-interrupted day. Hughes had not distinguished himself with the bat, making a five-ball duck batting at number 11 behind Reid, but was given the new ball with McDermott.

In the tour match against the Indians the previous week in Melbourne, Hughes had dismissed opener Kris Srikkanth cheaply, having him caught in the slip cordon after flashing at a widish delivery. Hughes felt Srikkanth had a weakness outside his off-stump and would test the hyperactive opener there when he began upwind. As for India's batting master, Sunil Gavaskar, the strict instructions from Border were to stay off his pads at all costs.

At the close of play, after bowling seven overs, Hughes' figures read 0–50. Srikkanth, who would make 86 from 89 balls in the second Test and a century from 97 balls in the third Test, had caned him on his way to 51 from as many deliveries.

When Hughes strained for extra effort against Gavaskar and slipped onto the little man's pads, the ball disappeared into the mid-wicket boundary before he had time to react.

'In Adelaide, I bowled the same way to Srikkanth that I had in Melbourne, and he belted me. I thought, "He didn't do this before".

'We came back on the next day and I had to come to terms with the fact I had given their openers my best shot, and ask myself, "What do I do here?"' Hughes says.

Gavaskar retired hurt, his overnight score at 39, to resume at the fall of the fifth wicket, while McDermott had dispensed with Srikkanth the night before, allowing Hughes to bowl at two new batsmen, nightwatchman Chetan Sharma and Dilip Vengsarkar.

Not long into his first spell on another rain-shortened third day, Hughes secured his first Test wicket, having Vengsarkar caught behind by Wayne Phillips for 7. It was to be his only moment of success as the Australians bowled until after tea on the final day, sending down 202 overs in all for the innings.

Australia had momentary hopes of running through the Indian innings at 4–187 but Gavaskar's return to the crease, coupled with strong support from Mohinder Armanath, Ravi Shastri, Kapil Dev and Roger Binny, pushed the score to an imposing 520. Gavaskar passed 9000 Test runs during the course of his 31st century as he gave an outstanding display of

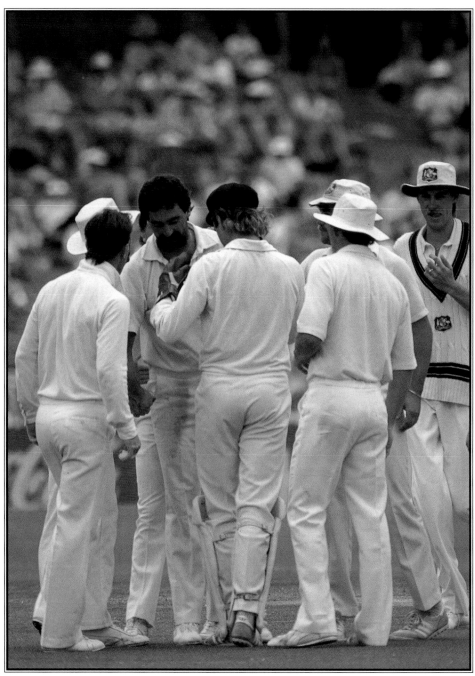

*Congratulations after Hughes' first Test wicket — India's Dilip Vengsarkar, caught by 'keeper Wayne Phillips for 7.*

batsmanship to the inexperienced Australian attack. With Hughes and Reid in their first Test and McDermott in his 11th, the Australians were feasted upon for an unbeaten 166.

As he tired, Hughes slipped onto the opener's pads all too often and the ball kept disappearing through mid-wicket. The fast bowler did suffer with three dropped catches and Border was impressed that Hughes never hid in the outfield at any stage and was always looking to bowl another over.

'When he had the ball in his hand, he was pretty menacing,' Border says. 'Merv started off quite well with good pace and had a little outswing going, but Srikkanth just teed off and Merv found that hard to cope with. I suppose he was trying too hard because it was a Test match, and his figures ended up not being that flattering. Once a few catches went down, that affected his overall results.

'He bowled quite well but there was certainly no indication then of the career he ended up having. Perhaps it was a bonus for him in the long run that he didn't have any instant results and so didn't have immediate pressure on him. It's a lot easier to build your reputation as you go.'

Hughes, in his debut Test, catches Indian tailender Shivlal Yadav, off the bowling of David Hookes.

Gavaskar could certainly bat and Hughes had found Test cricket was a major step up in class, which he had prepared himself for. What he had not expected though, was the level of public scrutiny and the way in which his shortcomings had been exposed so plainly.

Former Test captain-turned-commentator Ian Chappell, who would ride Hughes hard in the first few years of his Test career, was unimpressed with the way his action would fall away in his delivery stride and the ball would slide down leg side. As is Chappell's way, he clearly made his feelings about the new bowler known. From 38 overs, Hughes had finished with a return of 1–123. McDermott and Reid had each been more impressive with 3–131 from 48 overs and 4–113 from 53 overs respectively. Reid, in particular, had been a nugget the Australian selectors had unexpectedly stumbled upon as they searched for bowlers.

Hughes was dropped for the remainder of the summer but he was certainly still in the selectors' minds. His pace had not flagged during his heavy workload and Sawle would not be ruling a line through his name.

'Merv had a pretty tough initiation at Adelaide, which was always a pitch for batsmen at that time,' Sawle says. 'He did it very hard in his first Test but he showed enough for us to retain interest in him. We didn't push him along at that stage but that was a deliberate thing. We put him on hold for a while but we had long-term plans for him.'

Returning to the Victorian side, Hughes would finish his first full season with a more than respectable 37 wickets at 30.40 apiece, picking up his second five-wicket haul at the end of the summer. Bowling against Tasmania in Devonport, he would snare 5–53 to provide some confidence for the 1986–87 season.

Australia held on to draw the series against India, although the elements, rather than the skill of Border's young team, played a much more considerable role in that record. The Indians were just 67 runs short of victory in the second Test at Melbourne when torrential thunderstorms finished the match early.

Hughes would not be selected for the three-Test tour to New Zealand in early February, in which the Australians would lose the series 1–0 and Border would threaten to resign as captain unless performances improved. During the course of those nine Tests over an extended

1985–86 summer, the Test selectors chose 21 separate players to wear the baggy green cap.

It was obvious that such chopping and changing was doing the players no good and the selectors decided that a core group of players had to be chosen around Border and supported for some considerable period.

Former Test captain Bob Simpson had joined the New Zealand tour party as an observer and in 1986 accepted the job as Australia's first national coach. With a long-term plan to rebuild the side now in mind after the nadir of back-to-back losses to New Zealand, Greg Chappell said the Test selectors had firstly decided that Border was captain and those players with team qualities to support the reluctant leader would be preferred.

Among that group was Merv Hughes.

'In the first year that all the players went to South Africa, we tried something like 30-odd players in the Tests and One-dayers combined,' Chappell says. 'It was a high turnover and the realisation came that we couldn't keep doing that because we would obviously unsettle blokes. We had to have a look around and try to find the right sort of talent.

'We wanted not only the physical talent, but guys with good strength of character and the temperament to be able to cope with the travel, life away from home and all the other things that go with being an international cricketer. The initial decision was taken that Border would be the captain and we needed the right sort of people around him who would fully support his role as captain and not look to undermine him in any way.

'The first few guys on that list were Boon and Marsh and it was slowly added to with blokes like Steve Waugh and Merv Hughes. We had a look at a few people and then evaluated who had the best chance of making it. Merv was in that frame and he needed to learn what it was all about from AB and Simmo, and he needed time to develop,' he says.

Hughes would miss selection for Australia's tour to India (traditionally a difficult experience for fast bowlers) in September 1986. In that series, only the second tie in Test match history was played out at Madras, and Dean Jones demanded recognition with an epic knock of 210 in Australia's first innings of that game.

While Australia and India were playing out the third Test of their series at Wankhede Stadium in Bombay during the third week of October, Mike

Gatting's England squad had arrived in Australia. Unlike most previous tours that had begun in either Perth or Adelaide, the Englishmen would meet Queensland in Brisbane prior to heading to Adelaide and Perth for four-day games in each city, before returning to Brisbane for the first Test at the Gabba in mid-November.

Gatting had risen to the captaincy in June of 1986 after India had beaten David Gower's side at Lord's. Gower barely had time to jump before the axe fell after six successive losses under his leadership, five of those at the hands of the all-powerful West Indies in the Caribbean in early 1986.

When Gatting's side arrived in Australia, he had hardly done much better than his predecessor, boasting a record of two losses and three draws in his five matches as skipper. Like Border the previous summer, Gatting had been in charge when New Zealand had claimed their first-ever series victory on English soil.

If Australia was in poor shape, England wasn't doing much better with not a solitary victory from their last 11 Tests — eight unedifying defeats and three draws. However, the prospect of an Ashes series 'down under' raised English hearts, even if Australia felt they were unlikely to be beaten at home.

Coming into 1986–87, England had won four of the previous six Ashes rubbers and had surrounded Gatting with plenty of experienced hard heads — including Gower, Ian Botham, Allan Lamb, John Emburey and Phil Edmonds — for the visit to Australia.

The experience Gatting could call on would prove crucial. England was far from impressive in their lead-up matches and, in fact, were downright ordinary at times. Renowned cricket writer Martin Johnson, of the *Independent*, won a lasting place in history for his summation of how Gatting's side was travelling in their preparation for the Brisbane encounter.

Johnson wrote: 'England have just one problem: they can't bat, they can't bowl and they can't field.'

Hughes had started the season solidly with another five-wicket haul against Tasmania, again in Devonport, while burly left-armer Chris Matthews had destroyed England in the tour game at the WACA Ground.

Of the faster bowlers away on tour in India, only Reid had impressed, with both Gilbert and McDermott struggling terribly on the low, slow wickets. In fact, McDermott hit such a depressing low that he considered quitting as a fast bowler and turning to medium pace. His career, after such a bright start, would oscillate aimlessly until the summer of 1990–91 when a renewed dedication to his fitness would transform him into a spectacular performer.

The accepted theory leading into the first Test was that England was an ageing side still on the slippery slope downwards, whereas Australia had been through its trough and was heading back up the cricket tree. Added to that, the tourists were susceptible to left-armers and the Australian squad contained two: Reid and Matthews. Lawson was included in the XII, despite playing only two games since his return from back problems, but omitted from the XI on the morning of the match.

Border's new ball line-up could boast just nine Tests between them: Reid (eight), Hughes (one) and Matthews (nought). All in all, England could call on 378 Tests' worth of experience compared to Australia's 183, of which Border contributed the lion's share of 84. After Border had won the toss, on a rain-interrupted opening day, the greenish trio wasted the new ball on a typical Gabba wicket and allowed England to reach 2–198 by stumps.

Hughes had dismissed Gatting for 61 and added the scalp of Lamb before a run was added on the second morning, however Australia was worn down by a critical partnership between Gower and Botham. Gower, who was dropped before he had scored, added 51 in a stand of 118 with the great all-rounder, who went on to reach 138. Botham's final Test century led England to a tally of 456 and included a record 22 from one Hughes over, scoring 2, 2, 4, 6, 4 and 4. The faster the Victorian tried to bowl in the over, the further Botham hit him.

Cricketers have a black humour in the darkest times but Hughes was not cheered to hear his team-mate Jones' call when he tossed the ball back to him from mid off after Botham had pulled him for six.

'Geez Merv, that one went so far it should have probably qualified for frequent flyer points.'

From his 36 overs, Hughes returned 3–134, including two top-order wickets, but the only thing that stuck in the minds of everyone at the game was the mauling he had copped from Botham. At the tea break on the second day, Hughes had sat outside the dressing-rooms and considered where his international career was heading.

'I was inexperienced and Both got on top of me. During the break, I got kicked out of our rooms for causing too much trouble and I went and sat in front of the English rooms and was just sitting watching the rain come across the park.

'I was thinking that I played Test cricket but I wasn't a Test cricketer. I was trying to deal with what had happened, when Botham came out and asked how I was going,' Hughes remembers.

'He was at a coaching clinic I was at years before that in 1976–77 and I said, "You probably don't remember this, but I was at a clinic you did at a place called Benalla when you were playing for University, in Melbourne grade cricket".

'He looked at me and couldn't believe it and asked, "Did I pass on any words of wisdom?"

'I told him that back then I said I was right into cricket and wanted to become a fast bowler but he'd told me to give it away and take up tennis or golf because there was a lot more money in it and they were both far more enjoyable.

'He looked at me, stood up, and said, "You should have listened to me," and walked back inside.'

There would be no favours from the England side in an Ashes encounter and no-one was about to make Merv Hughes feel better about his bowling.

In defence of a man in his second Test, Border concedes that his captaincy hardly helped his bowler. Inexperienced as a leader himself, Border did not speak to Hughes at any time during his mauling and did not realise the benefits of trying to slow the over-rate or doing something different to frustrate a rampant Botham. Instead, he dropped his head and kicked the ground, betraying his helplessness to both his team and the opposition.

'We had high expectations after the Poms had had such a shocking lead-up. We were thinking we could turn things around after a couple of ordinary years,' says Border.

'Merv looked in great nick but Both came in and just teed off. I wasn't experienced as captain to cope with those situations. I had become a bit used to our bowling falling by the wayside under pressure, the same as our batting. I would start expecting us to fall over and that was hardly helping anyone. I wasn't confident enough, or upfront enough, to work out another strategy if we were struggling. I should have taken Merv off and perhaps brought myself on with a real deep field and let Both slog and see what happened. At the time, I just didn't think of these things. The faster and harder Merv tried, the further the ball was disappearing and I had no answers myself.'

Australia finished the second day at 1–33 and would be bowled out for 248, failing by 8 runs to avert the follow-on, which was enforced by Gatting.

In Australia's second dig, there was dogged resistance from Marsh (110) but England would be left with only a token target of 75 for victory, getting home with seven wickets in hand.

Hughes would claim the scalps of Bill Athey and Gatting in the second innings to give him a respectable five for the match, and had actually bowled much better than the left-armer Matthews, who had suffered terribly with nerves and sprayed the ball alarmingly.

However, despite some promising signs, the mauling from Botham could not be ignored and Hughes was dropped for the second time in his Test career. Again, he was shattered.

During his flight back to Melbourne, Hughes wondered whether he was up to international class. However, chairman of selectors Sawle remained convinced that Hughes could make it in time. Again, there would not be a line drawn through his name. He would just be removed from the firing line for a period.

'He won a lot of points with the selectors by the fact that he didn't drop his head when Botham was getting into him,' Sawle declares. 'He kept coming in and that convinced us he would be worthy of other chances later on. He was never the most accurate bowler, right from the word go, and often young bowlers that want to be quick don't start off very accurate. We weren't unhappy with his progress, even though he was not a regular member of the side in his early years.'

The view in the English camp was much harsher. Celebrating a 1–0 lead in the Ashes series and his first Test victory as captain, Gatting reveals now that he didn't expect to see Hughes again in Test cricket.

*Hughes' first wicket against England — Mike Gatting, bowled for 61.*

*Ian Botham blazes away during his final Test century, in Brisbane in 1986–87.*

Sure, the fast bowler had claimed Gatting's wicket twice but, because Australia was struggling, the England captain didn't expect the Australian selectors to have much patience with a wayward fast bowler.

'I can't think of any other bowler in my time in Test cricket who copped that bad a mauling early in their careers and came back from it to be a good player,' Gatting says. 'You could see as his over went on, that he was looking at himself and asking, "Where am I going to bowl the next ball?"

'Experienced players are able to cope with a shocking day like this one, which was why I expected Merv to disappear off the scene.'

Hughes missed the drawn second Test in Perth, but the abject failure of Matthews to cope with the mental demands of international cricket saw the Victorian win a recall for the third Test in Adelaide. And, while he was still to make his first Test run after four innings and three Tests, and could boast only eight wickets at almost 48 apiece, Hughes was retained for the fourth Test in Melbourne, starting on Boxing Day. He would play in front of his home crowd for the first time and would play in successive Tests for the first time.

In a pre-match interview for a Melbourne newspaper, Hughes said his two ambitions in cricket were to make a Test run and to play in a winning side. The first goal was a clear sign of the deficiencies in his game and the second of the deficiencies within the Australian team.

In coach Simpson, there was now someone on hand who would work as long and as hard as it took to make Hughes a better player. One thing that could be said of Simpson as soon as he stepped into the job, was that he ran a good practice session and fielding would be the first area in which the Australians should improve.

In Hughes, the coach could see a basic technique with the bat that could be developed. The bowler was embarrassed about his patent lack of results with the willow in the early stages of his career; he did not want to go into the nets at practice, fearing he would look foolish.

Simpson did not brook dissension in the ranks and offered a simple solution. If you don't want to bat at practice, you can run laps in your pads for the 15 minutes you would have spent batting. Hughes quickly acknowledged he would be better off if he went into the nets and set about improving.

Australia needed to win the Boxing Day Test at Melbourne to remain in the hunt for the Ashes and the Australian team resolved to be as positive as possible, attacking the bowling and attempting to take the initiative.

Unfortunately, their tactics backfired horribly with an innings defeat inside three days, forfeiting the Ashes and plunging the Australian side to another low. For Sawle, it was his worst moment in 14 years as a national selector.

'Things were looking very glum after Melbourne because it meant we had lost in 1981, 1985 and 1987 in quick succession to England,' Sawle says. 'That was my lowest point as an Australian selector. Something just had to be done and we needed to start rebuilding from that point. That set our minds — we would stick with that group of players and go with them for several years until they were established in Test cricket.'

Chappell had been impressed by a little-known off-spinner in Peter Taylor and lobbied hard for his inclusion in the final Test, to be played at Sydney. Taylor had caught Chappell's eye with his calmness in a tense situation for New South Wales the previous summer, and he was duly plucked from obscurity and named in the senior side.

Otherwise, the basics of a team for the years ahead had been put in place with Boon, Marsh and Steve Waugh surrounding Border in the batting line-up and Hughes and Reid nominated to fill two of the bowling positions.

Gatting declared that England desperately did not want to lose a major match on tour, but it can never be known whether his party subconsciously relaxed for the final Test. Regardless, Australia clinched a dramatic victory in the penultimate over on the final day when Peter Sleep bowled John Emburey with a skidding leg break.

Opinions within the team vary as to the significance of a hard-fought win over a good England side coming in a dead Test match. Some, such as Steve Waugh, viewed the result as immaterial, because the Ashes had been lost, while others, particularly Border and Sawle, took the victory as a major boost. It was Border's first win in 14 Tests and it renewed his spirit for the challenge of leading Australia. To that point, Border had led Australia in five full series, losing three and drawing two. Every morsel of success was cherished.

'The Poms were a good side then and we weren't experiencing much success. We'd win the odd One-day game but we had nothing in

**Above:** *English 'keeper Jack Richards (far right) and John Emburey appeal for the wicket of Hughes during the Victorian's first Test at the MCG, in December 1986.*

**Over page:** *The Australians celebrate a Hughes wicket in Sydney, during their only Test victory of 1986–87. Left to right: Dean Jones, Allan Border, Steve Waugh, Peter Taylor, Dirk Wellham (obscured), Tim Zoehrer, Hughes and Geoff Marsh.*

Test cricket. It was like we'd won the bloody series because we'd battled for a couple of years without any result. It felt great to beat a good side, even if the series was gone and I think that was a catalyst,' comments Border.

For a few members of the side (namely Jones, Marsh, Reid and Waugh), all had played in a loss, a draw and an incredibly rare tie for Australia before they had experienced the fourth result of a Test match — a victory.

Hughes would return to the Victorian side determined to finish the season strongly, after being passed over for January's One-day circuit. To play four Tests in a summer had been a major step forward and he could not afford to lose ground by slipping back into the pack with poor performances in Shield cricket. He would not disappoint himself or the Test selectors.

Playing against Tasmania at the Melbourne Cricket Ground over the Australia Day long weekend, he would return figures of 5–61 and 5–73

for the first 10-wicket bag of his career. Bowling with sustained pace for almost 60 overs for the match, Hughes also showed renewed control to lead Victoria to a six-wicket victory.

After several lean seasons at the foot of the Shield table, Victoria had risen to second position after their win over Tasmania, competing with Queensland for the right to meet runaway leaders Western Australia in the final.

Though Victoria would not secure a single point from their final three Shield matches, a traditional late-season collapse from Queensland saw Victoria earn the right to contest their first final, in Perth, to round out the season.

Western Australia had been outstanding under the captaincy of the newly-appointed Graeme Wood, winning six of their 10 matches outright and finishing a massive three outright wins clear of Victoria in second place. For Victoria to annex their first Shield title since 1979–80, they needed every ounce of luck to go their way.

When Hughes was shown this photo he replied with a smile, 'Almost the perfect dismissal, except his head wasn't in the helmet!' He quickly added, though, that the batsman, Western Australia's Mike Veletta (who was given out 'hit wicket'), is 'a real good bloke'.

The portents had not been good in the lead-up to the match, with Jones severely injuring a knee after a training accident involving Hughes. Jones remembers that the only team-mate to visit him in hospital, while he readied himself for an operation that would rule him out of the final, was Hughes.

On a benign pitch, Victoria reached 8–404 on the second afternoon before declaring their innings closed. As Hughes prepared to bowl the first over of the Western Australian innings, he called across to Tony Dodemaide at mid on for a bit of advice.

'Hey Dodders, is Swamp [Geoff Marsh] the guy we pitch shortish to over the off-stump and Waggy [Mike Veletta] the bloke we go just outside off-stump, or is it the other way around?' he asked.

Delaying the game for a minute or so, Dodemaide came across to Hughes and re-affirmed the match plans that had been talked through at the team meeting on match eve. He should not have bothered, as Hughes was drawing him in for a sucker punch.

'Fuck it. I'll just bounce both of them.'

Western Australia, led by Veletta and backed by Marsh, Wood and Tom Moody, would grind Victoria into the WACA pitch over the next three days. Victoria would spend almost three days in the field as Western Australia compiled their highest-ever first-class score of 654, thanks largely to Veletta's epic 12-hour knock of 262. Hughes would work through a marathon 42 overs for the innings, charging in relentlessly.

The opener stood up to everything thrown at him by the Victorian bowlers, as well as some considerable sledging from the field. The contest would do much for the reputation of both players. Veletta would win a tour spot to India and Pakistan for the World Cup later that year, while Hughes' whole-heartedness, even in the most trying circumstances, had impressed all who knew that Victoria was fighting a lost cause in this match.

In 15 first-class matches for the 1986–87 season, Hughes had taken 57 wickets at 28.47, including three separate hauls of five in an innings. While he would not be touring the sub-continent for the World Cup, the next challenge was to convert improved results at a domestic level into similar achievements for Australia.

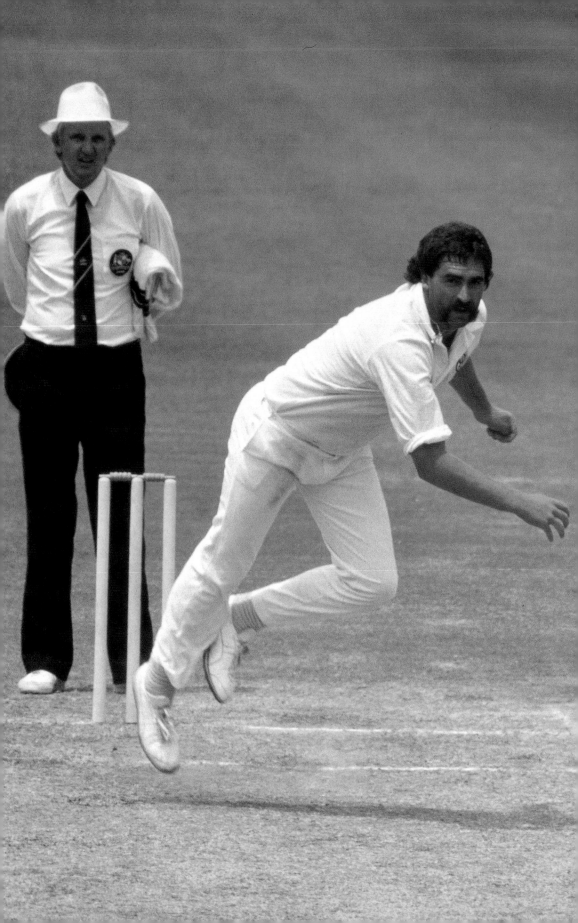

# CHAPTER FIVE

# HE THINKS HE'S A FAST BOWLER

The Australian season of 1987–88 had its latest start for some years, with the opening Sheffield Shield match of the season not scheduled until the second week of November.

Since the end of World Series Cricket in 1979–80, Australian fans had become used to getting their first cricket fixes by late October at the very least, with a Test match beamed around the nation by the middle of the 11th month.

The reason for the delayed start to Merv Hughes' seventh season of first-class cricket was the small matter of the fourth One-day World Cup, being played outside of England for the first time across the sub-continent.

Australia, despite being drawn in the weaker half of the draw with New Zealand, Zimbabwe and pre-tournament favourite India, was rated a 16–1 rank outsider to lift the trophy — unlikely to pose much of a problem in the semi-final stages if they managed to qualify in second place ahead of the Kiwis.

While home crowds in India and Pakistan prayed for the two host countries to set up a 'Dream Final', world cricket's pundits did acknowledge the chances of the West Indies and maybe even the experienced England side to upset the apple-cart. Australia was not in the frame.

By 1987, however, Australia had experienced some success in the One-day arena, even if Test victories were few and far between. Captain Allan Border and coach Bob Simpson had come to the realisation that One-day cricket was, essentially, a defensive game and the adherence to

*Opposite: Hughes in Sydney, fifth Ashes Test, 1986–87.*

a well-planned strategy would give a team an excellent chance of taking the tournament. Simpson's belief, from which he would never waver during his 10-year tenure as Australian coach, was that the team that took the most singles in a One-dayer would invariably win the match.

Slick running between the wickets had been the feature of Simpson's days as an Australian opener, particularly when paired with Bill Lawry, and the Australians were drilled remorselessly about the value of rotating the strike as often as possible. Four well-run singles put exactly the same number of runs on the board as one booming, crowd-pleasing drive to the boundary and provided the added bonus of frustrating a bowler's efforts to settle into a rhythmic line and length.

David Boon and Geoff Marsh were now a settled and successful pair at the top of the order while the electric Dean Jones, at number three, seemed born to play One-day cricket, with his frenetic strokeplay and peerless running between wickets.

Australia would win five of their six qualifying matches to march into the semi-finals, and then sent the whole of Pakistan into mourning with an upset 18-run win over the home side in the semi-final at Gaddafi Stadium in Lahore. The next day, India was plunged into a similar crisis when England defied the odds to reach their second final.

On November 8, 1987, there was finally real solace for Border as Australian captain when he was able to grasp the World Cup. After almost three years of heartache, the gutsy left-hander was able to bask in some well-deserved glory.

Border's next target would be his first victory in a Test series, preferably as soon as possible with the arrival of New Zealand in Australia in a fortnight's time.

New Zealand had twice won the Trans-Tasman trophy in the space of four months in 1985–86, thanks largely to the brilliance of Richard Hadlee. Hadlee had terrorised the young batting line-up and he had to be overcome. However, the New Zealand batting line-up also contained a young master in Martin Crowe.

Crowe had scored a superb 188 in the opening Test at the Gabba two years earlier, and, in 1987, would become the first batsman since English champion Len Hutton in 1948 to score 4000 first-class runs in a calendar year.

Crowe and Hadlee plagued Border's thoughts as he planned his strategy for the three-Test series, to be decided before the New Year. In early 1988, England would play a one-off Test in Sydney to celebrate the Australian Bicentennial and minnows Sri Lanka had been granted a Test at Perth to conclude the season.

While Hughes was not a factor in One-day discussions, he was still among the first three pacemen in the country, replacing Victorian team-mate Simon O'Donnell in the Australian line-up when the format switched from one-day to five-day cricket. O'Donnell would, in fact, miss the entire 1987–88 season after being diagnosed with lymphoma following his part in the World Cup win.

The Australians gathered in Brisbane in the first week of December for the opening Test match. Discussion of Hadlee and Crowe dominated the Australian team's tactics meeting the night before the match. Against Hadlee, it was imperative for the batsmen to leave as many deliveries as possible and frustrate the bowler by leaving many of his efforts

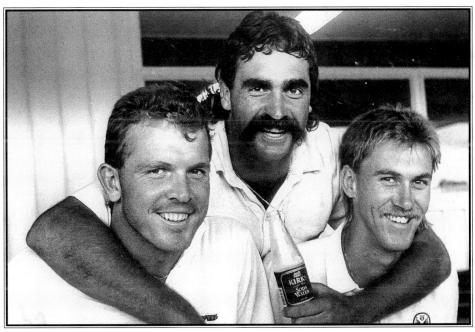

Craig McDermott (left), Merv Hughes and Bruce Reid, after the trio had reduced New Zealand to 9–181 on the opening day of the first Test of 1987–88, at the Gabba.

unrewarded. In regard to Crowe, the bowlers could not afford to pitch short because he would destroy them, either through the off side with the cut shot or on the leg side with powerful hooks and pulls.

Border sent the Kiwis into bat on a slightly under-prepared wicket and was thrilled to have the visitors reeling at 9–181 by the close. Bruce Reid and Craig McDermott had used the new ball well to secure early wickets while Hughes had backed them with 18 bustling overs, returning 3–40.

The Victorian had stubborn opener John Wright caught behind by Greg Dyer and also pocketed the dangerous Hadlee for 8, who had threatened to try to take the attack up to the bowling. Most importantly though, he accounted for Crowe for 67, who was comfortably the top-scorer for New Zealand and one of only two batsmen to pass 20 for the innings.

Crowe had never encountered anyone with Hughes' presence at the crease and the fast bowler's non-stop chatter had got under the outstanding batsman's skin. In his third year as an international player, Hughes was now unafraid to offer a few well-chosen words of abuse to a batsman and Crowe was decidedly peeved by his approach.

Martin Crowe, New Zealand's best batsman of the modern era.

How could someone, in just his sixth Test, have the gall to start sledging a batsman who was averaging almost 80 for the year and had the skills to destroy the Australian side if he was fired up by someone foolish enough to motivate him?

As it turned out, Hughes got Crowe so out of his rhythm as a batsman that he smashed a poor, wide delivery straight to Steve Waugh at point. As he walked from the field to the dressing-rooms, Crowe cursed himself for being taken in so badly.

'It was always frustrating to get out

to Merv because his antics would always annoy you. He would have the whole package when he was bowling: with stares, the odd swear word, the presence and everything he could possibly do to try to get you out. It was annoying to get out to him because he would get you out with his personality as much as anything, and that used to annoy me immensely. He was the sort of bowler that I just wanted to smash around the park because of his approach,' says Crowe.

By trying to smash him through cover for his 10th boundary, Crowe had paid the price of losing his wicket and condemning New Zealand to a total below 200.

Just as Hadlee depended so much on his rhythm as a bowler, Crowe was the same with the bat. He liked to retreat into his shell and worry only about what he was doing, shutting out the crowd, the conditions and the opposition. Here, in Hughes, was a bowler that he couldn't seem to keep out of his head.

'I liked playing against competitors like him because I'm a very competitive person,' Crowe continues. 'When he was carrying on with his stuff, I would stay in my shell and just steel myself to get on top of him as a way of shutting him up. Consequently, when a bad ball came along, I was perhaps overconscious of taking advantage of it and got myself out a few times. I wanted to dominate him to try to shut him up, but would occasionally end up getting out and he would win the battle. I would get so angry with what he was doing but it was working in that he changed my mental approach. To get me out was all the more galling because I had fallen into the trap.'

Chasing a meagre total of 186, Boon nearly eclipsed the New Zealand innings single-handedly with a superb knock of 143. While Boon did not have enormous support, there was enough from the other batsmen to lift Australia to 305 and a lead of 119. Boon had been enormously disciplined in leaving Hadlee's wider balls alone, forcing the great New Zealander to work through 31 overs for a return of only three wickets. The Tasmanian had been dropped against England in 1986–87 and his century, coming upon an outstanding World Cup, represented a triumph.

Border again stressed to his team the need to bowl tightly to Crowe, and felt confident of a victory to open the series. Crowe had reached 19 when

Hughes dropped short and was pulled for four. He gave the batsman a choice word or two, to which Crowe offered no response, but he steamed on the inside.

In slips, Border called up to his bowler not to pitch short again. Sure enough, the next ball was short and Crowe felt compelled to hook this upstart who would not shut up. Not quite inside the line, the catch flew comfortably to Dean Jones at square leg and Australia was well on the way to victory.

Border went straight to Hughes in the celebratory huddle. 'Don't you ever bloody listen at the team meetings? What did I tell you about bowling short to this bloke?' Border demanded, half-seriously and half-pleased with the result.

'You didn't mean *my* bouncers did you? I thought you just meant Billy (McDermott) and Chook (Reid) because they don't bowl them as well as me,' Hughes replied straight-faced.

Border had no answer.

As for Crowe, he had been sucker-punched a second time by someone he did not rate in his class as a cricketer.

'I was in real good nick both times and felt I had thrown away two really big innings. I tried to dominate him and got out twice by letting him distract me. What I eventually decided on, was that I had to put him out of my thoughts and stay in rhythm. I learnt that that was the best way to get the best out of myself, and Merv obviously knew straight away he had to distract me from that.

'He was certainly a thinking bowler in his different approach to various players to get them out of their preferred mode of batting. He could also bowl spells that, technically, would test me a lot.'

While Crowe would be annoyed immensely by Hughes' 'rural' approach to international cricket with his sledging and staring, he would be surprised again when he met the man off-field. After Australia completed a nine-wicket victory on the fourth day, Hughes was among the first into the New Zealand rooms to console the losers. The New Zealanders were impressed.

From Brisbane, the two sides headed directly to Adelaide to be confronted by a flat, brown wicket for the second Test and forecast temperatures above the old century mark on each day. Off-spinner Tim May had been drafted into the squad to support Peter Sleep and one of the pacemen from Brisbane would be squeezed out. Hughes had taken five wickets for the game, including the key scalp of Crowe twice, but would be the fall guy.

Reid and McDermott, who had played in the World Cup victory in Calcutta, had taken six and seven wickets respectively at the Gabba, and Hughes would, unluckily, be relegated to 12th man. He would end up fielding for two and a half days anyway, in the enervating heat, after Reid broke down with back problems inside the first hour of the opening day. (Reid would not play for three months and would play just one further Shield match for the season, in early March, during a 12-month rehabilitation from his first back complaint.)

Crowe, now free to build a cocoon that would not be disturbed by any of the other remaining fit Australian bowlers, would reach 137 in an imposing New Zealand total of 9–485. Australia replied with an equally mountainous 496 as the match drifted to a dull conclusion.

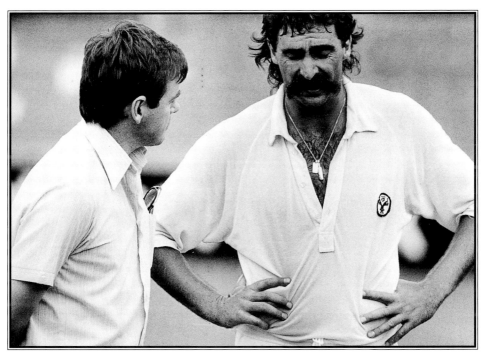

*Hughes and Australian selector Jim Higgs discuss the result of the fitness test that led to the fast bowler pulling out of the third Test against New Zealand in 1987–88.*

The only solace from the encounter was for the statisticians to record Border's ascension to top position on the all-time Australian Test-run list, surpassing Sir Donald Bradman (6996) and Greg Chappell (7110) during the course of his career-best 205.

Reid's unfortunate demise through injury had certainly opened up one spot in the Australian side for the third Test in Melbourne, and there was likely to be a second position up for grabs as well, given that two spinners were hardly likely to play at the MCG. Hughes would have the chance to impress against a full-strength New South Wales side at the SCG immediately before Christmas to decide if he warranted a return to the line-up.

Steve Waugh (170) and Mark Waugh (114 not out) highlighted a rain-affected encounter that did more to harm Hughes' Test chances than assist them. After 10 overs, he left the field with a damaged hamstring and would not bowl again for the match. With Victoria down a bowler, all-rounder Tony Dodemaide had to shoulder a considerable load and responded courageously by working through 45 overs for a haul of 5–114. Dodemaide had already had extra responsibility thrust upon him by Victoria in the absence of O'Donnell and his performance drew the attention of the national selectors.

Hughes was named in the XII for the Boxing Day Test, joined by the recalled Mike Whitney, but Dodemaide would stand by as 13th man in case Hughes' dodgy hamstring ruled him out.

Hughes had not been affected by leg muscle problems since his early days in first-class cricket and was unsure how to gauge his recovery in the lead-up to the Test. The advice of team physiotherapist Errol Alcott would be crucial as he could not afford to break down early in the match and leave Australia a bowler short (as had happened to the team in the previous Test in Adelaide when Reid departed the field).

Hughes bowled at full pace in the nets on Christmas Eve and again on Christmas Day, as Australia prepared to defend a 1–0 lead in the rubber, looking for Border's first series victory as captain. On Boxing Day, when the match was to begin, he felt some stiffness in the leg. Alcott felt Hughes should be able to get through the game, as some pain was to be expected during his recovery, but could not offer a 100 per cent guarantee against injury. There would always be the chance that the muscle could go again during the match.

Not yet consolidated in the Australian side, many would have been tempted to risk the leg and hope for the best. Hughes, however, would put the team before himself and withdrew, allowing Dodemaide to make his debut.

Dodemaide would prove a spectacular success, scoring an even half-century in his debut innings and bagging 6–58 in the New Zealand second innings — catapulting himself into the One-day side in the process.

Yet again, as part of the Test team but not of the One-day circuit, Hughes would be sent back to Shield cricket in early January of 1988 to prove that he was worth a spot in the side for the Bicentennial Test. McDermott, still riding on the crest of an excellent World Cup before losing his way again, was still ahead of Hughes, as now were Dodemaide and Whitney.

Returning to a Victorian side due to meet Western Australia in Perth, Hughes expected an open-armed welcome for the challenge of facing the

*Victorian all-rounder Tony Dodemaide during his Test debut, against New Zealand at the MCG.*

Sandgropers, who were well on the way to back-to-back titles. Instead, he was questioned as to his commitment to his State.

On the flight heading to Perth, close friend Jamie Siddons decided Hughes needed a rev-up. To that point of the season, the big fast bowler had taken just seven wickets for Victoria at 31 apiece, when his State needed him to be leading from the front, as he had in 1986–87.

Siddons struck a raw nerve when he questioned Hughes about his commitment to the Victorian team. Now that he was comfortable playing for Australia, did Victoria still matter to him?

To compound Hughes' anger, Siddons wanted to know why he seemed to be so nice on the field when bowling to his 'new Australian mates'. Where was the old Merv Hughes, the money man who delivered for Victoria in tight situations?

If ever a rev worked, it was this one. Dodemaide has never seen Hughes so angry, either before or since.

'Jamie didn't take any shit and Merv, being a country guy himself, respected what Jamie had to say,' Dodemaide says. 'For Jamie to have a go at him cut deeply.'

After an angry confrontation with Siddons during the flight, Hughes cut a swathe through the Western Australian top-order. Opener Mark McPhee was forced to retire hurt after being hit above the eye, opening a deep wound, while Greg Shipperd and Tom Moody were pounded on the body during brief stays for 17 apiece.

Captain Graeme Wood had his hand broken, but doggedly remained at the crease, while the sight of returned rebel captain Kim Hughes, batting in a cap no less, lifted Hughes to new heights. Hughes parted his namesake's hair with his first ball and then bounced him again, to which the elder Hughes swung an exploratory bat and top-edged a six straight over the wicket-keeper's head. No contemporary of Kim Hughes ever doubted his courage against fast bowling, but many questioned the sense of him then calling down the wicket, 'Forget it Merv, you're bowling to the big boys now.'

In Merv's following over, Kim would be trapped lbw for 7 and the bowler would not have time to get in a send-off, beaten to the punch by the entire slip cordon.

Siddons had never stood as far back from a bowler in his career and was pleased to see his mate back on track.

'We were on a flight to Perth and I just felt that he was getting a bit comfortable now that he was at the next level,' Siddons says. 'I got into him after he hadn't done that well in a game against New South Wales and asked him if the reason why he wouldn't fire up any more was because it would upset his Australian mates. I said that the mean Merv Hughes had disappeared and he really took it personally.

'He takes Victorian cricket very seriously and he spat it at me and gave me a huge spray. He bowled the quickest spell I've ever seen and, after each over, he kept telling us, "I'll give you friendly. I'll show you. I'll kill someone in this game".

'He hit Mark McPhee in the eye and split him open. As McPhee was lying on the ground, with blood everywhere, Merv walked up, looked at him and said, "He's not dead", so he grabbed the ball and waited at the top of his mark while the stretcher came out. We were a pitch and a half back from the stumps in the slip cordon and he was terrifying.'

The spell was enough for chairman of selectors Lawrie Sawle to be convinced that Hughes should be included in the XII for Sydney. Unfortunately though, two spinners would again be used in Sydney and the paceman was stuck carrying the drinks behind the preferred new ball duo of McDermott and Dodemaide.

A lay-off of almost a month, with just one first-class game in that period, was not good for the Hughes condition. He would stack on something like five kilograms during the period from lack of work, raising the first of real concerns for team management about his size.

Added to that, he was unable to be contained in the dressing-rooms, with so little to occupy his time — threatening to drive everyone mad. At the time of the Bicentennial Test, the second *Nightmare on Elm Street* horror movie had hit the big screen and Hughes was a devoted fan of the anti-hero, Freddy Kreuger. During the third morning's play, as Australia began their first innings, Hughes spent an hour using all of physiotherapist Errol Alcott's adhesive bandaging tape to secure five knives to his hand and create a shredding glove, just like the one made famous by Kreuger in the *Nightmare* movies.

After five minutes or so of 'slashing' at the waiting padded-up batsmen, he was banished to the toilets by Border and Simpson. The arrival of Prime Minister Bob Hawke, just over 10 minutes later, to greet the team during the lunch break saw one nameless Australian player meet the nation's leader with one hand held firmly behind his back.

By the time the fifth Test of the summer arrived in mid-February, against a weak Sri Lankan side in Perth, Hughes was obviously overweight. He had played just two first-class games since Christmas and the two stints as 12th man had seen his condition deteriorate dramatically.

Erroll Alcott recalls, 'The Test against Sri Lanka was the start of Merv's ballooning-out period. He loved the good times and when he would celebrate it wasn't just with drink, he would eat an enormous amount and then stick two Coronas down his gob at the same time. It was a crucial time in his career and I was trying to tell him this. He was enjoying the accolades of cricket and the benefits it was bringing, but you could see he was going to go for a downhill run at some point.

'We had come back from the sub-continent as World Cup champions and we now had some things in place to develop a good cricket team. It was an important time for him to show he wanted to be a part of that. He was a real talent man and a real heart man but he obviously hadn't kept up with what we had been doing while we were away. He was behind, and that showed up badly during that Test.'

A bouncy Perth wicket guaranteed Hughes a place in the final XI ahead of leg-spinner Sleep. Captain Border would be on edge throughout the match, despite a massive victory by an innings and 108 runs. Border would later liken the poorly-attended Test to a 'club match' and he was unhappy with a number of things during the three-and-a-bit days it took to wrap up proceedings.

Little things over the course of the Test brought the captain's occasionally volcanic temper to the boil. He made 88 himself but was furious to be bowled off an inside edge when he had the attack at his mercy during a 156-run partnership with Jones.

Later, Jones was on 98 in the final over of the day and had been tied down by some tight bowling. Rather than wait for the following day to

*Hughes (far right) gleefully explains the intricacies of a catch taken against Sri Lanka at the WACA in early 1988. His team-mates are (left to right): Greg Dyer, Dean Jones, Mike Veletta, Peter Sleep (with back to camera) and David Boon.*

score his hundred, the impetuous Jones launched a slog and was fortunate to be dropped, scoring two runs for his ton.

On the second day, Waugh flayed a bat at a wide delivery and departed for 20, causing Border to feel the young New South Welshman wasn't too worried if he was dismissed because the team already had nearly 400 on the board.

Finally, the attitude of the Australians in the field, as they dismissed Sri Lanka for 194 and 153, was decidedly blasé. One of the offenders was Merv Hughes.

Upon taking his fourth wicket in the second innings, Hughes joked in the Australian huddle about how disappointed he was to have taken three wickets in two overs on the fourth morning. The selectors would now probably pick him to go to Pakistan.

Border failed to see the joke.

Hughes would also claim the last wicket to fall to finish with 5–67 from 21 overs, his first five-wicket haul for Australia against a batting line-up patently unable to cope with the extra bounce in the wicket and the searing hip-to-heart bowling. However, much of his bowling was also directed down leg side and the Sri Lankan batsmen were happy to sway inside the line of the ball, thankful that another rearing delivery was posing no danger to life or limb.

A West Indian batsman would have been a different proposition and, up in the commentary box, Ian Chappell was unimpressed with what he was seeing. Memorably he would declare, 'The trouble with Merv Hughes is that he thinks he's a fast bowler,' as yet another ball speared down the leg side.

Hughes never forgot the criticism and it would return to haunt Chappell within the year. In the former captain's defence, he was not slighting Hughes' efforts, but rather what he was doing with the ball. Chappell's belief was that Hughes needed to be accurate and pressure batsmen relentlessly, rather than provide them with so many chances to score.

'In his early days, Merv would lay back and bowl the ball onto the pads a hell of a lot. I didn't see him as a strike bowler. When I first saw him in Test cricket, I didn't think he was that quick, that he could have blokes hopping around, but he certainly became that type of bowler. At the pace he was bowling when I first saw him, and being so inaccurate, I felt he should bowl in the same sort of style as Max Walker,' Chappell says.

The Australians had finished the summer 1–0 winners over New Zealand, winners over Sri Lanka and had managed a draw with England. For a side who had been previously starved of success, they were pleased to have played a summer at home without defeat for the first time since 1983–84.

The realist in Border though, could see that his side had been lucky to hold out the New Zealanders in the Boxing Day Test, had the worst of the drawn Test against England and hadn't proved anything at all against Sri Lanka.

In the hotel bar, and at his post-match press conference, the Australian captain boiled over. As his team sipped a few celebratory beers, Border launched a tirade at Jones, Hughes and Waugh.

He told Jones he was 'unrepentant', and should have put his head down to grind out a big century rather than slog recklessly in the 90s and risk giving away his hand. Waugh should do more for the Australian team and not just coast along offering glimpses of his rich potential. Hughes was plainly unfit and obviously not putting in the work to be a Test cricketer.

With the home team dressing-rooms now silent, the captain went upstairs and repeated his views to the press corps at the post-match press conference.

The journalists, bored by three days of writing about a one-sided Test the public had little interest in, were now presented with a red-hot news story — the captain of Australia blasting three of his players — and justifiably ran with it for several days.

Border does not regret what he said, only the fact that he took it outside the dressing-rooms:

'I realised in that Test that the media was not the right place to air your problems with a player. I should have just sorted it out with Merv and never taken it to the press. I gave Jones and Steve Waugh a bit of a bake as well. I thought Jones was irresponsible and I wanted Steve to take a greater role in Test cricket. I told the blokes to their faces but I shouldn't have gone to the media.

'I wanted more from Merv because I thought he was mucking around on the fringe of Test cricket,' Border says. 'I wanted him to get serious about it because there was too much "good times" involved in his preparation, and I wanted him to become a good Test cricketer.

'I wanted a good team and I was getting frustrated that guys weren't playing as well as I thought they could. I felt uncomfortable I had done it that way, but those three players turned out to be pretty handy cricketers for Australia from that period on.

'The good thing for me was that Merv is the most loyal bloke in the world. It bothered me that I had upset him but thank God he took it the right way.'

Waugh concedes he was enormously unhappy with Border for making his shortcomings public and felt betrayed for some months. In the long run, though, he says the captain got it right.

'After reading what was in the press, I wasn't sure what was going to happen to me,' Waugh says. 'It's always a dent to the ego to have bad things said about you in the press, and having it come from the captain was a tough pill. That was his way of saying what we had to do to become better Test cricketers, but I didn't take it that way at the time. I was really shitty and it annoyed me for a while but, looking back, it did me a favour and made me a better cricketer.'

Jones concurs. He can see the reasoning as he has grown older, but didn't at the time: 'I had a poor series and Merv had been hot and cold and AB didn't want one-off performances out of us.'

Hughes copped the worst criticism of the trio, however his respect for Border was such that his words were a wake-up call. He resolved to do the best pre-season of his cricket career. He would also quit alcohol for the winter and beyond, into the 1988–89 season, to ensure his weight was kept under control.

'AB pulled the three of us in and said, "I've got something to say about how I think you can improve". He said I had a future in the game but it was up to me.

'My first reaction was, "Allan Border's the boss and if he wants me to do something, I've got to do it",' Hughes says.

While Hughes had been given a clarion call regarding his long-term future in Australian cricket, the die had been cast in the short-term by the Test in Perth. Team management was far from impressed with his size. After playing four Tests against England in 1986–87, Hughes' status as a Test cricketer should have increased this summer, but it had not.

Instead, he had gained weight and played just two of a possible five Test matches, albeit taking his first five-wicket haul in one game. Injury had played a part in his absence from the Boxing Day Test match, but there was concern within team management about how committed he was to playing for Australia. Merv Hughes needed to show the hierarchy in Australian cricket he was serious about being a Test player.

The recommendation from Alcott, as team physiotherapist, to the national selectors was that Hughes should not be selected for the tour to Pakistan in September 1988.

'He was definitely not picked for the 1988 tour of Pakistan because of his size,' Alcott says. 'That was an issue for team management. I think the selectors realised pretty early on he was the kind of person who responded to a challenge, and they gave him a challenge by leaving him out of a tour. He responded to that by coming back stronger the following summer.'

Chairman of selectors Lawrie Sawle and fellow selector Greg Chappell both confirm that Hughes' size at the end of the 1987–88 season was a major issue with the selection panel.

'It wouldn't be any secret that Merv's bulk and size was always a problem,' Sawle says. 'While he performed, things were rosy but, when he didn't perform very well, he was exposed very quickly.

'AB gave him a barrel after the Perth Test and I thought Merv deserved that. The selectors were worried at the time and our interest had started to wane a bit because of his size. He had built up our hopes a bit, so we were pretty disappointed in him during that summer. He wasn't considered for Pakistan because of that.'

Chappell said the panel also felt, collectively, that the conditions in Pakistan would not suit a bowler of Hughes' style. Chappell had led the 1980 side to Pakistan and remembered how pitches had been doctored to blunt the effectiveness of Dennis Lillee, who managed just three wickets in three Tests. Chappell had declined to tour in 1982 but fellow fast bowlers Geoff Lawson and Jeff Thomson had suffered similarly bleak tours.

Hughes was a 'bang-in' bowler who relied on lift from the wicket to be an effective force and there was the worry he would be cannon-fodder.

Chappell comments, 'It was a combination of his size and the expectation of the conditions over there that saw him left out for Pakistan. It's a different thing in Perth where the ball is coming up chest-high and can still be a wicket ball. Guys can be intimidated with that sort of bowling, but to do it in Pakistan he would have been pasted from one end of the ground to the other. He had to get his act together and get fitter, or he would find that his career would be pretty short.'

The touring team to head to Pakistan would not be named until later in the year, well after Hughes had begun a rigorous preparation for the 1988–89 season.

The selectors were sweating on the health of left-armer Bruce Reid, hoping his lay-off would enable him to tour in September of that year. The spindly West Australian had played just one Shield game in early March after breaking down in December, nevertheless reports from Perth indicated his lay-off was going well.

If fit, Reid would be a certainty and someone would be squeezed out of the side. Speculation was rife that other changes could be made to the squad, particularly behind the stumps where wicket-keeper Greg Dyer had endured a horrid finish to the 1987–88 year.

Dyer had assumed the job from Tim Zoehrer for the 1987 World Cup tour but his season had been a nightmare from the moment he claimed a catch to dismiss New Zealander Andrew Jones during the Boxing Day Test. Replays showed the ball had clearly bounced and Dyer found himself under intense scrutiny.

Hughes and his close friend, Victorian wicket-keeper Michael Dimattina, were heading to Robinvale in north-eastern Victoria for the wedding of Jamie Siddons when the 15-man touring team was announced. Dimattina fancied his chances of replacing Dyer while Hughes was sweating on the possibility of his first overseas tour.

After captain Allan Border and vice-captain Geoff Marsh, the names were read in alphabetical order: David Boon, Tony Dodemaide, Ian Healy, Dean Jones, Craig McDermott, Tim May, Bruce Reid, Jamie Siddons, Peter Sleep, Peter Taylor, Michael Veletta, Steve Waugh, Graeme Wood.

'Ian fucking who?' was Hughes' incredulous reaction. Listening intently for the letter 'H' to hear his own name, he had nearly driven off the road when Healy's name was read.

Dimattina had expected his stiffest competition to come from Zoehrer or perhaps Queenslander Peter Anderson, not a replacement who had played a mere six first-class games to that point. As it happened, the Australian selectors struck upon another piece to fit in their long-term puzzle.

Reid had obviously forced Hughes out of the line-up and the disappointment of missing a tour to the sub-continent was extreme. The belief that Hughes was not suited to pitches in Sri Lanka, India and Pakistan would not change throughout his career. The only tour to that part of the world he would make would be the 1989 Nehru Cup visit to India, a short two-and-a-half week sojourn for five One-day matches.

'I knew then that I wasn't there yet as an Australian player,' Hughes recalls. 'I'm just disappointed in the career that I've had that I didn't go to the sub-continent once for a Test tour. But once I got left out, I knew I was going to be left behind as a possible Australian player if I didn't perform.'

As it turned out, the tour might not have been a bad one to miss. Australia lost the three-Test series 1–0, and the visit was every bit as rancorous as England's infamous tour had been a year before, with claims of poor umpiring and shoddy pitch preparation during the first Test at Karachi.

Siddons would impress with a dashing knock of 32 in his only One-day international, before being caught brilliantly at point, but would get so sick right at the end of the tour that he would not recover for more than 12 months.

At that time, Siddons was on the verge of national selection in the middle-order, however an average year in 1988–89 pushed him right back into the pack and cost him a tour of England the next year. His career never recovered.

McDermott would not play a Test for the entire tour and would struggle terribly with his fitness and confidence. Once dropped, yet again, during the summer of 1988–89, he would disappear from Australian selection for almost two years.

Reid would perform bravely as the side's strike bowler, taking 14 wickets in the three Tests, despite suffering terribly from dropped catches. However, with Australia on the verge of victory in the third and final Test at Lahore, Reid would again break down with back problems, ruling him out for much of the next two seasons.

Australia now had to face the all-powerful West Indies, undisputed champions of the world. Joel Garner and Michael Holding had retired since Australia had last met the West Indies in 1984–85 but Malcolm Marshall, the Windies' great paceman, was at the height of his powers. Viv Richards' squad also contained a spindly young quick by the name of Curtly Ambrose.

Little was known about Ambrose in his first year of first-class cricket, but good judges in the Caribbean expected him to go a long way. It would be a challenging season for the Australians.

# MERV MANIA!

The eighties was cricket's decade of fire and it was ruled by the West Indies. From March 1980, after leaving New Zealand, through to December 31, 1989, the Caribbean masters would not lose a single Test series as they regularly demolished all opposition that confronted them. The game-plan was simple — based around an imposing batting line-up capable of scoring at a run-a-minute and relentless fast bowling that battered both the bodies and the resolve of the opposition.

Three key prongs in the Windies' batting order were present through the entire decade: Gordon Greenidge, Desmond Haynes and Viv Richards, while the retirement of Clive Lloyd in 1984 was salvaged by the emergence of Richie Richardson at the same time.

Equal depth in the bowling ranks saw 1970s stars such as Andy Roberts, Michael Holding, Colin Croft and Joel Garner gradually joined, and then replaced, by the incomparable Malcolm Marshall and his proteges Courtney Walsh and Curtly Ambrose.

In support was a fielding and catching unit that has rarely been equalled in the history of international cricket. Under Lloyd, firstly, and then Richards, the West Indies would have no serious contenders to their crown until well into the 1990s. While sides would occasionally rise and consider themselves capable of stretching the champions, the challenge was always met and invariably put down without mercy.

Australia, on home soil, felt they had some chance of regaining the

*Opposite: Hughes at the MCG, World Series Cup, 1988–89.*

long-lost Frank Worrell Trophy in 1988–89 due to the confidence engendered by their 1987 World Cup title.

Lloyd, Garner, Holding and the indefatigable left-handed batsman, Larry Gomes, had all retired since the two sides had last met, while Australia had now begun to settle on a line-up to take them into the next five years. The Windies' journey around Australia for the lead-up to the first Test at the Gabba in late November was hardly memorable, but the tourists had mastered the art of switching up several gears when the Test matches began.

A seven-wicket loss to Western Australia was quickly countered by an emphatic innings victory over South Australia and followed by a rambling draw with New South Wales. Richardson and another key batsman, Gus Logie, had not posted a first-class half-century between them by the time the first Test rolled around. However, no-one was prepared to nominate Australia as favourites.

The wake-up call given to Merv Hughes by his omission from the team to tour Pakistan had certainly achieved its desired effect. Over the winter of 1988, the fast bowler had lost all of the excess baggage that he had been carrying during the Test against Sri Lanka in Perth and was back to a much trimmer 96 kg.

The unfortunate loss of Reid, due to his recurring back problems, had opened up a vacancy in the bowling ranks once again, however, form in the early part of the season deserted Hughes just when he needed it the most.

In back-to-back games against South Australia (in Adelaide) and New South Wales (in Sydney), the Victorian finished with disappointing returns of 1–66, 0–17, 0–40 and 0–59. Hardly the kind of evidence from which to demand a return to the international arena.

Left-arm bowler Chris Matthews had not played for Australia since his demoralising two Tests against England two summers before, but rocketed into calculations again with a double of 5–84 and 4–75 to bowl Western Australia to victory against the West Indies. It seemed certain he would join McDermott and Dodemaide in the line-up, unless Hughes did something spectacular against Queensland in the week before the Test match.

Hughes did, but a match haul of 10–121 was not enough to sway the selectors his way. Sure, he had skittled Queensland's first innings with

7–81 and he was much fitter, but had the lesson of the previous summer been learnt?

Better to leave him out for one more Test to keep him hungry, it was reasoned, and ensure that Merv Hughes continued to work hard at being a regular Australian Test cricketer. Matthews, McDermott and Dodemaide would fulfil Australia's new ball duties for Viv Richards' 100th Test match, in Brisbane.

Any visions of seriously challenging the West Indians had disappeared from Australian eyes by stumps on the opening day, with the home side dismissed for a meagre 167. The West Indies had been robbed of the services of the intimidating Patrick Patterson, who succumbed to a thigh injury, yet were still able to rely on Marshall, Ambrose and Walsh to finish the Australian innings inside 70 overs.

Faced with a deficit of 227 on the first innings, some clean hitting by Steve Waugh (90) and unyielding tailend resistance from Matthews (32) and McDermott (32 not out), at least enabled Australia to avoid the humiliation of an innings defeat.

But bowling again would put paid to Matthews' Test career once and for all. He had struggled in the first innings with figures of 0–62 and he was terrible in the second innings, sending down a horrid assortment of wides and no-balls in 3.5 overs, before breaking down with a side strain.

Changes were demanded for the Test in Perth, with the new ball attack under most scrutiny. Hughes' 10-wicket haul against Queensland would rocket him past the vanquished Matthews in the pecking order, while the up-and-down McDermott, in a trough after the tour of Pakistan, would be dumped for Lawson, who had taken 19 wickets at 17.63 from four matches in 1988–89 for New South Wales.

At their absolute peak in the mid–1980s, the West Indies never paid a lot of attention to the opposition's make-up, aside from targeting the captain for harsh treatment. The reasoning was simple — if the captain was bereft of confidence and in danger of losing his position, the rest of his side would soon be in tatters. Australia had lost a captain, Kim Hughes, in this manner in 1984–85, and England went through four in a single series in 1988!

For this Perth Test, the selection of Merv Hughes did cause some discussion in the tourists' ranks. As the two squads trained side-by-side the day before the game, Marshall and Walsh could not believe the physique of Hughes. Matthews had, plainly, looked unfit to them in the first Test and now the Australians had erred again by picking another bowler who was too big. The West Indies' expectation was that Hughes would be quick for a few overs and then quickly wilt.

'We hadn't heard much of Merv Hughes before 1988–89,' Courtney Walsh recalls. 'We were quite surprised that a guy of his size could bowl for so long with the same pace. He got a lot of lift and hurried the batsmen along. For someone who was relatively new to put in that kind of performance, it was a big effort and very impressive.'

Captain Allan Border won the toss and the traditional promise of life in the WACA pitch convinced him to send the tourists in to bat. Lawson provided experience in the attack, compared to the disastrous opening day of the series against England two years before, while Hughes offered fire. Both bowlers found the edge often enough in the early part of the day, however shoddy catching in the slip cordon would ruin Australia's hopes of coming back to square the series.

Haynes (2), Greenidge (5) and Carl Hooper (0) were all dropped before they were set — these three errors would cost the home side a little in runs (70) but much in the way of confidence.

By stumps, the West Indies had powered to 4–280 with Richards marching regally to 95. Having already posted his 100th first-class century in the game against New South Wales immediately before the first Test, Richards would power through the 90s the next morning to finish with 146. His 51 runs on the second morning occupied only 40 minutes and his 146 was laced with 21 boundaries and three sixes.

For Merv Hughes, bowling to an in-form Richards was a sobering experience. To put it bluntly, Richards plainly intimidated Hughes with his sheer power — even just the West Indian captain's presence at the crease was daunting. It would not be until the 1990–91 series that Hughes would be able to view Richards as he did any other player — just another opposition cricketer.

'I really did find Viv intimidating the first few times I played against him,

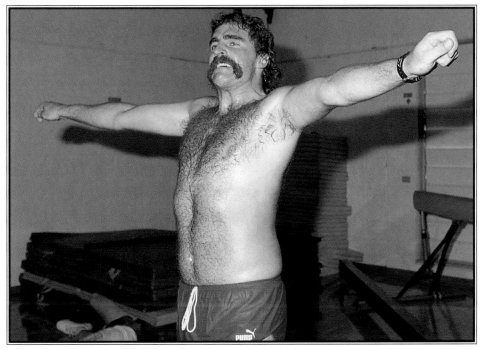

*Hughes, as fit as he'd ever been, at the start of what would prove to be one of the most important summers of his cricketing life.*

because you felt he didn't have a weakness,' Hughes says. 'He was the master of body language and nothing ever seemed to worry him.

'I had watched him on TV, taking on Lillee and Thomson, and he is probably the hardest hitter of a ball that I've ever bowled to. At times, you would nearly consider wearing a helmet when bowling to him — and that was no way to approach trying to get a bloke out.'

Hughes had taken some punishment from Richards, but neither his pace nor his effort had flagged through a marathon 36.1 overs. For the second consecutive innings in a Test at Perth, he would lead the team off with a five-wicket haul, finishing with 5–130.

Haynes and Richardson had been the best of Hughes' wickets and he had cleaned up the lower-order, claiming Ambrose and Patterson off consecutive deliveries from the last ball of his 36th over and the first of his 37th.

Dodemaide had been caned for almost 5 runs an over through the innings, forcing captain Border to use Hughes and Lawson for the vast majority of overs from the pacemen. The pair had certainly dished out a liberal number of bouncers and repayment in kind was expected when Marshall and his cohorts got hold of the ball.

In reply to the West Indian tally of 449, Australia reached a position of strength at 4–367 before the innings tumbled in spectacular and controversial fashion. Ambrose accounted for both Graeme Wood (111) and Steve Waugh (91) after their partnership of 200 for the fifth wicket, and then rifled through the middle- and lower-order. Keeper Ian Healy and spinner Tim May were both peppered about the body before being dismissed, as the lanky Antiguan recorded his first five-wicket haul in Test cricket. The score was now 8–395. With only Lawson and Hughes to come, Ambrose was chasing a big bag of six, or even seven, wickets to announce his arrival on the international scene.

Lawson joined Dodemaide and was greeted immediately with a searing short ball from Ambrose. Batting in a helmet, but without the protection of a facial grille, Lawson tried to hook a second short ball but was horribly late on the shot, collapsing onto his stumps as the ball crunched into his face. His jaw badly smashed, Lawson lay on the pitch bleeding profusely as several West Indians tried to help him before medical assistance rushed onto the field.

In the viewing room, Border seethed as he watched yet another member of his team go down with a serious injury. Through the 1980s, a litany of Australian players had missed Test matches after sustaining all manner of injuries at the hands of the West Indian quicks. Border and his team-mates were united in their desire to support a fallen comrade.

To strike while this angry feeling was at its highest, the Australian captain declared. Hughes would not bat and instead the charged-up Australians would go out and bowl for a couple of overs in the hope that adrenalin could make early inroads.

During the 10-minute changeover of innings, the injured Lawson was placed on a bench in the middle of the dressing-rooms to rest while he waited for an ambulance to arrive.

'Henry came back into the rooms with a huge indentation in his cheek the size of a cricket ball,' Steve Waugh remembers. 'Before we went out, he was lying on the bench and Errol had put a beer jug next to him. Henry was spitting out blood and had filled this jug a quarter of the way up, while he was choking and gagging away. His face was an absolute mess and it shook a lot of players to see a guy in that condition. We were thinking about Henry and Merv just charged out there and got into them.'

Hughes took the new ball, his eyes were spinning like the maddest of defenders in an up-country footy game. His first ball rocketed into Greenidge's pads, the entire side went up in unison in a raucous appeal, and umpire Terry Prue's finger acknowledged the successful appeal.

'Fuck off!' Hughes screamed at Greenidge.

Greenidge had never taken kindly to on-field exchanges and shot back at Hughes, 'What did you say?'

'Fuck off! Get off!' Hughes screamed at the departing batsman again.

In the drama of Lawson's injury, everyone had forgotten the fact that Hughes had taken two wickets in consecutive deliveries to finish the first innings. Now, he had completed the most convoluted Test hat-trick in the history of the game — spread over three overs and two innings.

After play, team manager Ian McDonald had other concerns. He told the fast bowler he thought he had stepped over the line with his barrage at Greenidge and that he should apologise as soon as possible.

A still-pumped Hughes said he couldn't actually remember saying anything to the batsman and wasn't sure if he had done anything that serious. A view of the replay quickly showed him just how far he had gone in an excitable moment. As he had been taught, he had to acknowledge a mistake and apologise.

Grabbing a couple of cans of Coke for himself and a six-pack of beer for Greenidge, Hughes headed to the West Indian dressing-rooms, accompanied by Ian Healy. David Boon had already gone to the tourists' rooms to seek out good friend Jeff Dujon and had been talking to the West Indian 'keeper for some moments when Hughes arrived.

Boon recalls: 'Merv had calmed down after stumps and he knew that he had to apologise. He always kept things between 11 and six and, as far as he was concerned, there was nothing personal in it at all between him and Gordon. I was sitting with Duje and asked if anything had been said by Gordon because Merv was coming into the rooms to sort it out. He just said it would be really interesting to watch.'

Through his long career, Greenidge was a solitary and often surly character in dealing with his West Indian team-mates, let alone opposition players.

Born in the West Indies but raised in England, many have speculated that his isolation stemmed from the fact that he felt he was never truly accepted in the Caribbean because of his time spent in England. He rarely communicated to anyone outside the hours of play and certainly was not one for light banter on the field.

When Hughes arrived and moved to apologise, Greenidge turned his back on him and faced the locker. When the fast bowler walked around to face him, Greenidge turned a second time and snubbed him.

'Look Gordon, I didn't mean what I said out there and I don't want you take it personally,' Hughes tried a third time.

'I don't believe you. I don't want your beer because you don't mean a word of what you're saying,' Greenidge replied. With that, he turned his

*Like Hughes, Mark Waugh (right) made his One-day International debut for Australia in 1988–89.*

back on Hughes yet again and headed out to sit in the team bus, where he stayed until it departed for the hotel some 45 minutes later. The blatant snub was witnessed by nearly all of the West Indian team and several Australians.

It was a defining moment for Merv Hughes the Test cricketer. In Shield cricket, he regularly blustered away and sledged his opponents but the Australian way was to have a beer at the end of the day to clear the air and then resume battle the next morning. Plainly, that was not the case at international level where different cultures had a different view of the way Australia played the game.

When he relayed his disappointment at Greenidge's snub to captain Border, Hughes got a most surprising answer.

'Merv has always been a great believer that on-field stuff is not taken off-field,' Border says. 'If you feel you've stepped over the line, you seek out your opponent and you sort it out. I think the reaction he got from Gordon was important for him at that stage of his career. It taught Merv to say, "Stuff it, I can't get worried about what they think of me",' Border says.

In the absence of Lawson on the fourth day, Hughes would reveal a side of his character previously unseen at international level. In Shield cricket, Hughes had been the money man for Victoria and had often bowled for up to a session at a time when his side had needed wickets or aggression. Now, with Lawson sidelined and Dodemaide at the mercy of an aggressive line-up, Hughes would have to shoulder the load.

He did so unforgettably, taking six wickets for the day from a marathon 34 overs to finish at stumps with figures of 7–78. An eighth wicket would be added on the fifth morning for a final return of 8–87 and only Richards' declaration prevented him from taking 9 for the innings.

In one spell, Hughes would bowl unchanged for 19 overs — from before lunch to 15 minutes before the tea adjournment. In the final session, very nearly out on his feet, television replays would show Hughes walking back to his mark, eyes closed to conserve every available amount of energy. At the top of his mark, or sometimes well past it if he hadn't opened his eyes again soon enough, he would charge in yet one more time. Through his epic spell, his pace never flagged.

Richards, who swaggered at the crease against fast bowlers from Lillee through to Waqar, seemed visibly shaken by Hughes' aggressive barrage.

*This was award-winning cartoonist Ron Tandberg's reaction to Hughes' heroic 13-wicket performance in the Perth Test against the West Indies in December 1988.*

A streaky loft down the ground was followed by an ordinary effort to get in behind a ball that was up and he was trapped lbw for five, giving the fast bowler some measure of revenge for his first innings treatment.

Hughes led his team-mates from the field at the end of the fourth day, but the West Indies had built an imposing lead of 385 with a day to play. Despite Australia's parlous position, the effort had struck a chord with former Test players who were present, many of whom were moved to seek out Hughes in the dressing-rooms and tell him how proud they were.

After his first Test, when criticised heavily by Ian Chappell, Hughes knew in his heart that he was not a Test cricketer, but rather someone who had just played Test cricket. Chappell's further biting comments in early

1988, which Hughes had to acknowledge as correct, had only motivated him further.

Now, his idol accepted him as an equal. There could be no higher accolade.

'From the moment Lawson went down, Merv seemed to grow in stature,' Chappell says.

'In that Test, he went from being someone who had played a number of Tests to an accredited and accomplished Test performer.'

Each time Border had thrown the ball to Hughes for a new over, during Hughes' marathon spell, he waited for a moment to see if the bowler would throw it back, unable to continue. Finally, in the lead-up to tea, Border relieved him. Hughes asked his captain if he could leave the field early to have an extended tea break, he would then be willing to bowl again straight after the resumption of the final session. Border agreed, though it was his general rule that players should never leave the field unless forced to do so.

Hughes trudged from the field with applause ringing in his ears, and then collapsed onto the bench in the dressing-rooms where Lawson had lain less than 24 hours earlier.

'Hooter, I need ice,' he told physio Errol Alcott.

'Where?'

'My hammys, my groin, my back and my shoulder.'

Hughes lay there, covered in four separate ice-packs, and then called the physio over again.

'Hooter, why is it that my hamstrings, my groin, my back and my ankles are all telling my stomach it shouldn't eat so much?'

Maybe the message had got through, Alcott thought.

'Luckily, my stomach has told them all to get stuffed and get on with the job.'

No chance he would be eating less.

Despite Hughes' match heroics of 13–217, Australia would tumble to a second consecutive defeat, losing by 169 runs. However, his efforts in a losing cause had transfixed the nation. Suddenly, there was Merv-mania. Wherever he went across the nation, he was the focus of adulation.

*Hughes leads the Australians off at the end of the fourth day of the West Indies Test at the WACA.*

In contrast to previous years, Hughes would also find a role in the One-day side during 1988–89, playing nine of Australia's 11 One-day matches for the summer. Encouraged by the crowds mimicking his every action at his home ground, the MCG, he was very quickly becoming Merv Hughes — cult figure.

On the One-day circuit, Hughes would secure 14 wickets at 22.07 and conceded around 4.5 runs per over. His contribution was solid, even though Australia would lose the World Series finals 2–1 to the West Indies. It remained a bone of contention for him throughout his career that he did not play more One-day cricket.

With a total of 14 wickets in seven One-dayers but only one wicket over the remaining three Tests, in Melbourne, Sydney and Adelaide, after his heroics in Perth, the selection panel came to a conclusion. In their eyes, Hughes the One-day bowler had affected Hughes the Test bowler and the selectors much preferred the Test bowler. McDermott, Reid, Simon

O'Donnell, Terry Alderman and others were better suited to One-day cricket while Hughes was obviously a Test firebrand. From 1988–89 onwards, Lawrie Sawle and his panel decided that Hughes would only play One-day cricket when the selectors were short of bowlers.

'The selectors were a little worried about Merv in the field in One-dayers, but the main reason he wasn't selected was that we never wanted him to change any aspect of his bowling,' Sawle says. 'A lot of bowlers have to alter their bowling for One-day cricket and we wanted him to stay purely as a fast, tearaway.

'We didn't want him to try to alter his style to suit One-day cricket by slowing down or bowling containment stuff. We just wanted him to be the fiery Merv and blast blokes out.'

Australia took another Test match hiding, their third in a row, over the Boxing Day Test match at the MCG. On an up-and-down wicket that made batting extremely difficult, Patrick Patterson bowled faster than he ever had before to destroy the Australians on the final day.

Patterson took 5–39 in Australia's meagre tally of 114 and did as much damage with the number of painful bruises he inflicted on the batsmen. Healy was twice struck in the testicles, Jones was X-rayed for a cracked rib and both Border and Wood suffered cracked fingers.

Thrashed 3–0 in three Tests after beginning the summer with high hopes for the Worrell Trophy, the beaten Australians signed a pact in alcohol that night. Nursing their bruises, the 12 players and team management gathered in a room at the Hilton and vowed that a line had to be drawn. As a unit, the side could not back down and had to start standing up to the West Indies. (They would lose 1–2 in both

*Despite the Windies' victory in Perth, there was no doubt as to who was the man of the match.*

1990–91 and 1992–93 before the drought broke in 1995, when the Worrell trophy was finally regained. Only three players from 1988–89 — Boon, Waugh and Healy — would be able to convert that drunken promise into reality.)

Border's 11 wickets in Sydney set up a consolation victory in the fourth Test but, of more importance for the long-term success of the team, was the positioning of Mark Taylor. The selectors decided to break up the reliable opening partnership of Marsh and Boon, shifting Boon to number three to accommodate the inclusion of Taylor, and in Taylor's first full calendar year in Test cricket, he would become the first player from any country to post more than 1000 runs.

After the fourth Test turnaround, many critics argued that the West Indians had relaxed since the third Test at Melbourne. Whatever the Windies' approach, for the Australians the final Test in Adelaide in early February would be played for pride and for selection on the 1989 Ashes tour.

Hughes' 13 wickets in Perth made him a certainty for the England trip in the eyes of most, but not his own. Mike Whitney was enjoying a stellar season for New South Wales, Terry Alderman had returned from exile after touring South Africa while Geoff Lawson was expected to be fit in time for selection after his broken jaw. As well, Queensland's Carl Rackemann was in excellent form.

Hughes had played four Tests in succession but he still did not feel he had a lock on a Test berth. However, if he was hoping for wickets in Adelaide to shore up his position, a match return of 0–106 from 24 overs did him no favours at all. Despite his performance, his standing with the public would increase again during the Adelaide Test, all because of his deeds with the bat.

Border won the toss and Australia moved impressively to 3–283 by the close of the first day. Dean Jones had starred with an unbeaten 131, dominating a fourth-wicket stand with Allan Border that would grow to 214 in all. Jones seemed much better suited to a role in the middle-order in his second coming as a Test player, rather than at number three, and was on target for the second double-century of his career before a middle-order collapse on the second morning. From 3–289, the Australians subsided quickly to 7–333. Tim May made a dogged 24 out of a stand of 50 for the

*Hughes with Steve Waugh in Sydney, after dismissing the West Indies' Gordon Greenidge caught and bowled.*

eighth wicket but Jones was still some 28 runs short of 200 when he was joined by Hughes. The only batsman to come after Hughes was Whitney.

Hughes' batting, thanks to the constant work of coach Bob Simpson, had improved markedly from his first days in Test cricket, but his approach was still very much based on a liking for the huge slog. Repeatedly, Simpson would tell Hughes that the time would come when his team-mates needed him for either runs to win a match, or for support.

Jones needed him now, although he didn't hold great hopes of making a second double-century to add to his epic innings which he scored in Madras.

'Merv walked out and I was thinking I was no chance at all. His highest score was about 8 to that point and Whit was only good for three balls or so,' Jones says.

As he left the Adelaide dressing-rooms, Hughes was reminded, by some unfeeling team-mates, that the job ahead of him would not be easy. Steve Waugh produced a cardboard cut-out of Merv, vowing to mark every

*Hughes bowls to Richie Richardson in front of a packed house — by the summer of 1988–89 all fervent Merv fans — at the MCG.*

spot where Hughes would be hit while batting.

Before he headed to the crease to face Ambrose, Hughes spoke briefly to Jones. No-one knew why until much later.

'Merv walked up to me and said, "Deano, we started playing for Victoria together on this ground. We've represented Australia together and we've been through some tough things. I'm going to be here when you get your 200",' Jones recalls.

'I thought that was bloody inspirational.'

Ambrose's first ball struck Hughes in the midriff and the second on his arm guard. After allowing the third ball to pass, the fourth struck him a

*Hughes with some more of his fans, including (far left) team-mate Mike Whitney, in Adelaide during the final Test of 1988–89.*

painful blow on the inside of his thigh. Unwilling to show any pain, he would not rub the spot where he'd been hit, instead he buried his head in his chest and awaited the last ball of the over.

Ambrose pitched short again for the last ball of his over, hitting Hughes for the fourth time in five deliveries.

'He tried to duck the last ball, but it didn't get up and it hit him on the helmet,' Jones remembers. 'There was such a crack I thought they'd killed him. I raced down to the other end but he got up, turned around and asked me, "Are you 200 yet?"'

Hughes was going to take a pummelling if he stayed at the crease for any length of time so he had to decide on a shot or two that would work reasonably effectively, both to get him off strike and to defend himself. He decided he would hook. He began to play his shots and the tourists were frustrated by a succession of balls lobbing over fieldsmen in the ring or short of the men in the deep. In the 90 minutes to tea, the stand had grown to 70, Jones was nearing 200 and Hughes a maiden first-class half-century.

Courtney Walsh would bowl the final over before tea and, on the second-last delivery, Jones sent the home crowd into uncontrollable delight by completing 200. After acknowledging the crowd, Jones walked down the pitch to thank his partner for holding up an end.

'I've given him the biggest hug of all time because it was a fabulous day for us. I've said to Merv, "The crowd have gone spastic for us. You should block this ball out from Courtney and we'll walk off together with all the cheers",' Jones says.

Instead, Hughes would pull a short ball for a huge six over mid-wicket. Having got one up on his partner, he would chide him as they left the field together.

'Get your bat down Deano. They're not cheering your 200 — they're all yelling about my six.'

On the other side of tea, their stand would stretch to 114 and Jones would reach 216 before running himself out trying to retain the strike. Hughes would be left unbeaten on 72 when Whitney duly fell quickly for 2.

'I was pretty chirpy when I got back in [to the dressing-rooms] and I thought I may as well tell everyone how well I'd done.

'You can hear everything from the rooms out in the middle and all I could hear was the laughing, every time I got hit. They were all cheering the replays showing me getting hit so when I got in there, I ripped into a few of them.

'They all took it pretty well, except for AB, who spat it when I said I would take him down to the nets and show him how to hook Curtly Ambrose.'

Hughes made his team-mates' life a misery for the next few hours until he was silenced for good by Jones in the bar that night. After yet another whinge that Jones had cost him a maiden ton by running himself out, his Victorian team-mate told him he had done it deliberately.

'I had to get out Merv. It would have been a slight on the game of Test cricket if you had got a century. It would also have taken the gloss off my innings.'

Hughes finished the Test series poorly, in terms of his bowling, but at least his first-class form had not deserted him totally. In the lead-up to the fifth Test, he scythed through a full-strength New South Wales line-up on the last day of the Shield game in Melbourne to finish with 6–36.

Hughes bowled with his usual sustained pace and demonstrated that there would be no favours for Test team-mate Steve Waugh, bouncing him five balls in succession after Waugh had spent all summer facing exactly the same kind of bowling from the West Indians. Needless to say, a jaded Waugh made only 10 and looked a sorry figure heading back to the pavilion.

Despite Hughes' own doubts, provided he could finish the domestic season strongly, his place in the team to go to England, for his first tour, looked assured. However, Victoria would complete their season with games against Tasmania, South Australia and Western Australia on their way to a disappointing wooden spoon.

Simon O'Donnell had made a brave comeback from his battle with cancer to captain the side, but there had been precious little on-field

*Bay 13 at the MCG, 1988–89.*

*Dean Jones during his superb 216 against the West Indies at the Adelaide Oval.*

*Jones' partner in an extraordinary ninth-wicket partnership of 114 ... Merv Hughes!*

success. Hughes would struggle similarly in the last three matches, taking just five wickets at a prohibitive 63.80 apiece. To add to his woes, he was fined $750 after being reported by umpire Robin Bailhache for obscene language and disputing decisions during the game against South Australia.

Finally, in April, the Ashes side was announced and Hughes was included in the squad of 17. Alderman and Lawson provided experience while young Tasmanian paceman Greg Campbell had been a bolt from the blue. Rackemann and Hughes had won the other two fast bowling spots with Whitney omitted, despite taking 7–89 in the fifth Test and 58 first-class wickets for the summer.

Border felt England were ripe for the picking, if only because Australia had been hardened by a summer of cricket against the West Indies. On a personal note, he resolved to present a much harder visage to England. As captain in 1985, he felt he had too often allowed himself to be a soft touch and his good mates Ian Botham, David Gower (who would lead the Englishmen throughout the 1989 series) and Mike Gatting had run roughshod over him at crucial times in the series. Winning the Ashes would be Border's solitary focus for 1989 and friendships would be addressed later. His side would play their cricket very hard indeed, just like the West Indies did.

The Australians arrived in England on May 1, with just over three weeks to prepare for the three-match One-day series and almost six weeks before the first Test. The party had been drilled carefully to be wary of the English press corps and, at all times, to present an image worthy of an Australian touring team.

Hughes had signed a radio contract with Melbourne station Fox FM for the duration of the tour and, for his first report back to Australia, dropped in a line, 'We've already had our first half-century of the tour after David Boon had such a big trip on the plane'.

The fall-out from that one sentence was both immediate and spectacular.

The ACB offices in Melbourne were inundated with callers demanding to know what Boon had done, prompting chief executive David Richards to get on the phone to team manager Sawle and demand answers.

Hughes, one day into his first tour, was read the riot act by Sawle and Simpson and told that another step out of line would see him on a plane

*Hughes and Jones in Adelaide at their post-partnership media conference.*

home. He was here to play cricket, not to be a media star and create further problems. The last thing Australia needed was to have the English tabloids on the trail of an off-field story.

Hughes did not play a part in the One-day series, but injury to Rackemann and the inexperience of Campbell guaranteed him the third fast bowler's place behind Lawson and Alderman for the first Test at Headingley.

Wisely, team management had decided that during the build-up to the Test series Alderman would act as Hughes' tutor while Lawson would do the same for Campbell. Alderman had taken 42 wickets in England in the 1981 Ashes series and his influence on Hughes was profound.

Immediately, Hughes' run-up was further refined and he was delivering the ball from closer to the stumps, enhancing both his chances of winning lbw decisions or drawing an edge to the slip cordon.

'Playing and training with players at a higher level, such as Alderman and Lawson, was great for me,' Hughes says. 'I wanted to be competitive and not be left behind so I had to get better. They worked on my run-up but mostly on my state of mind. Terry Alderman told me the key was to be a relaxed bowler, whereas I tended to get too tense and try too hard.'

Alderman would be the decisive factor in the first Test with match figures of 10–151, leading Australia's unexpected last-day charge to victory. Centuries to Taylor (136) and Waugh (177 not out) had built a tally of 7–601 but victory looked out of reach once England fought their way past the follow-on.

An aggressive second innings established a lead of 401, before Border's closure left 83 overs in which to dismiss England and claim victory. The home side collapsed so badly that 27 overs were not required. Hughes would manage three wickets in the second innings to

*Hughes at Headingley in 1989 — his second Test 70-plus score in a row.*

back Alderman but also distinguished himself with his second consecutive Test knock in the 70s, reaching 71 out of a stand of 147 for the seventh wicket with Waugh.

Waugh was in peerless form and the instructions to Hughes were to put his head down and support the specialist batsman. Border was none too impressed when Hughes soon pulled Gooch for an enormous six and demanded an explanation when he returned at the tea break.

'Sorry AB. I went to block it and followed through a bit strong and it just went for six.'

Hughes' ability to take a lend of his captain, even at the most inopportune occasions, was becoming legendary.

England's batting had offered precious little resistance in the second innings, aside from a knock of 68 from Graham Gooch and 34 from a

*Above:* Hughes bowls to England's 'keeper Jack Russell and a six-man slip cordon on the final day of the first Test of the '89 Ashes series.

*Middle:* Russell, caught Ian Healy bowled Hughes, 2.

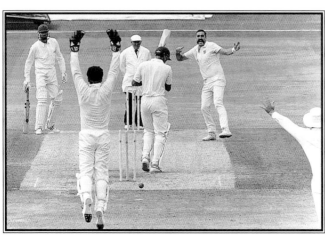

*Left:* Australia go one-up in the series — DeFreitas, bowled Hughes, 21.

greenhorn named Robin Smith. Smith was new to the Australians, a late replacement for the injured Mike Gatting, but had proved a combative character. Raised in South Africa, he quickly became known to Hughes because he didn't mind the odd verbal exchange.

Smith murdered anything pitched short, especially outside off-stump, but he lost the mind games with Hughes. He made the mistake of telling Border, over the rest day, of his tactics to deal with Hughes' sledging. Knowing that Hughes would eventually have to go back and bowl, Smith told Border he would stare Hughes down until he turned and he would consequently win the mind game. Border told his bowler and set him thinking about how to combat this plan.

'AB had told me of Robin's plan to stare me down so I spent most of the night and the rest day thinking about how I could get under his skin the next time I bowled,' Hughes says. 'In the first innings, when I stared at him, he'd stare at me for a while and when I sledged him, he would say something back. Now he was going to keep staring.

'After I bowled, I looked at him and would say something like, "weak prick", and then quickly turn around and walk away. As I was walking back to my mark, he'd be sledging me back for what I said to him.

'With the next ball, I'd bowl and then follow through and say, "If you're going to say anything to me, I'd appreciate it if you say it to my face," and quickly turn around and walk off again before he could say anything. That really annoyed him, because he wasn't getting the chance to get a word in. It was all designed just to get under his skin.'

Hughes was settled upon as the side's enforcer. Alderman and Lawson would probe away relentlessly at the batsmen whereas Hughes was a wildcard — capable of anything. When the captain wanted something done, he would call upon the Victorian for a combination of speed, bouncers, stares, sledging and anything else he thought of.

While it may seem simplistic, team-mates were convinced it worked on the English batsmen through 1989.

'When AB wanted things to happen, Merv would stick it up them, give them the chin music and the stares and the body language and all that stuff. The Poms didn't like it at all and it certainly does affect some guys. There were a lot of players who would turn their back on Merv so they

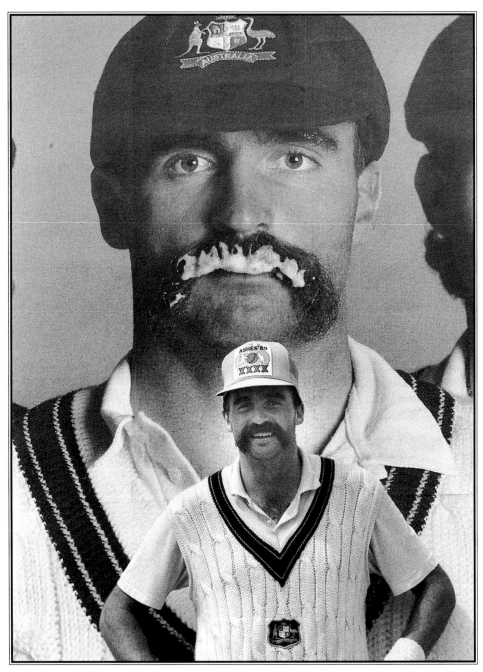

*Throughout the 1989 tour, the Australians featured in a promotional blitz for Fourex beer. Inevitably, Hughes played a pivotal role in the campaign.*

couldn't see him and get distracted. Once a batsman was worrying about Merv and sledging him back, he was often on the road back to the sheds,' recollects Dean Jones.

Hughes had come a long way since he had last played against England in 1986–87, forcing a hurried re-think on the part of the English hierarchy. In England's pre-match planning, Gooch, who was not a part of Gatting's tour, had not even bothered to ask about Hughes because of the derogatory reports he had received from Gatting and Botham.

'Merv wasn't held in high regard by our side after 1986–87 and a lot of our guys were quite pleased to see his name in the touring party,' Gooch says.

'We didn't think a lot of him pre-tour but that changed quite quickly. He could always produce the wicket-taking ball when you least expected it and he continually put the batsmen under pressure.'

A second victory at Lord's had Australia leading 2–0 and well on the way to regaining the Ashes before England had even got a foot in the series. Gower would fight hard for 106 and Smith would continue his running battle with the Australians for 96 but Australia achieved victory with six wickets to spare.

If Smith had lost the sledging duel in the first Test, he would regain valuable ground here. As he and Gower added 139 for the fifth wicket to offer some hope of saving the match, Hughes peppered him with short balls and vitriol.

'You can't fucking bat,' Smith was told as one short ball whistled past his nose.

When the next ball disappeared for four through point, Smith would get to even up.

'We make a fine pair, don't we Merv?'

'What do you mean?' asked the chastened bowler.

'Well, I can't fucking bat and you can't fucking bowl.'

When the monarch arrived for her traditional visit, even she could not help but notice the feeling between the pair.

'It appears you do not have many friends out there,' Queen Elizabeth noted of Smith during their meeting on the ground.

By the end of the series, England would be a rabble with only Smith and 'keeper Jack Russell able to say they had enhanced their reputations during the 1989 series.

The Australian team of 1989. **Back row:** E.L. Alcott (Physiotherapist), T.V. Hohns, T.B.A. May, G.F. Lawson, C.G. Rackemann, T.M. Moody, M.G. Hughes, T.M. Alderman, G.D. Campbell, M.K. Walsh (Scorer); **Front row:** R.B. Simpson (Coach), T.J. Zoehrer, M.A. Taylor, D.M. Jones, A.R. Border (Captain), L.M. Sawle (Manager), G.R. Marsh (Vice-Captain), D.C. Boon, S.R. Waugh, M.R.J. Veletta, I.A. Healy.

But for the interference of rain in the third Test, at Birmingham, and the final Test, at The Oval, Australia could have considered a 6–0 whitewash, as England ploughed through 29 players during the rubber. Injury and defections to a rebel South Africa tour had hardly helped, but the English players seemed devoid of the desire the Australians showed under Border.

Alderman (41 wickets) and Lawson (29) took the lion's share of the spoils; however Border and Simpson contend that Hughes' role has been vastly underplayed by history. The bare figures of 19 wickets at 32.36 apiece from six Tests do not seem earth-shattering but Hughes was developing a propensity for taking the big wicket.

When Gower was holding up the push for victory at Lord's with a second-innings century, it was Hughes who produced a vicious lifting ball out of nowhere to entice an edge to leg gully. On the rare occasions that England began to build a partnership, it was Hughes who was called upon to break the deadlock.

Sawle would return home to tell his fellow selectors that the glimpse of light shown in Perth the previous summer had become a new dawn.

'The bowler who went away and the bowler who came home were two different people,' Sawle says. 'Merv only got 19 wickets compared to what Alderman and Lawson did but the wickets he got were in pressure situations where we needed someone to come in and blast someone out. That was exactly what we had wanted out of him for a couple of years.'

Strangely enough, Hughes felt the overwhelming success of the new-ball pair had held him back for part of the series. Alderman and Lawson were often so successful with the new ball that Hughes would come on to bowl with England less than 50 on the board but already with three, and sometimes four, batsmen in the pavilion.

After such a strong start to the innings, he would fall into the trap of trying too hard to create wickets, instead of bowling with patience as Alderman had stressed. It was a valuable part of his education as a bowler.

The Australians meet the Queen at Lord's. The players are (left to right): Mike Veletta, Allan Border, Trevor Hohns (obscured), Greg Campbell, Merv Hughes, Terry Alderman, Geoff Lawson, Carl Rackemann.

*The Australians with the Ashes at The Oval, after the final Test.*
*Left to right: Tim May, Merv Hughes, Tom Moody and Greg Campbell.*

As England turned through the sods of county cricket in the search for a decent XI, they did manage to discover the odd nugget. Angus Fraser would make a solid impression in three Tests after debuting at Birmingham, while a 21-year-old Michael Atherton would be tossed in to bat at number three in the fifth Test at Trent Bridge. Atherton debuted with a second-ball duck — lbw to Alderman — but top-scored with a fighting 47 in the second innings. Young, fresh-faced and very inexperienced, he was given the rounds of the kitchen by all of the Australians.

For once, Hughes, Border and the other talkative members of the side would be poor judges of who to sledge and who not to. Gooch and Gatting were two players to whom Border instructed his team never to speak, because, like him, it only motivated them to do better. Atherton seemed like a soft touch . . . but this was later proven most definitely not to be the case.

Coming from Cambridge University, Atherton had never experienced an approach like Australia's and had to learn quickly. By the end of Australia's next tour of England in 1993, he would be the England captain.

'There was no-one at all like Merv in county cricket, and he was a real eye-opener for me,' Atherton says.

'Our selectors were just casting around anywhere for people to play, and the chance to play against the Australians and Merv was my introduction to sustained, aggressive sledging and a really full-on style of cricket. As a new, young player, I was a pretty obvious target to give it to.

'When facing Merv, it also required

*Hughes with the famous English umpire, Harold 'Dickie' Bird, after the sixth Test.*

a good deal of physical courage to play against him because he was very fast and he would not hesitate to test you out. I wasn't sure how to feel about Australia's approach because it was so new to me and I didn't know the form. I thought they were all like that off the field but, as you play a bit more, you realise that nearly everyone playing international cricket is a good bloke and pretty easy to mix with. It took me some time to learn that because it was hard to differentiate between what I was getting in their on-field approach and meeting them off-field.'

At the end of the 1989 Ashes series, Hughes could feel he was well on the way towards becoming an established member of the Australian side. As long as he was fit, he could command a place as one of three pacemen in the XI. Added to that, by this stage Merv had revealed his true colours. Most obviously, Hughes was an old-fashioned 'snarly' fast bowler who made it very obvious that the batsman was not wanted at the crease.

It was now Australia's task to consolidate the gains they had made in England — it was time to embark on a long-term plan to eventually upset the West Indies.

# CHAPTER SEVEN

# SLEDGING

The issue of sledging has been a vexed question throughout the recent history of Australian cricket. It has been the view of Australia's elite cricketers that anything that happens on the field is not continued after 6 p.m. when stumps are drawn. If there is a serious difference of opinion, it is to be resolved over a beer in the dressing-rooms. From park cricket all the way up to Shield cricket, this has been the unspoken way the game has been played.

Sledging, of course, is an all-encompassing term that covers a range of actions, from mild through to extreme. At the mildest end of the spectrum, a simple, 'Gee, you're struggling out here, mate' can be taken as a sledge, while the more extreme can extend to deeply personal abuse — even racist exchanges.

Certainly, no-one could condone the extremes of abuse, but the question of when sledging crosses the line from legal gamesmanship to unfair cheating has never been ruled upon in cricket's law book, and is certainly very difficult to define. Exchanges between players is not a recent innovation to the game. Cricket's history is littered with reports of run-ins, originating in the early days of Test cricket and continuing from there.

The term 'sledging' first gained wide coverage in Australia, according to Ian Chappell, from the late 1960s. In his book, *Chappelli: The Cutting Edge*, the former Australian captain wrote that the New South Wales Sheffield Shield team were having a party in the room of right-arm bowler Grahame Corling when Corling swore in front of a waitress.

*Opposite: Hughes farewells Graeme Hick, first Ashes Test, Manchester, 1993.*

A team-mate admonished the former Test fast bowler, saying he was as subtle as a sledgehammer.

Over the next few weeks, Corling was called 'Percy', in reference to Percy Sledge, who had released the song 'When a Man Loves a Woman' at the time.

'From that moment on, any cricketer in Australia who made a faux pas in front of a lady was said to be a "sledge", or guilty of "sledging",' Chappell wrote.

Problems in relation to sledging have arisen in two areas over the last few decades.

Firstly, Australia's approach can be at odds with other countries and cultures at international level and misunderstandings can quickly become serious stand-offs. Players from other countries often don't say a word on the field and to be subjected to any form of exchange, be it mild or serious, can be unexpected and not received well. Never let it be said though, that Australians are the only players with anything to say on the field.

Secondly, the rise of the electronic media has made on-field happenings plain to those off the ground when, previously, it was kept among those on the field. Under constant surveillance, players have had to become increasingly aware of the image they present of themselves.

Merv Hughes was a cricketer who believed that you played it hard between 11 and six. The next day, you went hard at it again. Yes, he swore on the field but, no, he never crossed the line into racist abuse.

While batsmen were certainly sworn at by Hughes in both domestic and international cricket — and occasionally umpires too, which landed him in hot water — not every exchange was fierce.

In researching this book, opponents and team-mates alike have all stated that Hughes was one of the funniest men on a cricket field, as well as one of the most intimidating. His skill in defusing a moment, or particularly when winding-up Allan Border, was legendary. Of the many international cricketers I spoke to, not one held a grudge against Hughes for an on-field exchange.

In Shield cricket, Merv Hughes was also a fearsome prospect to many batsmen. He had a sharp tongue and could back it up with some serious fire power in the form of dangerous, short-pitched bowling.

Off the field, Merv Hughes didn't hold a grudge against any of his opponents but, while he had a ball in his hand, he hated anyone who was gripping a bat at the opposite end of the wicket. During his State and international career, he would invariably pick one batsman in the opposite team who would become his 'target' for the match.

The chosen player would be the subject of his fiercest bowling, plus a verbal tirade, for no other reason than that it helped to motivate Hughes. That player could have been the opposition's star, one who played the short ball poorly, one who was supposedly mentally frail when sledged or one who just annoyed Hughes with his on-field manner. It was a very subjective judgement and was often based on little rhyme or reason.

When representing Australia, Hughes would noticeably lift a gear when Mark Greatbatch arrived at the batting crease for New Zealand, Carl Hooper for the West Indies and either Graeme Hick or Mike Atherton for England.

The opening batsman, Steve Small, and all-rounder Greg Matthews inevitably copped the brunt of a Hughes onslaught in games against New South Wales, while middle-order batsman Wayne Andrews was the target in the Western Australian side, and opener Trevor Barsby received the harshest treatment in the Queensland side.

However, one player stood out above all others — if any one player would bring on the red mist in Merv Hughes, it was James Brayshaw.

In a 75-match career (during which he played for both Western Australia and South Australia), which only concluded during the 1996–97 season, Brayshaw scored a very respectable 4934 runs at 42.53, including 10 centuries. His record against Victoria was particularly outstanding. Six of his 10 centuries came against the Vics and, as a predominantly back-foot player, he could handle a Hughes short-pitched barrage as well as any Shield player.

For all of that, he was bounced and sledged remorselessly from the time he first played against the Victorian fast bowler. Now in retirement, Brayshaw cherishes every memory of playing against Hughes.

'I reckon Merv's fantastic and playing Victoria was nowhere near as much fun when he was gone. The game is a poorer place without him. I never thought I'd say that about Merv Hughes, but it was like playing New South Wales after Mike Whitney retired. I don't know why I copped it from him and it was something I never asked him. I probably strutted around a

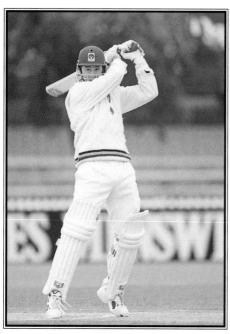

*James Brayshaw ... Merv Hughes' public enemy No. 1.*

bit when I started and thought I was a bit better than I was, especially as a kid. He probably didn't like that, and he might have thought I would wilt under what he was giving me. He wasn't the only bloke who had ever tried it, mind you.'

Brayshaw first crossed paths with Merv Hughes in 1987–88 in Perth in the game where the fast bowler flattened Mark McPhee and experienced a run-in with Kim Hughes. Brayshaw was 12th man and was secretly quite pleased he wasn't picked after watching McPhee being carried into the rooms on a stretcher, and Graeme Wood have his hand broken.

Brayshaw would not bat against him until a Victoria–South Australia game at the MCG in 1991–92, when Hughes was at his fastest. Brayshaw was at the non-striker's end when Hughes broke close friend Jamie Siddons' cheekbone during a fierce 11-over spell. It was a sobering experience, and provides welcome illumination as to what Hughes would do and say during a long spell.

'Merv came on for his second spell after lunch, with Jamie and I batting, and here's the great man at the top of his mark ready to go,' Brayshaw remembers.

'I thought to myself, "This is it. I'm now finally going to face him, after five years of playing. He's only starting his spell and he'll take a couple of balls to warm up so I'll warm up with him".

'The first ball just disappeared past my nose and [Darren] "Chuck" Berry has taken it eight rows up above his head. 'I thought, "Oh fuck, that's real fast".

'I waited for about two seconds and then this barrage has just come. It was the most personal vitriol I have ever, ever received: "You faggot, you cocksucker, you dirty little prick" he's called me, and I'm just standing at the crease thinking, "Fuck, what have I done to this bloke?"

'This went on all day. It was amazing. Every ball was half-way down the wicket and every ball was followed by the best quality sledging I've ever copped. It was the most personal and nasty stuff of all time.

'We were having drinks and I was standing in the middle of the MCG thinking, "How can I have annoyed a guy — who I haven't ever officially met — that much, for him to come out with stuff of such high quality?" Eventually, we finished the day and I walked off a shattered man.'

Brayshaw had survived the most hostile spell of bowling he had encountered, but the verbal barrage he endured had destroyed his confidence. By the end of the day, he was happy just to keep Hughes out and wasn't looking to play any sort of attacking shot against him.

Hughes may not have got his man but he had certainly changed the way Brayshaw batted and destroyed his effectiveness. In effect, Brayshaw realised Hughes had partly won the battle anyway.

'A lot of blokes try to sledge but just aren't particularly good at it. They say something stupid and you end up laughing at them, or some of their own fielders laugh at them. Merv was not only a great fast bowler, he was a great sledger. Everything he said was right on the money and he said it with such passion and venom. I felt myself believing what he said. I would walk off thinking, "I must be a real cockhead",' says Brayshaw.

In the dressing-rooms, Brayshaw sat next to Hughes' Australian team-mate Tim May and related the day he'd had out in the middle with Hughes. He had been harangued after nearly every ball he faced, whereas the other batsmen had hardly a word spoken to them. Everyone told Brayshaw that Merv Hughes was a great bloke, but it was hard to see how he had won that reputation.

'Maysie just laughed and said, "He's like that with everyone",' Brayshaw recalls. 'Five minutes later, and five minutes before any other Victorian had come in, Merv was the first one to bowl into the rooms and I was the first one he bowled up to.

'I thought, "Here I go, I'm going to get some more". I was sitting there and he said, "Well played. I called you a cocksucker — but that's first-class cricket". He handed me a beer, had one of his own and we sat there for about five minutes.

'I was shaking my head but it turned out, over the next 10 times I played against him, that that was Merv. He was exactly the same the next day and the next night after play. While I don't think Merv would count me as one of his special friends, I certainly have a lot of respect for him. He plays it hard but he's a terrific guy off the field and a great bowler.'

Once Brayshaw knew the barrage would be coming in every game, it was much easier to deal with. However, he would certainly try not to upset Hughes because the bowler had the ability to deliver on his threats of mayhem.

'I always thought that if you made runs at the MCG against Merv when he was having a real crack, you were fairly entitled to be reasonably pleased with yourself,' Brayshaw continues. 'It was a pretty thorough examination of your ability to handle that kind of situation. As a batsman, I think you have to cop everything and it's no-holds-barred. That's part of the game and if you're not capable of copping it, you shouldn't be out there.

'With Merv, after the first time, you knew it was all just on-the-field stuff. He wasn't going to take it off the ground and not speak to you. It was just part of his bluff and bravado and the psyche of Merv Hughes.'

In matches against South Australia, Hughes would never say a word to their aggressive opener, Paul Nobes, because Nobes was capable of taking on the short ball and scoring quickly. Equally, he would never direct his baiting at either Allan Border or Geoff Marsh, because they thrived on sledging for their concentration.

Most batsmen were able to block it out, including Brayshaw, although he did react during one game in 1994–95 — and the response he received from Hughes was surprising.

'The last time I played against Merv,' Brayshaw recounts, 'I was batting and really struggling. I had made a few runs but I was nicking them, or playing and missing. I was getting shittier and shittier with myself because I was playing worse and worse and scratching about with a hell of a bad display of batting. As I was going, Merv was getting shitty with me and giving me gobfuls.

'Finally, he bounced me and I tried to hook it, didn't get there and the ball bounced off my helmet and went to third man. As I'm half-way through the run, Merv has climbed into me and I just snapped, "Merv, it's been fucking 10 years, why don't you shut the fuck up and we'll both get on with the game. I've heard it all before so fuck off".

'I wasn't angry at him, I was angry at the whole situation because I was going so badly the ball was hitting me. He turned around with a big smile on his face and said, "All right". He laughed at me and not another word was said for the rest of the game.'

In the whole time he played for Australia, Merv Hughes played every Test of his career under the captaincy of Allan Border. Border's leadership became more aggressive as he grew into the job and Hughes became more aggressive as he settled into international cricket.

While Hughes, as a Test player, was twice reported by the umpires and once by the referee, Border knew that everything Hughes said and did was carefully orchestrated.

'I felt he was always in control and knew what he was doing. When you went up to talk to him, to see how he was going, when he was giving someone a serve, he was always skylarking around. Nothing was bothering him and he never looked like the beans had gone or he had lost the plot. When he was at the top of his mark, he carried on like a nuisance — like a 12-year-old — not like someone who needed to be pulled into line,' Border says.

Bowlers fall into two categories — those who do speak to batsmen and those who don't say a word. The West Indies' Curtly Ambrose, for one, is renowned for virtually never speaking to an opponent and strongly disapproved of Hughes' actions.

In contrast, Pakistani pair Wasim Akram and Waqar Younis said they copied much of the Australian bowler's approach after playing against him in 1989–90.

'I totally agree with Merv's approach — 100 per cent,' Akram says. 'I don't have a problem with the words and the stares, as long as you are not going overboard. You have to try to make the batsmen annoyed with you, and sometimes it works and sometimes it doesn't. As a tactic, I think you have to do it because cricket is professional and you need to try everything you can.'

Waqar, who was on his first overseas tour in 1989–90, said he was prompted to grow a moustache after playing against Hughes in the belief that it might make him look a bit more fierce.

'You have to give a look to the batsmen,' says Waqar. 'You can't be a fast bowler and not do that. Merv had the best look of all. I think batsmen would occasionally get really scared, because he had the big moustache, a really mean look and the eyes that were really fierce. I think that's good because a bowler needs to be aggressive.'

That is not to say that every team-mate of Hughes supported his actions. Geoff Marsh, for one, always maintained that too much was said at times on the field. A batsman is a lonely person on a cricket field and needs to be left alone.

'Everyone has their own personality on the cricket field but I believe that, as Australians, we sometimes sledge too much,' Marsh maintains. 'I have always thought that silence is the biggest fear.

'We say things when we'd be better off putting our concentration into the next ball. From a batsman's point of view, most players at international level are there because they have a real toughness about them and sledging backfires sometimes.

'As an opening batsman, I loved being sledged. One of the disappointing things towards the end of my career was that no-one ever sledged me, because it was good for my concentration.'

While Marsh held the view that often too much was said, another long-time team-mate, Ian Healy, felt the wrong things were said. Healy, a keen student of body language and the mental strength required to be an elite sportsman, felt Hughes should certainly speak out, but needed to make a better impact with what he was saying.

'I would like to see bowlers come out with some comment that gets a batsman thinking, "What's he saying that for?", and distracts them,' Healy says.

'That's the type of comment a bowler should make, rather than just calling them a "fucking prick". In my view, Merv was an ordinary sledger. He was pretty basic and just swore a lot.

'At the same time, though, I was right behind him when he was getting up batsmen and I was thinking, "Go for it Merv". James Brayshaw was

*Sledging is pointless without the missiles to back it up — Hughes bounces Graham Gooch at Trent Bridge in 1993.*

right in believing that batsmen knew Merv was just going to come at them with the basic stuff, but Merv did have some pretty good armoury to back up his words. In the back of James' mind, and any other batsman, he wouldn't want to get Merv fired up and would be hoping to sneak through without the barrage.'

Hughes had some spectacular failures with his sledging, notably Mike Atherton through the 1993 Ashes series, but he did have some pretty impressive successes as well. While Atherton may have scored more than 550 runs in 1993 and not reacted to anything said to him, New Zealand's champion batsman Martin Crowe never scored a century against Australia in a Test in which Merv Hughes played.

Hughes knocked Crowe over far too many times for his liking.

'He was the sort of bowler that I just wanted to smash around the park because of his approach. I would get so angry with what he was doing, but it was working in that he changed my mental approach. To get me out was all the more galling because I had fallen into the trap. It was annoying to get out to him because he would get you out with his personality as much as anything. Merv was certainly a thinking bowler. He had a different approach to various players to get them out of their preferred mode of batting.'

Hughes struggled to retain his confidence when he first encountered West Indies captain Viv Richards in 1988–89 but made significant progress in 1991, getting his man in a decisive psychological battle in the third Test at Port of Spain.

Richards, like Crowe, didn't rate Hughes as an opponent and sledging the West Indian was the wrong track to head down because he thrived on a verbal exchange. Rather, it was important to upset Richards' ego — that could lead to a false stroke. Richards hated a bowler staring at him, especially one he didn't rate, because he felt it was a slight on his status.

At Queen's Park Oval, Hughes disposed of Richards in five balls in the midst of a spell of 4–19 from 33 balls. He upset him without even saying a word. After his first delivery flew past the outside edge, Hughes gave Richards a long glare.

'Get back and bowl, man.'

He had got a reaction. Hughes followed with a bouncer and another long stare.

'Don't you be staring at me, man. Get back and bowl. This is my island. This is my culture. Don't you be staring at me. You have no place here to be staring.'

The third delivery missed the outside edge and another long glare was offered to Richards.

'This is my culture. This is my island. You get back and bowl.'

Another bouncer would certainly draw a shot from Richards and the ball had to be over off-stump to ensure he top-edged to the two men in the deep. The bouncer and the edge both came, but flew wide of Craig McDermott at fine leg, enabling Richards to steal two runs.

Another glare.

'This is my culture. You can't come to Vivi and stare.'

Expecting a bouncer, Richards instead received a full-pitched, slower ball and had his feet totally out of position when he went forward to drive, spooning a catch to an exultant Steve Waugh in the gully.

As Hughes went past Richards, he celebrated.

'In my culture, we say, "Piss off".'

Since Hughes departed from the first-class scene, there has been no-one with such overt aggression to step into his shoes. Glenn McGrath, who has developed into a fast bowler of the highest quality, can provide a searching examination of a batsman's technique but does not get into a batsman's face as much as Hughes did.

Former Test batsman David Boon and long-time Shield player Jamie Siddons both feel the absence of a Hughes-type bowler holds back the development of young Shield batsmen.

'When you're batting, you've got to be able to cop everything,' Siddons says. 'It's a part of the game and I reckon it's a good part of the game. You don't get the physical contact that you do in football but there is a certain challenge that needs to be met. It's a tough man's game.'

'Merv stuck it up me in Shield cricket and I loved it,' Boon says. 'I wanted him to do it to our young players because it's the best way to learn.'

The major problem for Merv Hughes was the fact that his actions were never going to remain purely on-field because the advancement in technology took him, close-up, into homes across the nation. Where once it was only ever suspected that a player had had something to say, since the late 1970s it has been apparent whenever an exchange has taken place.

Youngsters mimic their heroes and Hughes could set a poor example — when either giving or receiving a burst from an opposition player. Whether he had lost control or his actions were carefully planned, it all happened in front of the eyes of thousands. As such, he simply had to tone it down as he progressed.

Cricketers can rightly argue they are judged by harsher standards now than their predecessors were, but the game also offers rewards today that weren't available in a bygone age.

The final word should go to Hughes.

His on-field personality was aggressive and demonstrative but he prides himself on the fact he never took an exchange off the field.

'Cricket was business and what you saw happening on the field was me trying to win,' he says. 'At the end of the day, when it's over, you try to sit down with everyone because there's no point being enemies. I like to think I did that.'

# CHAPTER EIGHT

# A MOUNTAIN OF A MAN

**A**t the conclusion of Australia's 1989 tour of England, Allan Border asked the journalists who had followed his side throughout their historic 4–0 success what the reaction had been like at home. When assured that the decisive victory in Manchester had dominated news bulletins and newspapers across the country, Border confirmed he had also heard that the response had been 'pretty positive'.

In fact, the reaction was overwhelming.

Border's unheralded tour party were given a ticker-tape parade in Sydney on their return home and then paraded around the MCG on VFL Grand Final Day. A series of welcome-home dinners and civic receptions were duly held as Australia loudly celebrated their best result in England since that achieved by the immortal 1948 combination under Don Bradman.

The Australians had played well and, despite England's deep-seated problems (which would not become plainly obvious to most until another few Ashes beltings), many at home were prepared to nominate Australia as second only to the West Indies. A trifle premature, certainly, but home soil was expected to prove enough of an advantage for the 1989–90 meetings with New Zealand (one Test), Sri Lanka (two Tests) and Pakistan (three Tests).

Alderman and Lawson had produced stunning results on the 1989 tour but both were ageing and were not expected to be major players when Australia next confronted the West Indies in early 1991. It was time for other bowlers to step forward — and Merv Hughes had provided much to

*Opposite: The Australian team at Sydney's Darling Harbour in 1989, after their ticker-tape parade along George Street.*

please the selectors during his visit to England. Tour manager Sawle would report back to the rest of the panel that the Victorian was now ready to step forward. In his eyes, a fit Bruce Reid and a fiery Hughes at the other end was the new ball combination to lead Australia into the 1990s. All that needed to be done was to get Reid back onto the park and ensure that Hughes kept his weight under control.

Craig McDermott remained in the background, but he would still be serving his penance throughout 1989–90 and would have to do much to earn a second chance.

'After the England tour, Merv had arrived as a Test bowler. That was very pleasing for the selectors as Terry [Alderman] and Henry [Lawson] were both getting towards the end of their careers. In England, Merv had stepped into the role we wanted,' Sawle says.

Across Australia it was wrongly expected that New Zealand, Sri Lanka and Pakistan would simply be steamrolled as Border's side continued on their unstoppable path from England.

Instead, Australia were unable to close out victories in either of the first two Tests of the summer — against New Zealand in Perth and Sri Lanka in Brisbane. With no variation in the Australian attack (with Reid still unavailable they had four right-arm pacemen bowling over the wicket), in each game a batsman was able to hold up Australia — Mark Greatbatch in Perth and Aravinda De Silva in Brisbane. Greatbatch batted for just under 11 hours for an epic, unbeaten 146 while the tiny De Silva caned the Australians to the tune of 167 at the Gabba.

Obviously, there was still a piece or two missing in the puzzle to complete the line-up of an Australian side capable of stretching the West Indies.

Prior to 1989, when Australia had struggled, Hughes had been one of those bowlers unable to maintain his output. His head would never drop but his line and length would disappear and he would be punished, forcing Border to relieve him from the attack. Now, in 1989–90, amid the disappointments of the two draws, the signs were that Hughes was quickly becoming the spearhead to the attack.

While Lawson would be dropped after Australia's two disappointing draws, never to reappear in Test cricket, and Alderman would concede more than 30 runs apiece for his seven wickets, Hughes would be the standout bowler with 10 wickets at a little over 26.

Aside from his improved line and length and undoubted stamina, Hughes had now developed a habit of taking wickets in bursts at international level, breaking through the middle-order of a side and quickly changing the course of a match. In Perth, a spell of 4–6 on either side of tea on the third day wrecked the New Zealand innings and made a lasting impression on Greatbatch (who in the second innings saved the match with the best performance of his Test career).

'Merv was a mountain of a man and playing him in Perth for the first time, first up on a quick wicket, was a handful indeed,' Greatbatch says. 'Because of his size and the fact that he was a fast bowler, he seemed bigger again.

'He kept bowling fast, even up until the last half-hour of the match, and he was easily the most demanding bowler in the game. There was never a moment where you thought you could just play him and bide your time without having to worry, even after 11 hours or so.'

In Brisbane, the one disappointment for Hughes had been his failure to hold a sharp return catch from De Silva in the early stages of the Sri Lankan's innings. As the little dynamo powered past his century and on towards 150, Hughes had bowled for some 16 overs consecutively in draining Brisbane humidity when the second new ball was due.

'Do you want me to keep bowling with the new ball?' Hughes asked his captain, prepared to continue if asked.

'You dropped him. You're the one who's going to bowl to him,' was the succinct reply.

Sri Lanka fought equally hard in the second Test, at Hobart, and Australia only prevailed in the final hour on the last day, winning by 173 runs after the tourists narrowly fell short of a 10-hour task to save the match.

A hard-fought 1–0 series win over a team that had been thoroughly belted just two summers ago showed how far Australia still had to come, and that overcoming Pakistan would be no easy task at all.

The Australians would claim the series 1–0 against Imran Khan's men but it could not be argued the margin was either decisive or that impressive. In the solitary victory in the opening Test, in Melbourne,

Pakistan lost six batsmen to lbw decisions in their second innings and suffered defeat with only 22 minutes left to spare on the clock.

In Adelaide, Australia dominated the early part of the match before stunning centuries from Imran and his young protege, Wasim Akram, turned the match and actually forced the home side to dig in on the final day to earn a draw.

Rain then ruined the third Test in Sydney, and few Australian reputations had been enhanced during the rubber. Akram had starred with 17 wickets at just 18 to stamp himself as a player of rare international quality, leaving Australia to rely on the batting of Dean Jones and Mark Taylor, and the bowling of Alderman and Hughes for their series success.

The Pakistanis had not played against Hughes before the series, but he had made an immediate impact in Melbourne, rifling through the middle-order to finish with 3–34. His liking for the short ball and his aggression had a number of batsmen disinterested and hopping at the crease.

When Pakistan were set an imposing 429 to win in the second innings, senior batsman Javed Miandad promised his young team-mates he would take care of Hughes for them.

*Terry Alderman (left), Steve Waugh (centre) and Merv Hughes at the 1989 Hawthorn–Geelong VFL Grand Final, where the Ashes-winning Australians were paraded before the full house.*

*The Hughes–Wasim Akram incident at the Adelaide Oval in 1989–90. Umpire Tony Crafter is the man in the middle.*

According to Akram, the feisty right-handed veteran declared he would go out of his way to upset the bowler, in the hope of putting him off his game, and thereby reducing his effectiveness. When Javed set his mind to upsetting someone, he rarely failed.

'The bounce that Merv was getting was often too much for many of our batsmen,' Akram recalls. 'Merv's short ball was very good, coming in towards the batsmen, and it was something our players could not deal with.

'Javed knew this so he went to say two magic words to Merv to make him go overboard. He would call Merv "bus driver", because he thought he looked like one and would talk to him all the time to annoy him. Merv did a good job not to get angry and still bowl well.'

When Hughes pitched short, Javed would walk almost to the stumps at the other end and pat down an imaginary spot on the wicket while Hughes glared at him. When he pitched wide of off-stump, he would cock a leg at the ball, making his thoughts on Hughes' standards obvious.

Through it all, he kept repeating, 'Hughes, you're a bus driver. You should not be out here.'

Hughes did so well in resisting Javed's baiting that he worked through 42 overs for a return of 3–79, prising out both openers and century-maker Ijaz Ahmed deep in the last session to ensure Australia's victory.

When he finally claimed his man Javed in the next Test, the 'bus driver' had a winning comeback: 'Tickets please,' he called to the departing batsman in Adelaide.

Never having been sledged so blatantly by a batsman in a Test before, the surprised Hughes held up well to the novel tactics. While the West Indies batsmen relied on intimidating bowlers with sheer power, Javed was one of few batsmen with the confidence to open a sledging battle.

In Adelaide, for the second Test, Akram and a very young Waqar Younis (on his first tour) would try a different tack again. Akram and Younis both realised they were losing the fast bowling war, not because of their own efforts but because of their batsmen's unwillingness to face Hughes, so something had to be done.

The situation reached crisis point in the second innings when an inspired Hughes burst of 4–6 reduced the innings to 4–22. The series was fast disappearing.

Hughes dispatched Shoaib Mohammad (0), Rameez Raja (2), Salim Yousuf (1) and Ijaz Ahmed (4), prompting Akram to put Plan B into action.

At stately Adelaide Oval, scene of previous cricketing mayhem such as Bodyline in the summer of 1932–33, Akram decided his plan would be to swing from the hip with the bat, run into the bowler a few times, jam the bat into Hughes' ribs and see if he could make him lose his temper.

He certainly succeeded in his goal on the fourth afternoon, provoking an unseemly slanging match between the pair that would have drawn the ire of a match referee, had there been one in cricket at the time. As it was, umpire Tony Crafter was required to step between the duo to keep Akram and the aggrieved Australian apart as the insults flew.

'I was cocky as a batsman and that would annoy Merv. In the Adelaide Test, Australia looked like they would win and I came out to bat with Imran. I decided to play my shots and everything I was hitting was going for four and Merv was getting very annoyed. We wanted him annoyed and I hit him for a three and he was standing right in the middle of the pitch. He didn't move and I had the bat up high so I just banged into him, with the bat under his ribs. He was very strong and didn't move, but there were a lot of words exchanged. It was quite funny,' recalls Akram.

The Australians didn't see the funny side but Akram's tactics succeeded so well that he had raced to 123 and swung the match before the opposition reacted.

Hughes would secure 2–63 and 5–111 for the drawn encounter but, rather than the loss of a minor battle with Akram, the story of this match for the Australians was Hughes' effort to even get on the field.

A busy workload through the summer leading up to Melbourne's Test in mid-January had significantly increased the strain on Merv Hughes' right knee. He was never one to complain but on the morning of the Test in Adelaide, his knee locked and left him barely able to walk, and certainly unable to bowl. The panicked Australian side had less than an hour before the start of match and were without one of their remaining new-ball bowlers, having lost Alderman to a groin strain the previous day.

Rookie Greg Campbell had been called in overnight to replace the injured Alderman but team manager Ian McDonald was now faced with the prospect of putting Cricket Academy novice Phil Alley — a 19-year-old net bowler — on stand by to play a Test match.

A quick examination by team physiotherapist Errol Alcott determined Hughes could do no more immediate damage and would be able to play, if he was prepared to have an injection to deaden the pain. With Alderman out, Hughes declared he was prepared to have an injection. And so began a mad scramble by Alcott to get the fast bowler to a nearby doctor in North Adelaide and back in time for the start of the Test.

Captain Allan Border was told to stall the toss for as long as possible, to allow Alcott time to get the fast bowler ready for the match.

'We jumped into one of the team buses and went straight up to the hospital. I was more worried about dying in a car crash than any needle I might get,' Hughes remembers, after Alcott charged through the Adelaide

Oval car park at top speed and over the gutter to get onto the road and then ignored a succession of red lights in his haste.

Upon reaching the doctor's rooms, Hughes was assured again he could do no long-term damage but Alcott knew he would need minor clean-up surgery at the end of the season. As Hughes' right knee was his weight-bearing knee in his bowling stride, Alcott was also certain that Hughes would have further problems as his career progressed, especially with his family history of knee troubles.

'The doctor had the injection ready to go as soon as we got there and we got out again as quick as we could,' Alcott says.

'I remember saying, "Geez, have a look at that, that needle is huge", which didn't really help Merv, who had to put his white floppy over his face so that he couldn't see what was happening.

'We jumped back into the van, without even waiting to dress the knee, drove over the gutter and back down the hill to beat the traffic and headed straight to the nets so he could bowl a couple of balls. Once he had done that, we told the captain that he was fit.

'That was the biggest effort of all-time of any player associated with the Australian team while I've been doing the job.'

Alcott was hoping Australia would bat, to give Hughes more time to recover, but Border lost the toss under Murphy's Law and Pakistan decided to bat.

Hughes went straight out and bowled 18 overs on the opening day, leaving Border and Alcott in awe of his courage. In the second innings, he wrecked Pakistan's top-order with a sustained burst and forced Akram to do something out of the box in a bid to upset him.

A further three wickets in the rain-ruined final Test gave Hughes a return of 34 wickets for the summer spread over six matches at 22.91 apiece. Unquestionably, he had now established himself as a valued member of the Test side.

Unfortunately though, his right knee would require surgery before the start of the upcoming short tour to New Zealand in March 1990, ultimately ruling him out of the one-off Test, in Wellington.

In the One-day arena, Hughes played Australia's first five matches in the World Series before disappearing from the side. For the rest of his career,

*Hughes during the winter of 1990, fighting off the calories.*

his One-day international appearances would be intermittent, only being required when one of the more regular members of the side was unavailable or struggling for form.

The fast bowler suffered no complications with his keyhole knee surgery in February 1990 but Australian team management were becoming concerned about his size.

When inactive, Hughes tended to gain weight quickly and Alcott and coach Bob Simpson would forever be onto him that extra weight increased the strain on his knees and threatened to cut short his career. In the winter of 1990, he heeded the advice and cut his weight again — just as he had done in 1988 — starting the Ashes summer in peak condition. For the arrival of Graham Gooch's side in Australia, Hughes would weigh just over 95 kg and was in fantastic fettle. Added to that, his pace was now at its peak and his control was such that batsmen were given no respite whatsoever during a long spell.

In Shield cricket, Hughes went just as hard as he did for Australia and the national selectors now looked upon him as a measuring stick for other players. Assured that Hughes never let his guard down in State cricket, as some other Test players unwittingly did, any runs scored against him were hard-earned.

During the period between 1990 and 1992, Hughes was Australian cricket's ECG — he tested the hearts of up and coming batsmen.

'We always wanted to look at the footwork of young batsmen when they were up against Merv when he was bowling very fast for Victoria,' Lawrie Sawle says. 'If they had a good back-foot game and could handle the sort of bowling that Merv would dish up, the selectors were impressed.

'A lot of batsmen who struggled against Merv just stayed in the queue for a Test spot or disappeared from the reckoning altogether. He was someone we used a lot to gauge the performance of other players.

'There was great store placed on whom the runs were scored against and how players handled a better bowler such as Merv. A lot of guys get runs when they should get runs but it counts as to how many they get when the conditions are much harder.'

One player who won a Test berth on the strength of his excellence against Victoria, and Hughes in particular, was Mark Taylor. Taylor averaged just over 40 when he was first picked for Australia in 1988–89

*Above and below:* South Australia's Jamie Siddons, who a year before had scored more than 1000 first-class runs for Victoria, has his cheekbone broken by Hughes at the MCG in 1991–92.

and, at the time, other batsmen were posting better scores. The tubby left-hander had been around the scene for some four years by then but had been steady and consistent, rather than piling on 1200 runs a summer and demanding selection.

Sawle had been particularly impressed by a knock by Taylor of 73 against Hughes at the SCG early in 1988–89. The fast bowler had peppered Taylor, who stood up and played several pull shots and was never flustered at any stage. That was enough for Sawle to convince the rest of the panel

*Hughes on home turf during the second Ashes Test of 1990–91.*

the opener was worth a punt, and Taylor was set on the path to the Australian captaincy.

'Around that time, Merv was the most feared Shield bowler,' Taylor says. 'Craig McDermott was one of the best Shield bowlers, because he had the ability to swing the ball, but Merv was probably the most feared because of the way he bowled and the hostility he bowled with.

'I remember the particular innings at the SCG because he hit me on the helmet but I saw him off and hit a couple of good shots while I was there — a hook and a cut over point for four.

'I was hitting them pretty well and people said to me, when I got picked, that that innings had counted for a lot. I didn't doubt it because my average was only 40-odd at the time and I had it confirmed by some people in the know a few years down the track.'

If Taylor jumped the queue, as did Mark and Steve Waugh, for efforts against Hughes, then the most obvious loser in this game of selection snakes and ladders was Jamie Siddons.

Decades from now, cricket fans will look up the record of Siddons and wonder how he played just a solitary One-day international for Australia and never won a Test cap. Siddons had all the shots as a batsman and completed his game by being rated as a slip-catcher and all-round fielder who vied with Mark Waugh for the title of Australia's best. However, a combination of bad luck and Merv Hughes ruined his international dreams.

In 1987–88, as a 23-year-old, Siddons blasted four centuries during a season in which he scored 1077 runs and averaged 67, winning a place on the Australian's 1988 tour of Pakistan.

Siddons fought his way into the One-day side but, while on tour, contracted a stomach bug and would not fully recover from illness for 18 months, ruining his chances of breaking into the Australian side during 1988–89.

Once completely fit, he put himself back into selection calculations with more than 1800 runs for Victoria at almost 60 in 1989–90 and 1990–91

*Hughes, inevitably, is at the centre of the Australians' celebration after the Ashes had been retained in Sydney, after the third Test was drawn.*

combined and, playing for South Australia, centuries against Queensland and Tasmania to start the 1991–92 season.

Against Victoria at the MCG, Siddons faced Merv Hughes in the third game of the 1991–92 season and could not avoid a searing bouncer which smashed his cheekbone. A Test opportunity floated away once more and, when he returned, a subsequent change in his footwork meant he was never considered again.

'I don't think I've ever been the same player since, even though I've made good scores and 1200 runs in a season,' Siddons admits candidly.

'It certainly changed my game and turned my career in the wrong direction. I had been on a bit of a roll with four hundreds or so in my last six games but I never made another run for the rest of the year. It ruined my chances of playing for Australia and it was my worst moment in sport.'

But Siddons does not blame Hughes for his broken cheekbone. He had a bat in his hand and couldn't get out of the way or defend himself. That made the error his own. The fact that Hughes went so hard as a bowler against a best mate, even though he unintentionally caused serious injury, defined him as an elite sportsman in Siddons' opinion.

'The fact that Merv bowled as fast as possible against me is the approach I would want from my players,' he says.

'I expect people to treat me just like any other batsman in the game because there are no friends on the field.

'We've never really spoken about it but the one thing he did do was — the first ball he bowled to me in a game after that was a half-volley on leg stump.'

When Siddons was hit, the blow resounded around an almost empty MCG as he fell back onto his stumps. In the instant after the ball struck, the Victorians celebrated his dismissal before realising Siddons was in serious trouble. A call over the PA system for a doctor to come to the South Australian rooms hardly helped Hughes' composure as he waited for the lunch break to check on his friend's condition. However, despite what had happened, Hughes continued to bowl in his usual way. If ever his desire to bowl fast was tested, it was then.

'I'd known Jamie for a long time and it made me feel a bit sick to see him like that,' Hughes says. 'If it had been any one of the other South

*The Australians in Antigua in 1991, waiting for coach Bob Simpson (to Hughes' left) to get behind the steering wheel.*

Australians, it wouldn't have worried me. He had a bat in his hand and a helmet on so I had to get on with the business. If you're going to be worried about hitting someone as a fast bowler, you may as well bowl spin.'

England were duly dispatched 3–0 in the summer of 1990–91 but Australian eyes were focused towards the West Indies tour that followed that series. England, with Gooch and Allan Lamb absent at crucial periods, had offered only stuttering resistance, so none could be sure where Australia stood in the pecking order until the champions were confronted.

Hughes finished with a respectable 15 wickets at 24 apiece for the Ashes series to sit third in the averages, and the presence of Reid and McDermott as the two ahead of him prompted much confidence for the series in the Caribbean.

Reid had played just four Tests to secure 27 wickets at 16 apiece, while McDermott had completed his long rehabilitation to return for the final Tests in Adelaide and Perth and snare 18 wickets at 20. Hughes had renewed acquaintance with Michael Atherton and Graham Gooch but his expected battle with Robin Smith had been a total fizzer. Smith had a shocking tour of Australia and could not manage 250 runs for the series in 10 digs, leaving the load to be shouldered by the experienced Gooch and Gower.

A fit and in-form pace combination of McDermott, Reid and Hughes, with Alderman still in the background, provided hope of regularly dismissing the West Indian line-up.

Australia were now in a position to determine if their improvement since 1988–89 was real or imaginary. On a personal level, Merv Hughes would soon discover where his own career stood.

He had muscled out the Sri Lankans and Pakistanis the previous summer while a weak England side had put him beyond 100 Test wickets. To reach three figures for Australia had seemed impossible when Hughes debuted but he had set out to prove that he wanted to be a part of Test cricket. He had taken 13 wickets in a Test against the West Indies, but then slipped back dramatically over the rest of that rubber with just one scalp in three matches. To play the West Indies in the Caribbean offered the sternest challenge in the game.

Viv Richards had never lost a Test series as captain since taking over from Clive Lloyd in 1985 and, into his final year in Test cricket, was determined to maintain that proud record, no matter the cost. Experience would be a byword in the West Indian camp, with an ageing Gordon Greenidge, Malcolm Marshall and Jeff Dujon preferred to younger rivals, including the likes of Brian Lara.

Australia's tilt at the crown suffered a body-blow before the first of the five Tests had even been engaged. On the long flight to the Caribbean, via London, Reid's back had seized again and would trouble him terribly in the early part of the three-month tour. Reid's self-confidence was affected badly; he would claim just five wickets in two Tests. In the final warm-up match in Jamaica, fellow fast bowler Craig McDermott had also been injured — struck over the eye by Courtney Walsh while batting. McDermott would be pounded through the series, but while his batting would degenerate terribly, his bowling remained unaffected. In fact, McDermott, along with Mark Taylor and Mark Waugh, could justly claim to have advanced his reputation on this most difficult of tours.

After rain had washed away Australian hopes of victory in the first Test in Jamaica, the tourists' hopes in the series — and of regaining the Frank Worrell Trophy — were effectively dashed in one exhilarating three-hour session on the second day of the second Test in Guyana. Border's side had fought long and hard to reach 6–328 by lunch on that second day, however, just 24 hours later, the tourists were trailing by five runs overall and had taken just two West Indian wickets.

Upon being bowled out for 348, Australia had the West Indies lurching at 1–10 when Richie Richardson joined Desmond Haynes at the wicket for the final session. Border's side were compelled to bowl 41 overs for the session due to the fact that, under a since-discarded rule, they had to fulfil the over requirement left vacant by disgraceful West Indian over-rates.

Richardson caned the Australians in the final session for 106, on the way to an eventual 182 from 242 deliveries. The last man to bat regularly without a helmet in Test cricket, Richardson hooked two sixes and thrashed 27 boundaries, mostly to the square boundaries past Geoff Marsh, who feared for his safety at times while fielding in the gully.

*Hughes in the Caribbean — not always the paradise the 1991 Australians were searching for.*

McDermott could hold his head high but the rest of the frontline Australian attack took a pasting as the West Indies charged to 569 from 153 overs. As Richardson raced to his electrifying 182, scored during just 81 overs at the crease, Hughes would bowl 10 of those overs and be pummelled for 71 runs.

From the time he established himself in the Australian team in 1988–89 until his last Test in 1993–94, no-one would treat Hughes with such contempt as Richardson did in Guyana in March 1991. Every other time, both before and after, that Hughes received some serious punishment, he would always answer with a wicket when Border asked something special of him. He could always make something happen.

Here, he had no answers — and neither did anyone else — as Richardson tore the Test from Australia's grasp. Australia had taken a long time over their runs and Richardson, perhaps sensing the tourists were unsure how to grasp the momentum, took hold of it himself.

'I bowled three overs for 20, another three overs for 20 and then another four overs for 30 on the second day he batted. By the time he got out, I was just shellshocked,' Hughes remembers.

'I was thinking, "What went wrong?", because I didn't think I bowled that badly. It was unbelievable batting but I went away from that match really doubting my ability.

'Terry Alderman was fantastic for my recovery because he kept telling me you don't lose your ability overnight. The batsman had won this day, and played well, but I had to come back at him.'

After stumps, Richardson told the Australian press corps he always enjoyed a match against the Australians, because their chat and approach motivated him to do well.

While Hughes and McDermott blasted away with short balls and occasionally with angry words, Richardson simply led the way in an even-time stand of 297 for the second wicket with Haynes. For Border, it was a brief return to the bad old days against England in 1986–87 when he could not stop the tide flowing against his team.

'We were in a reasonable position but Richie destroyed us. All Merv's histrionics were useless because this guy was taking him on.

Merv's battery is good corridor work and some intimidating bowling but Richie blew him away. He didn't worry whether anything was being said at all and it wasn't often Merv got treated like that in the latter part of his career,' recounts Border.

Hughes, for the sake of his battered confidence, needed to hit back quickly. He bowled well in the rain-ruined third Test, in Trinidad, taking 4–48 in the West Indies' only innings, and did so again at Barbados, in the first innings of the fourth Test.

Australia had surprised by choosing only three specialist bowlers but Hughes and McDermott claimed four wickets apiece as the home side tumbled out for 149, their lowest score in a home Test since 1972–73.

Importantly for Hughes, he had managed to claim a key wicket in Haynes, who had starred to that point in the rubber, as well as the scalps of Dujon and Carl Hooper. When Australia finished the day at 2–56, trailing by 93 runs overall, they entertained visions of a substantial lead and squaring the series at 1–1.

It was here that the bowlers made a considerable mistake. As a group, McDermott, Reid and Hughes joined an Australian supporters' tour group for a party that night and celebrated well past their normal bedtimes. A number of other members of the Australian side were also present. The bowling trio, having worked hard to dismiss the West Indians in the space of 61.1 overs on a ground where they had not lost for more than 50 years, were expecting at least a full day's rest and did not look after themselves as well as they could have done.

Instead, the West Indians promptly rose from the canvas to fire out Australia for 134 on the second morning and led by 153 runs overall at stumps, having reached 1–138.

Greenidge and Haynes benefited from poor bowling from all three pacemen and coach Bob Simpson was ropeable that a chance at the Frank Worrell Trophy had been allowed to slip by through complacency. The Australians had assumed they had the West Indies on the mat, without delivering the knockout punch.

'We had always worked on a trust system and never had a curfew at all in the Australian team,' Simpson says.

'You have to have faith in your players to do the right thing and for them to have done that was absolutely stupid. We were talking about professionalism and that was totally unprofessional. I think they were just so delighted with what happened that they got carried away and over-confident.'

Border would not learn of the incident for some years, most probably because his players all knew how strongly he disapproved of going out during a match. In the captain's eyes, a night out had to be earned — by winning a Test match.

Merv Hughes had always put his hand up when he had been in the wrong and had to do so here. But that wasn't going to bring Australia back into the match, or the series.

'We were feeling happy about life on the first night of that Barbados Test,' Hughes says.

'A few in the tour group asked me what we were doing and we were saying, "We'll be right, we won't be bowling tomorrow".

'We were expecting to bat for two days but, all of a sudden, we were bowling by lunch and it's, "Oh shit". By stumps on the second day, the series was just about gone.'

Just about gone. An out-of-form Greenidge had been under enormous pressure to retain his place in the side but had been given one last chance on home soil to prove himself.

Taking the lead role, he raced to 85 by the close of the second day and would be joined by Richardson on the third morning. Australia had to get back into the match by lunch or they could forget about the Worrell Trophy for another few years.

Luck, though, would turn its back on Merv Hughes at Kensington Oval, Bridgetown. Richardson, who had

*Moustaches all round in Barbados, during the '91 tour.*

made centuries at both Kingston and Georgetown, joined Greenidge inside the first 45 minutes of the morning's play. A compulsive hooker when in form, he top-edged McDermott to Hughes at fine leg with just a single to his name and the overall lead at less than 170.

Hughes moved quickly but the ball reached him low and bobbled out of his hands, giving the right-hander a life he would turn into an innings of 99. By the time Richardson departed four hours later, Greenidge was on 179 and the overall lead was nearing 400.

Simpson, who was never one to mollycoddle his players at any time in either his captaincy or coaching reign, bluntly told the big man he had cost Australia the series.

'You can't change lbws but the dropped catch was something that could have been changed. To get told, in front of the rest of the side, I had cost them the Test series hit me pretty hard. I was pretty disappointed as I came off for the break but I didn't want to think I had cost the team a Test match. Being told that was like rubbing salt into the wounds and I couldn't find a hole big enough to throw myself into,' says Hughes.

His confidence shattered, Hughes made absolutely no impact for the rest of the innings, as the West Indies raced the match away from Australia's grasp. Greenidge would power on to 226 and Richards would allow the total to climb to 9–536, an impossible target of 552 for victory, before he finally called a halt on the fourth day.

Hughes' return of 1–125 from 36 overs had left him, for the second successive Test in which the West Indies had stepped up the pace, short of the standards set by the best in the world. Australia were hammered by 343 runs on the fifth day, forfeiting the series, and any hopes of challenging the best team in the world would have to be laid to rest, at least until 1992–93. Merv Hughes, like most of his team-mates it must be said, could star against every other team in the world but often struggled against the West Indies.

Australia won a consolation victory in the final Test at Antigua but the lasting memory would be of the bitterness between the two squads. Richards had launched an unprecedented tirade against Simpson in the aftermath of the fourth Test victory and squabbling between various players was apparent to all in the fourth and fifth Tests.

After the tour of the Caribbean, the Australians headed to Bermuda for a well-earned 10-day rest. Hughes was joined by 27-year-old Sue Kelly, a mothercare nurse he had known since 1984.

On the occasion of their first meeting, at the Castle Hotel in North Melbourne, Hughes was too shy to say hello and sent over a female friend, to tell Sue he would like to meet her.

Sue, who had no interest in cricket or cricketers, declined that invitation. However, despite that initial hiccup, the pair developed a platonic friendship over the next few years. In late 1990, the relationship changed and they began to go out. After less than six months as a couple, Hughes proposed and Sue accepted. They were married in May 1992.

Hughes had done a reasonable job in the Caribbean, as evidenced by four separate hauls of four wickets in an innings during the Test series, but he had also been found wanting on two crucial occasions when the pressure had been raised. In his favour, by the end of the tour he weighed 98 kg, just six kilos more than new-ball partner McDermott, and none could fault his commitment on tour or his dedication to improving himself.

The Australians on the beach in Antigua, the day after winning the final Test. Left to right: Mark Taylor, Geoff Marsh, Merv Hughes and Terry Alderman.

Unfortunately, at the end of the series, he would go right off the rails. So much so that his next summer of cricket would be affected.

After being hounded by Alcott and Simpson throughout the Caribbean for his dietary habits — most notably after news spread of a 'Hughes and McDermott eating exhibition' at KFC in Barbados one day — Hughes lashed out. Within 10 minutes of the fall of the last wicket in Antigua to secure victory, Hughes fronted Alcott with a full plate of eclairs, feigned to offer him one and scoffed the lot. Washed down with a few cans of coke, he declared his tour and his diet were now over.

In his time for Australia, Hughes would never see two figures again in the weight department. And this, obviously, would increase the stress on his knees.

'From the time we left Antigua, I put on 13 kg in six weeks,' Hughes says. 'I really let myself go and I don't think I ever recovered.'

Alcott and Simpson would now hound Hughes about his weight up until the time he was omitted from the Australian team some three years later. The extra weight he carried certainly had no effect in the short-term as India were blitzed 4–0 in the home summer of 1991–92. McDermott again starred, being named International Cricketer of the Year, but Hughes backed him superbly with 22 wickets at 23.22 apiece.

Just as they had for the visits of Pakistan and Sri Lanka two summers beforehand, the majority of batsmen from the sub-continent found Hughes far too difficult a prospect to deal with.

Players who had arrived in Australia with enormous reputations, such as Kris Srikkanth, Sanjay Manjrekar, Dilip Vengsarkar, Mohammad Azharuddin and Navjot Sidhu, were totally unable to cope with the bounce of Australian wickets. Between them, the quintet scored a miserable 784 runs from 40 Test innings and averaged just 19.60 collectively.

It would be harsh to label the group as scared on the bouncier Australian wickets but when captain Border wanted a wicket, he could call on Hughes at any time in this series and it seemed that none of the batsmen were too interested in staying around for long.

'In the series we played at home against sides such as India, Pakistan and Sri Lanka, there were a few guys who fell into the category that Merv could sort out,' Border says. 'There were guys who were good Test cricketers but, when they were put under the acid, you felt like you had got them.

'Merv always exposed those guys very well by his sheer presence. He looked menacing and you knew you were going to face a lot of difficult bowling. I just knew I could bring Mervyn on and he would get the better of those guys we would try to muscle out. Unless you were prepared to stand your ground, he would steamroll you.'

The two exceptions to the rule explained by Border were veteran opener Ravi Shastri and a kid in the middle-order by the name of Sachin Tendulkar. Shastri pounded a double-century in the third Test, at the SCG, while Tendulkar revealed his undoubted class as a prodigy of 19, with centuries in both Sydney and Perth. Critics could point to the fact Shastri had cleared a path for the boy genius at Sydney but the Australians were awestruck by his knock of 114 out of 171 scored while he was at the wicket in Perth. For the last Test, he had been raised to No. 4 in the batting order, ahead of veterans Vengsarkar and Azharuddin, and none could dispute his class.

By the end of the summer, Hughes would be nearing 150 Test wickets but was still well over 100 kilos. The haranguing from Simpson and Alcott was answered simply by Hughes in the form of his results. His weight could not be an issue, as far as he was concerned, because he was match-fit, bowling well and taking wickets.

For Victoria, Hughes was still the money man. Even though he was only playing four games at most a year, due to international commitments, his presence in the State team meant volumes in terms of spirit and effect.

Young pace bowlers Paul Reiffel and Damien Fleming both benefited with wickets from his presence at the other end while a tyro leg-spinner, Shane Warne, watched the confidence of Hughes in the middle and modelled his approach on him.

Reiffel made his Test debut in the fifth Test, at the WACA, while Warne was thrown in (in this case, before his time), to suffer as Shastri and Tendulkar peeled off their big centuries in the third Test. Warne perhaps suffered early from copying a few of Hughes' eating habits but his selection was to be the last piece in the puzzle for Australia.

Victorian teams had not enjoyed much of their cricket in the mid–1980s, due to so many losses, but fresh from a Sheffield Shield victory in 1990–91 and with a jovial Hughes in their side, 1991–92 was a rewarding season, even though they did not reach the Shield final.

A pre-season trip to England, as Shield champions, to meet county champions Essex resulted in a draw, with Hughes starring with the bat and adding to the growing repertoire of legends involving him.

As he and Tony Dodemaide fought for a draw on the last day, Hughes survived a confident caught-behind appeal from Test spinner John Childs and then went down to discuss the decision with his partner.

'Geez, I hate that.'

'Yeah. It's a bloody disgrace when they try to cheat you out like that,' Dodemaide sympathised.

Hughes at the WACA in October 1991, during an FAI Insurance Cup match against Western Australia.

'No. If I'd got a bit more wood on it, it would have gone for four.'

Against South Australia, in mid-November, captain Simon O'Donnell instructed his fast bowler to go out and have a look at the bowling for a while before taking a few swings, in preparation for a declaration.

Spinner Tim May had posted a long-off and a long-on on the fence and tossed up the first ball in case Hughes fancied a swipe down the ground. Sure enough, he rose to the bait and was caught by Glenn Bishop on the long-on fence for a golden duck.

'What the bloody hell were you doing? Don't you listen to anything your captain tells you?' O'Donnell raged when Hughes returned to the Victorian rooms some two minutes after his departure.

'Oh what's your problem Simon, never got a good one early?' Hughes replied, dissolving the room into paroxysms of laughter.

Fleming and Warne both fell victim to the Hughes room service feasts on tour, and Warne was also nailed during his second Test match, in Adelaide. Unable to sleep, Hughes rang room service at 2 a.m. and ordered two cheeseburgers, two club sandwiches, two serves of fries and a couple of milkshakes before waking Warne and asking him what he wanted. Warne, who was decidedly porky in his first few Tests before paring down over the winter of 1992, joined him for a couple of toasted cheese sandwiches and a milkshake.

At 3 a.m., having consumed everything from their 'diet of champions', Hughes gave the rookie the assignment of pushing the room service trolley down the hall and placing it in front of another person's room to ensure they would not be discovered in the morning by either Alcott or Simpson. Naked, Warne had to be let back into his room by a kindly concierge after Hughes slammed the door on him.

As for Reiffel, his first Test would be made memorable by batting with Hughes. The debutant joined Hughes in the middle at 7–290 after the dismissal of Ian Healy. Reiffel blocked his first ball from Javagal Srinath and then joined his partner for a mid-wicket conference.

'How are you going?' Hughes asked.

'No problems. I've got Simon covered.'

'What are you on about?'

'Simon O'Donnell got a golden duck in his first Test innings. Even if I get out next ball, I've done better than him,' Reiffel told Hughes.

Having considered such a statement for a moment or two, Hughes told Reiffel he had made a five-ball duck on his debut for Australia back in 1985–86.

'Well, you're my next target then, in the next over.'

In Srinath's next over, Reiffel got a thin inside edge to the second ball he faced and the Indian side went up in unison for a huge appeal.

As umpire Tony Crafter answered in the fortunate batsman's favour, all he could hear from the bowler's end was Hughes.

'He's hit that. Give him out, he's hit it.'

Crafter did not change his decision and, unfortunately for Hughes, Reiffel got away from him to make 9 in his maiden innings for Australia.

*Hughes on Shane Warne: 'A spin bowler is only as good as the quick bowling from the other end.'*

# CHAPTER NINE

# THAT'S THE WAY HE LIVED

n the four-and-a-bit years between November 1987 and March 1992, after their victory over England at Eden Gardens in Calcutta, Australia were officially classified as the One-day champions of the world. After winning the World Cup, Australia certainly justified the title in the years that followed, dominating One-day cricket as they gradually built a strong Test side.

Captain Allan Border showed a rare flair for One-day tactics and the highpoint of Australia's One-day success was probably their emphatic 4–1 victory over the West Indies in the Caribbean in 1991. No side had ever beaten the West Indians in a One-day series on their home soil but Australia dominated them, their only loss coming with the interruption of rain.

Unfortunately, Australia's aggressiveness and willingness to take risks in One-day cricket was not converted into the Test arena on that tour and the West Indies held on to their unofficial title of world Test champions.

Merv Hughes played only a minimal role in the One-day side in that period, being stuck behind the likes of Terry Alderman, Bruce Reid and Simon O'Donnell in the initial stages of his Australian career and then a rejuvenated Craig McDermott and Mike Whitney.

Hughes had an impressive summer against India in 1991–92, intimidating the majority of their batting line-up, however few expected him to be named in the 14-man Australian squad for the World Cup, to be played in Australia and New Zealand.

*Opposite: Hughes at Australian team training, 1991–92.*

Whitney, McDermott and Reid had three pace bowling spots parcelled up, leaving Hughes to contest the final spot with 1987 World Cup hero Simon O'Donnell and the emerging Paul Reiffel.

Reiffel had yet to make a major impact in One-day cricket but was expected to become a regular in the future while O'Donnell had long been a key member of the side but was suffering from a shoulder injury. In the end, Reiffel's lack of experience counted against him and Hughes was preferred to O'Donnell when the selectors were unwilling to risk the all-rounder's fitness.

Merv Hughes did not expect to play much of a role in the four-week tournament and joked he was on a Kontiki tour with Mark Taylor. Taylor, had also been regularly omitted from the One-day side at that time, was included in the 14 along with Hughes, prompting the fast bowler to tell the world, 'He's Kon and I'm Tiki. We're the Kontiki brothers'.

Australia had a poor World Cup, starting with three losses from their first four matches, and were never able to settle on their best line-up. Their previously successful batting order was shuffled around endlessly while the bowlers were also turned over in a bid to find the best combination. By the time Australia were playing their final qualifying match against the West Indies at the MCG and had regained some semblance of form, they knew they could not qualify for the semi-finals and fifth spot was their best hope.

Hughes played just the one match for the tournament, remaining unbeaten on 0 and finishing with 1–49 from his nine overs against India in Brisbane.

Off the field, coach Bob Simpson, physiotherapist Errol Alcott and team manager Ian McDonald were less than happy with the weight he gained during the month on the road.

Hughes had always needed regular work to remain match-fit and the inactivity of the World Cup saw him blow out by some five kilos. It would cost him dearly.

Just as in 1988, the recommendation was again made that he should miss Australia's next tour, meaning he was omitted from the 14-man squad to tour Sri Lanka in August of 1992. The outstanding work he had done in the Test arena since 1989 had been destroyed in the space of a month, and he would have to start from scratch to win a place against the West Indies for the summer of 1992–93. Steve Waugh would also be omitted from the Australian touring team, a decision that set him on a determined path to become the best batsman in the world.

Aside from Hughes' poor report card from the World Cup, chairman of selectors Lawrie Sawle said the panel also believed that the conditions in Sri Lanka would not be conducive to a bowler of Hughes' style. Joining McDermott and Whitney in the tour party was Victorian all-rounder Tony Dodemaide — a naggingly accurate bowler who would be able to tie down an end in difficult conditions.

As it turned out, the wickets Australia were presented with in Colombo seamed appreciably at all three Test venues and the squad badly missed Hughes' venom. But for a colossal error of judgement from Sri Lankan vice-captain Aravinda De Silva on the final day of the first Test, Australia would have lost the series 1–0.

Sri Lanka needed just 54 for victory with eight wickets in hand in the first Test when De Silva attempted a wild slog at McDermott and Allan Border held a brilliant catch, prompting a collapse of 8–37 to give Australia victory by 16 runs.

Border tossed the ball to Shane Warne in the closing overs, even though he had been smashed out of the attack in the first innings, and the young leg-spinner defied his then-Test record of one wicket for 332 runs to wrap up the innings with a burst of 3–0.

Warne had arrived.

The perception that Merv Hughes would automatically struggle on the sub-continent grated mightily with the fast bowler through his career and he remains deeply disappointed he never played a Test in either Pakistan, Sri Lanka or India.

'I had a short tour to India in 1989 with a One-day tournament and the wickets were certainly slow but I did get a few wickets in the games I played,' he says.

'It was hot and it was difficult, but I certainly would have liked to have tried myself in that part of the world, and known how I would have gone, rather than always be left wondering.'

After being omitted from the tour party to Sri Lanka, Hughes would soon get his chance to seek atonement with a first-up meeting with a

*Hughes with umpire Steve Randell at the Gabba, first Test against the West Indies, 1992–93.*

full-strength New South Wales side in the opening Sheffield Shield match of the 1992–93 season.

The fast bowler had performed superbly against India in 1991–92 and finished the season with 53 first-class wickets overall at 25. However, he had not taken a single five-wicket haul during the previous summer and this, too, had been noted by the selection panel.

His pace and aggression were undoubted but did his size allow him to come back just as hard at the end of the day and mop up the tail? Team-mate Tony Dodemaide pointed out exactly this fact when Hughes searched for reasons to explain his omission.

Dodemaide's words hit home and Hughes was in peak condition for the meeting with international team-mates Mark Taylor and the Waugh twins at the SCG.

He roared through the Blues' innings to secure 6–83 and dismissed Steve Waugh first ball with a vicious delivery aimed straight at his throat. If anyone was going to question his ability to last a day, they had been shown quick smart.

The effort impressed the national selectors enough for them to name Hughes in the Australian XI side to meet the West Indies in Hobart, a fortnight before the opening Test at the Gabba.

For this tilt at the champions, Hughes' experience and aggression would be vital but he was not going to be handed his position in the side on a platter. The panel had also decided on a policy of stroke-makers in the middle-order for the series against a Windies' side now captained by Richie Richardson and would give Steve Waugh a chance to impress in Hobart.

Under their plan to wrest the Worrell Trophy, batsmen had to try to score runs at a reasonable rate because, in a war of attrition, they would eventually be dismissed by the class of Curtly Ambrose, Courtney Walsh and new paceman Ian Bishop. As such, the Waugh twins would take two spots in the middle-order, while youngster Damien Martyn was also slotted into the team.

Hughes and Steve Waugh both won spots for Brisbane by impressing in Hobart. Waugh contributed a double of 95 and 100 not out while Hughes bagged 3–76 and 3–44, including the wickets of top-order batsmen Richardson, Desmond Haynes, Keith Arthurton and Gus Logie.

While Waugh won back his Test position after some 18 months on the sidelines, he remembers the match for other reasons. After being dismissed for 95 on the opening day, he came across an item of useless trivia in the *Hobart Mercury* which declared that the average person broke wind 14 times a day.

Waugh told Hughes, who was padded up waiting to bat, that there must be a lot of people in the world not pulling their weight because of the work Hughes was doing in that area. To rub it in a little further, he declared Hughes was capable of notching 100 in a single 24-hour period.

The fast bowler rose to the challenge.

'Merv spent the night loading up on fizzy drinks and all kinds of food that would help him the next day for his assault on the record,' Waugh says. 'He thought 70 would be reachable and he was farting away like a trooper the next day in the field. He was tearing them off and got to the average in about an hour and a half. By the end of the day, he was up to 50-odd and then he went out to dinner and I went out separately.

'I came back and there were about six messages under my door. I opened the first one and it said, "Just lodged number 62 at 7.36 p.m. Message taken by Cherie".

'I opened the next one and it said, "68 and still feeling strong".

'He was updating me with messages every half hour or so. I was about to go to bed and I get a phone call. All I hear is this huge fart, and then Merv saying, "that's 81". He just killed it and he was really proud of himself.'

Waugh has still got the phone messages from the Grand Chancellor.

The first Test match, at the Gabba in Brisbane, would be a much more serious affair, though.

Gordon Greenidge, Jeff Dujon, Viv Richards and Malcolm Marshall had all retired from the West Indian side since the 1991 tour, while it was felt Australia's best chances of victory would come in the second and third Tests in Melbourne and Sydney, where the pitches were less conducive to fast bowling. The Brisbane wicket had begun to change character from its old seaming days under the excellent new curator Kevin Mitchell jnr but there was still the worry Ambrose and co. could run through the side if conditions assisted them.

Ironically, with pace expected to dominate, it was the spin of Carl Hooper that played the major role in limiting Australia's first innings total to 293. Hooper claimed 4–75, including both David Boon and Mark Waugh.

In reply, the West Indies had reached Australia's total with six wickets down and only the bowlers to support century-maker Keith Arthurton. It was imperative for the tail to be cleaned up as quickly as possible and Australia begin their second innings to put pressure on the visitors.

Instead, Arthurton fashioned an important lead of 78 by cobbling together the support of the pacemen for long enough to reach 157 not out. After that, Border could not consider a declaration and Australia batted into the final day, eventually leaving a target of 231 from a minimum of 65 overs when they were dismissed for 308.

The most likely result seemed to be a draw, with a West Indies victory a definite possibility. To bowl the visitors out in just over four hours did not look feasible, but there was the slim chance that either Haynes, Richardson or Brian Lara could get going and carry the West Indies to victory. The pressure that only a Test match can bring was well and truly on.

In a crazy 20 minutes before lunch, the West Indies collapsed sensationally to 3–3 and were 4–9 within two overs of the resumption. Now, it seemed that only Australia could win and they had four hours to take a 1–0 lead in the rubber.

However, Richardson, who had hooked a six from McDermott for his second scoring stroke, and survived a contentious lbw appeal, would not be moved. His four-hour 66 frustrated the home side and he elicited the support of Ian Bishop, 16 not out in 107 minutes, to earn a draw.

As Australia's frustrations grew on the final day, Hughes snapped while bowling to Bishop. When another raucous lbw appeal had been refused by umpire Steve Randell, the bowler asked him, 'How come that was out yesterday but it's not out today?'

After Randell chatted with fellow umpire Terry Prue, Hughes would be reported for the first time in his Test career, under the International Cricket Council's newly-introduced Code of Conduct. Captain Border would also be reported by Randell for a separate incident during a tension-filled last day.

'I took exception to what Merv said because it implies that I'm cheating,' Randell says.

'I've been to many hearings where what is said on the field has changed a bit by the time we've got to the hearing, but Merv was very matter of fact, owned up to it and didn't deny one word.'

Under the ICC's new code of behaviour, a player could be fined up to 75 per cent of his match fee for an offence or suspended for up to three Test matches. Hughes appeared in front of match referee Raman Subba Row, from England, with the umpires to give evidence. As is allowed, Hughes was joined by coach Simpson and team manager McDonald.

Hughes, who had always put his hand up when in the wrong, pleaded guilty and was fined the minimum $400 — 10 per cent of his match fee.

According to Subba Row, Hughes' honesty saved him from any stiffer penalty.

'He came in to the hearing and said, "I said that, but you know me don't you? I don't bear any malice to anyone. I'm a bit of an idiot for doing that and I'm sorry,"' Subba Row says.

'He was so nice that we were all laughing and joking and chuckling. That was in contrast to Allan Border, who failed to turn up for his own hearing. These days, Border wouldn't have played again until he had the courtesy to appear at the hearing.

'As a referee, Merv didn't worry me greatly at all. It all happened in a moment with him and then was forgotten straight away.'

While Subba Row did not view Hughes' offence in any serious light, it was still an official mark against his record. Also, Australia had been unable to close out an important Test match and the side had allowed their frustrations to take a hold, underlining a trend that had been developing for some time.

Australian tempers had frayed at times during the World Cup, when things were not going well, particularly in a match against Pakistan in Perth. The 1991 tour of the West Indies was also clearly in the minds of cricket's followers as a tour in which bad blood was evident. The behaviour of the Australian players was on the lips of cricket followers, and in the mind of the new ACB Chairman, Alan Crompton, when he was elected in September 1992.

Crompton, a lawyer by training, had played many years of club cricket in Sydney and is an engaging and amiable personality. He felt the national team had often been unjustly treated by the media with regard to their behaviour, but certainly had to agree that standards on the field were an issue.

'Prior to my coming in as Chairman in September 1992, I had a concern about the Australian team being seen as "ugly Australians" when this judgement wasn't really justified,' Crompton says.

'I didn't necessarily agree they deserved that reputation but it was a fact that they had that reputation. I felt the team were often accused of sledging-type activities when no such thing had occurred. People were often content to accuse them of behaviour that fitted the reputation, rather than fitted the facts.'

Australia had been unable to complete a final-day victory in Brisbane because spinner Greg Matthews posed no real threat to the tourists. Border bemoaned the absence of leg-spinner Warne, who had played for the Australian XI in Hobart and performed solidly, but was not considered for the Gabba.

Warne's lack of experience (four Tests to that point) had counted against him in Brisbane but he was subsequently included in Matthews' place for the Boxing Day Test on his home turf at the MCG. The blond 23-year-old would take 7–52 on the last day to spin Australia to a 1–0 lead in the series. He would not be omitted from the Australian team again and, within 12 months, was being hailed as the best thing to hit international cricket in decades.

Hughes had started the West Indies series well and continued his good form at Melbourne, ripping through the top-order in the first innings and securing the key wicket of Haynes in the second innings.

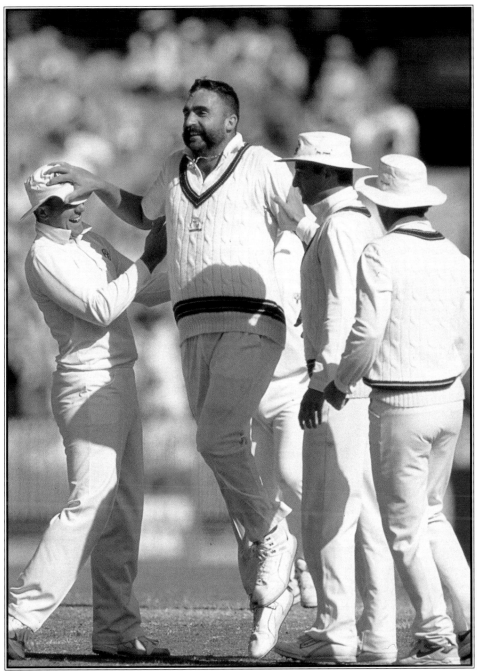

*Jubilation at the MCG in late December 1992, during Australia's only Test victory over the West Indies that summer.*

The fast bowler reduced the West Indies to 3–33 but his right knee continued to cause him problems. Alcott told him he was certain he would get through the Test series without inflicting permanent damage but would, again, be likely to need minor keyhole surgery after the tour of New Zealand in February and March. It was a matter of whether he could deal with the pain.

By now, the ache in Hughes' knee had become chronic but could be blocked out with a combination of painkillers and courage. At the start of each session in which he would be required to bowl, Hughes would pop two tablets into his mouth and take the field.

'Merv was a chronic digesic pill-popper, which are the ones that are now banned,' Alcott says. 'He would take two before a session and then go out and bowl and field for two hours. Before the next session, he would take another two and then another two at the next break. This went on for the last few years of his career. He knew he would suffer some discomfort and he would take these pills and it wouldn't hurt as much. That's the way he lived so he could play for Australia.'

The West Indians were also well aware that Hughes was struggling, just by looking at him when he arrived at the ground in the morning and departed at night.

Walsh, who has carried injuries as well as any bowler in history, said the tourists fully expected Hughes to withdraw from the Australian side during the course of the rubber and they were amazed he kept fronting up. The fact that he was taking wickets as well only heightened their admiration for him.

'You can tell when a guy is struggling and he's not 100 per cent fit. In 1992–93, we thought Merv was in trouble with his knee and was getting over the hill,' Walsh recalls.

'He still got wickets though, and then he had a tremendous series in England. You could tell his injuries weren't healing but he would not stop. That takes a lot of guts.'

The drawn third Test at Sydney was a bat-a-thon with the 19 wickets taken for the match costing the bowlers a massive 64.50 each. Three centuries and six half-centuries were scored on a flat SCG wicket with the undoubted highlight being Lara's peerless knock of 277.

A much more bowler-friendly wicket at the Adelaide Oval promised a result, so Australia's 1–0 lead would either become an unbeatable margin or a tied result going into the final game at Perth, where conditions traditionally favoured the West Indies. In fact, Adelaide would host one of the great Tests in history and Australian hearts would be shattered late on the fourth day with a 1-run loss — the narrowest defeat in 115 years of Test cricket.

On the opening day, Hughes rifled through the order to claim 5–64 — his sixth such bag for Australia — but the West Indies tally of 252 comfortably headed Australia's reply of 213. In that Australian innings, Hughes' gutsy knock of 43 would be the only time he would top-score for Australia in his Test career.

Recalled spinner Tim May then claimed a stunning 5–9 to fire out the visitors for 146 in their second innings and Border's side began the fourth day a mere 186 runs from claiming the Worrell Trophy.

Ambrose, who had taken 6–74 in the first innings, enlisted the support of the able Walsh to reduce Australia to 7–74 when Hughes was trapped lbw for 1. As the fast bowler paced dejectedly from the ground, he felt he had failed to support young Justin Langer at the other end. Langer had shown commendable guts in his Test debut, but it seemed it would be nigh on impossible for him to gather 112 more runs for victory with only Warne, May and McDermott in support. However, as it happened, the foursome made 110 of them and lost the Test by just one run.

When May and McDermott's heroic 88-minute 10th-wicket stand of 40 was broken by Walsh, Border hurled a ball at the floor of the Australian dressing-room so hard that it bounced back up and hit the roof.

The anger and disappointment in the Australian rooms was overpowering, and these emotions boiled over when the West Indies (who had also won the World Series Cup finals) blitzed Australia inside three days on a greentop in Perth to retain the Worrell Trophy for the seventh consecutive series.

At the WACA, Hughes and Border were both reported for the second time that summer. This time, Hughes was reported for swearing by umpires Col Timmins and Steve Randell but maintained he was only swearing at himself.

*Over page: Hughes top-scoring for the only time in his Test career, against the Windies at the Adelaide Oval.*

With a reputation for owning up to his mistakes, he was reprimanded only.

Hughes' knee ached and his heart hurt after coming so close to upsetting the best side in the world. A New Zealand tour beckoned in a fortnight's time, as did an Ashes series in late May, and, physically, he was struggling.

Alcott decided Hughes should have surgery after the tour of New Zealand and, with the month's break before the tour of England, he would then be right for the start of his second Ashes tour.

Alcott was also determined that Hughes would not fall into the old trap of again gaining weight rapidly and requested team manager McDonald buy a set of scales so he could monitor Hughes' weight daily.

Hughes took the purchase of the scales as a huge insult, but had no comeback when ordered to get on them by McDonald and Alcott during the last warm-up game, in Nelson, before the Test against the Kiwis.

'Jump on the scales!' McDonald yelled after Hughes had repeatedly refused to get on.

Hughes duly jumped, and an imported $150 set of German scales were promptly rendered useless. McDonald's subsequent explosion of temper at the fast bowler cleared the Australian dressing-rooms. However, Hughes succeeded in his goal because another set of scales wasn't purchased on tour.

Australia were expected to regain the Trans-Tasman trophy — lost at Wellington in 1990 — on the basis of their perceived fast bowling strength and depth in batting. However, New Zealand had always proved to be a difficult opponent on home soil.

It was uncertain what effect Warne would have on the series after he had been harshly treated by Crowe in a warm-up game. Admittedly, though, Warne had bowled nothing but standard leg breaks to Crowe and had not shown him his flipper, top-spinner or big-turning leg break. The New Zealanders had fatally under-estimated the young spinner's tactical nous.

Australia duly won the first Test in a canter by an innings and 60 runs, made doubly memorable for Border's achievement in becoming the highest run-scorer in Test history. Warne proved he had double-bluffed Crowe and the Kiwis by snaring match figures of 7–86 to be named man of the match. Hughes was also an overwhelming success: the fast bowler claimed 2–44 and 4–62 and enjoyed himself immensely with a knock of 45 from 46 balls in Australia's imposing total of 485.

Coming to the wicket at 6–363, Hughes joined the new world-record-holder, Border, and was given a licence by his captain to play some shots. Having been invited to slog, Hughes duly struck three boundaries and four huge sixes. Off-spinner Dipak Patel was twice put on the Lancaster Park grandstand roof while the quick bowlers, Chris Cairns and Murphy Su'a, were each lofted over the boundary.

While Merv Hughes enjoyed every one of his 212 Test wickets, he got a rare pleasure from hitting sixes, especially with a recognised batsman up the other end he could skite to at the end of an over.

'I do like hitting the ball a long way in the air and when you've got a few runs on the board, you've got the leeway to do it. When I was batting with "batsmen", I enjoyed hitting a six more because I knew it would annoy them more. They'd be working hard on their techniques and pushing the ball around for ones and twos and then I'd come out and just swing and plant one for six,' says Hughes.

Australia started the series in dominant fashion and New Zealand looked to be in total disarray midway through the second Test at Wellington when Crowe offered to resign the New Zealand captaincy.

Plagued by poor press in his home country, Crowe fronted a media conference on the second night of the Test and demanded to know from one local journalist why his paper had run a story on AIDS rumours and whether the journalist thought Crowe was gay.

Sir Richard Hadlee, who was working for the series' sponsors as a liaison officer, had to call a halt to the slanging match between Crowe and the journalist which bemused all the Australians who witnessed it. Amazingly, the outburst galvanised the New Zealand team, which fought back strongly in the second Test to earn a draw.

New Zealand required victory in Auckland to square the series and went through the Australians on the first day, dismissing the tourists for 139.

Paceman Danny Morrison, who had starred in the second Test with 7–89, was dominant again with 6–39, as a combination of excellent bowling and a mis-reading of the pitch by Border put paid to a decent Australian first innings.

*Mark Greatbatch, the New Zealand left-hander who had a highly-publicised on-field spat with Hughes in 1993.*

New Zealand scrambled to a lead of 85 and Australia's second innings of 285 left the Kiwis with a target of 201 for victory in five sessions. Unless rain came, time would not be a problem — whether the home side could score the runs required was the only discussion point.

Up to the second innings of the final Test at Auckland, the enigmatic Mark Greatbatch had had a poor series indeed. Famous for his epic unbeaten 146 at Perth in 1989–90, Greatbatch was in the midst of a horror slump that had seen him post successive Test scores of 4, 0, 61, 0 and 32 for a total of 97 runs at 19.40.

His Test place had been in grave danger and, in the opinion of seasoned cricket observers in the Shaky Isles, he was paying the price for his electrifying 1992 World Cup. Greatbatch had been one of the sensations of the tournament with his free hitting at the top of the order but an attempt to take a similar approach into Test cricket had been a sorry failure. Still, with a target of 201 for victory, he would stick with his game plan and play his shots.

Like Hughes, Greatbatch is an emotional cricketer who wears his heart on his sleeve. His highs are very high and his lows can be equally so. But when he is in form, he is an extremely difficult player to counter, as he was on this fourth day.

Almost immediately, the left-hander put Hughes onto the roof of the square-leg grandstand and smacked McDermott for a pair of boundaries. On his way to a breezy 29 from 30 balls before he was bowled by Hughes, Greatbatch was more than happy to exchange words with both Australian opening bowlers.

'I had gone out there with the deliberate intention of trying to be positive and hitting McDermott and Hughes off their line,' Greatbatch says.

'Things were pretty fiery and I decided to go out and upset the apple-cart by being positive. I wanted to attack and I decided on the approach that had worked during the World Cup by lifting a few over the top early.'

During Hughes' third over, at the height of an exchange between the pair after Greatbatch's third boundary, the Australian fast bowler spat down the pitch.

Due to the distance between bowler and batsman, Hughes' spittle fell well short of Greatbatch but the camera shot from over the batsman's shoulder made it appear as if he had been spat at from only a metre or two. The incident would be replayed endlessly for the remaining three hours or so of play, both in New Zealand and at home in Australia.

Greatbatch and New Zealand captain Martin Crowe both felt Hughes' actions set a poor example to children but, equally, both knew there was considerable distance between the pair.

'At the time, I wasn't that impressed with what Merv was doing because of the example it was setting but, at the end of the day, we got together and sorted it out over a beer. I think a lot of people couldn't believe we were talking after what had gone on out on the ground, but Merv was a different bloke on the field. He came and apologised and it was forgotten by the next time we played against each other,' recounts Greatbatch.

Crowe, who always enjoyed a run-in on the field with Hughes, felt it was the one time the bowler had stepped over the line in his meetings with Australia.

'Merv's antics in that game could be seen clearly by young kids and the crowd and they were unacceptable. He got so fired up with Greatbatch and it got a bit ugly there for a while. It was like big-time wrestling on the old black-and-white TV and these two big blokes were going at it hammer and tongs.

'It was probably a sigh of relief for the whole crowd when Paddy got out and we were all able to go back to normal cricket.'

Hughes felt he had been stitched up by the television coverage of the day's play. Yes he had spat in the batsman's direction but not *at* the batsman.

Equally, Greatbatch's desire to upset both bowlers with a few well-chosen words was underplayed because little could be detected from under his helmet.

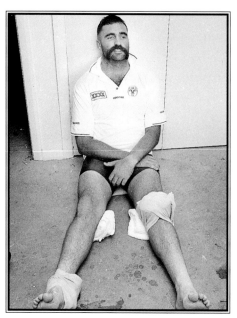

*Hughes in New Zealand in 1993 — ice on the right ankle, ice on the back of the right knee, ice on the left knee ...*

'It was an aggressive moment but I would certainly never go out and spit on a person,' Hughes says.

'We were both talking to each other and as I said a few things, I spat down the pitch in the middle of what I was saying. Because it seemed like there was nothing between us, it seemed a lot worse than it was.'

In Alan Crompton's view, the fast bowler did not think enough about the image he was presenting. He would speak to Hughes before the team's departure for the Ashes tour.

'Three very early isolated incidents spread over the day were packaged together and made to look like a very ugly day at the cricket,' Crompton says. 'I believe that was grossly unfair to Merv and the coverage did him over in that sense.

'One of those incidents was the spitting affair and the camera coming over Greatbatch's shoulder made it appear as if they were only a few feet apart. Merv spat out of the side of his mouth and not in the direction of Greatbatch at all.

'I felt it was greatly unfair but it did highlight to me that, with nine, 10 or 11 cameras at the ground on the game, no player could ever expect to do anything of even a mildly unacceptable nature and get away with it. My concern that the players should understand this, Merv in particular, prompted a subsequent conversation I had with Merv at the team's farewell dinner to England.

'I was sympathetic to the way he had been treated and the way he had been portrayed but I wanted to make the point that nothing he did on the field would escape scrutiny.'

Neither umpire made a report of what had gone on and match referee Majid Khan did not feel the run-in between the pair was worthy of a hearing. However, team manager Ian McDonald was aware of the growing controversy in Australia over behaviour. In his view, the team needed to be aware that such behaviour would not be tolerated but he also knew the danger of further inflaming what could become a media storm.

Hughes was fined $500 and the penalty was never made public, so the incident would die a quick death.

'In those days, we preferred to handle it that way,' McDonald says.

To cap off a shocking day for Hughes, he dropped a crucial catch in the half-hour before stumps. With New Zealand wobbling somewhat at 5–162, vice-captain Ken Rutherford attempted a square drive at Warne and the ball ballooned to Hughes at point.

If he held the chance, the Kiwis would still be 39 short of victory, with only the bowlers to come. Instead, Hughes misjudged the looping catch and it dropped out of his hands as he came forward.

In these situations, the gallows humour of your team-mates hardly helps.

'What's up Merv?' asked Paul Reiffel as the pair trooped into the team's hotel an hour or so later.

'I was thinking about that catch. It could cost us the series tomorrow,' he replied.

'Don't worry about it. We all drop catches.'

'Thanks mate.'

'Although, I can't remember anyone ever dropping a catch as important as the one you put down.'

'Get stuffed, Pistol.'

The following morning, New Zealand reached their target with five wickets still in hand. After the disappointment of only squaring the Test series, Australia then finished their tour of New Zealand with five One-day internationals.

Due to the fact that McDermott had to return home for groin surgery, Hughes played all five One-dayers as the tourists squeaked home 3–2.

Of more importance though, was the fact that, during the fourth game, in Hamilton, the fast bowler again felt severe pain in his right knee.

He underwent minor surgery as soon as he got home, which proved successful, but if Merv Hughes was to have any impact on the 1993 Ashes series, he would have to be nursed through the early part of a very long tour.

# CHAPTER TEN

# PLAY UNTIL YOU DROP

Youth and recent form were at the forefront of the selectors' minds when they sat down to name a squad of 17 for the 1993 Ashes tour. While the spine of the Australian team contained plenty of experience through the likes of Allan Border, Mark Taylor, David Boon, Ian Healy, Steve Waugh, Craig McDermott and Merv Hughes, a decision was made to infuse some new blood.

After the disappointment of yet again being unable to defeat the West Indies, a long Ashes series offered the chance to blood a few players in the hope they may play crucial roles by the time the 1995 series for the Frank Worrell Trophy rolled around.

Leg-spinner Shane Warne was still a babe with only 11 Tests to his name. Leg-spinners had traditionally never done that well in either New Zealand or England but Warne had defied the pundits in New Zealand and it was hoped he could hold down the spinner's berth for the six Ashes Tests.

Boon, as the side's best player, had to bat at number three, with a new partner to be found for Taylor. Consistent Queensland opener Matthew Hayden, after two seasons in Shield cricket, earned his spot with sheer weight of runs, while New South Wales' Michael Slater was a dramatic bolter after scoring more than 1000 runs in his first full season. One of those two would partner Taylor, with Boon never to be moved again from the number three spot.

In the bowling ranks, McDermott and Hughes were obvious spearheads while Reiffel had been on the fringes for several years, despite playing

*Opposite: In 1993, the Australians had their own 'Terminator'. Hughes poses for publicity shots during his second Ashes tour.*

only four Test matches to the start of the 1993 tour. Their support would come from in-form youngsters Wayne Holdsworth and Brendon Julian, who had both finished the Sheffield Shield season in strong form.

Australia could consider themselves as favourite to retain the Ashes if only because, in Border's opinion, they were fresh off a series against the West Indies.

'Playing the West Indies was always a great lead-in for a series against England,' Border says. 'England was a little off the pace of what the West Indies were like and each time we've gone to England in the last few series, we've just been ready to play and get into them.'

Suitably, the Australian tour party arrived in England on Anzac Day 1993 with just over three weeks to prepare for the three-match One-day international series and a further two weeks before the first Test at Manchester.

Hughes' right knee was causing him further problems during practice at Lord's, upon the team's arrival in London, so it was decided he would not be a starter in the early matches. Straight away, Alcott determined that Hughes would not play in any of the three warm-up one-day matches.

Hughes knew he would have to pace himself through the tour, although this could often be difficult for an exuberant character such as Merv.

'For the first couple of days in England, I was just having treatment all the time from Errol and hardly training at all,' Hughes says.

'The other lads probably got a bit shitty about this.

'Early in the tour, I was supposed to be wrapped up in cotton wool but I went to the rugby league final at Wembley and then went out with Cracka [Wayne Holdsworth] later that night, had a few beers and got home late.

'I was on the fines committee and Cracka put his hand up and said, "I want to fine Merv". He said it was great I couldn't train for four days but managed to get on the piss after a rugby game, on the dance floor and up onto the bar.

'Hooter and Simmo were sitting together and staring at me.

'I said, "Okay, five-pound fine", but he just kept going and going with what I had done, telling them both how my knee locked up while dancing and how I had struggled to get home. That wasn't received well.'

Hughes' exuberance left him on the sidelines for the encounters with an England Amateur XI, the Duchess of Norfolk's XI and Middlesex but proved a blessing in disguise when he was forced to miss the three-dayer at Worcester.

At the New Road Ground, the Australians would cross paths with Graeme Hick. Hick was high on Border's hit-list for the 1993 Ashes series, along with Graham Gooch and Mike Atherton.

In Border's eyes, Hick, Gooch and Atherton were the three batsmen who could win the Ashes for England, so they would come in for heavy treatment when the series started. If a bouncer was to be bowled, it was to be sent down at one of these three. In Gooch's case, he wouldn't be sledged because he thrived on it, but Hick and Atherton were to get the rounds of the kitchen in the major matches. With this in mind, the Australians didn't consider it such a bad thing that Hick wouldn't sight Hughes before the real stuff started.

'I always thought I could get under the skin of Atherton and Hick,' Hughes says.

'The whole point of saying anything to anyone is to make them play differently and I specifically targeted those guys in 1993 because I thought they were a major threat to us. It was a waste of time going at Gooch because he used it well to his advantage.'

While Hughes would not play at Worcester, leg-spinner Warne was named in the Australian side. He was quickly dismissed as a threat by the English media, who were in large attendance at the match, after he finished with second innings figures of 1–122 from 23 overs.

Hick, who thrashed 187 from only 220 balls, belted the leggie for six sixes over the short square-leg boundary and most English observers felt Warne would now play little role in the series.

Unbeknown to them, Warne had similarly bluffed Martin Crowe in New Zealand earlier that year. And, against Hick, Warne had again hidden his flipper, top-spinner and big-spinning leg break from view — only bowling standard leg breaks, six of which disappeared into the crowd.

Alcott took Hughes out of cotton wool in the second week of May, a fortnight after the team's arrival in England, for the encounter with Somerset at Taunton in the south. From 15 overs in the first innings and

11 in the second, the only thing Hughes could console himself with was the fact he had at least got through the match.

Figures of 0–63 and 1–32 aptly summed up his lack of form. Added to his struggle for rhythm, he had also been plagued by no-ball problems. It was not a happy return and there was some distance to travel to be right for the first One-day international in 11 days time.

'At Somerset, they didn't come out at all well,' Hughes says. 'I just hadn't had any bowling and I needed a lot of work.'

Fellow fast bowler McDermott had struggled likewise, bowling more than 30 no-balls for the game. Usually, he would rarely overstep more than two or three times in an innings. McDermott's unhappiness at his own form prompted him to give Border a curt send-off when the captain asked what was going on and, unfortunately for both, their spicy conversation was taped in its entirety by an off-ground directional microphone placed there by an Australian television station.

Border had already run into trouble on tour for knocking over the stumps in the one-dayer against Middlesex at Lord's and a second media storm,

*Hughes with David Boon on the streets of London, hamming it up for the tour sponsor's photographer.*

*Members of the Briars Sporting Club from Sydney, watching Michael Slater and Mark Taylor score hundreds on the opening day of the Lord's Test.*

combined with the form of his fast bowlers, threatened to drive him into his shell.

Holdsworth had struggled to adapt to English conditions and the occasional waywardness of both Reiffel and Julian left Australia with a decidedly inconsistent attack if either one of the frontliners was off key. Both Hughes and McDermott had to be right for the One-dayers.

If Hughes was to have any chance of making the side for the One-day internationals, he would have to play in both the three-day match at Sussex and a one-dayer at Northampton and bowl through his lack of form.

At Sussex, he bowled 26 overs in a rain-affected match and still the wickets would not come. The scalps of middle-order batsmen Colin Wells and Peter Moores would hardly terrify the English camp. McDermott again struggled also, but if there was one small consolation, at least Julian had secured his first five-wicket haul on tour.

Hughes felt he was gradually gaining confidence in himself and his knee had not hurt since he had resumed playing. However, at Northampton, on

May 16, just three days before the opening One-day international, that new-found faith in his fitness would disappear in a moment.

As he walked onto the field to warm-up 15 minutes before the game, Hughes' right knee locked totally for the second time in a month and he could not walk. He could barely put any weight on his right-hand side.

'I was just walking onto the ground and AB told me to get ready because I was bowling,' Hughes says.

'The knee locked and I couldn't do anything. It scared the shit out of me. I looked at AB and said, "I'm in trouble here. I have to see Hooter". I went straight off.'

Alcott manipulated the knee and freed it up in the space of several minutes. His immediate diagnosis was that there was floating debris in the joint but that it would not get any worse on the day and he could bowl. However, he would need to see a specialist the next day just to make sure there was nothing else going on.

Hughes sent down nine overs and, with his confidence now in tatters, bowled poorly for a return of 0–52. He would be on tenterhooks when Alcott accompanied him to London the next day for a second opinion.

'I told Merv to carry on because he couldn't do any more damage,' Alcott says.

'We got a surgeon's opinion to make sure and he said the same thing. He couldn't do anything worse to that injury but the "chronic" part of his knee certainly got worse over time.'

With no real form to speak of and a knee scare behind him, Hughes was still named in the Australian side for the opening One-dayer, at Old Trafford.

Hughes, Border reasoned, was still bound to be a better bet than either the inexperienced Julian and Holdsworth, while Warne was also left out of the One-day side to shield him for the Tests.

Half-centuries to Taylor and Mark Waugh led Australia to 9–258 from their 55 overs and England could manage only 254 in reply, with McDermott and Steve Waugh each claiming three wickets.

Australia's under-prepared bowling attack had come through and the injection of confidence would do so much that the One-day series was to be swept 3–0. A brilliant run-chase by Mark Waugh and Border would set

*Hughes takes the final wicket of the One-day International at Lord's — Richard Illingworth, caught Healy for 9 — to complete an Australian clean sweep of the three-match series.*

up victory at Birmingham while an English lower-order collapse handed the tourists victory in the final game at Lord's.

In Hughes' three outings, his returns of 1–40, 0–51 and 2–41 would not be particularly outstanding but at least he was getting through matches. Of far more importance would be his game against Leicestershire immediately before the first Test.

In the run-up to the start of the Ashes series, Australia were scheduled to play Surrey and Leicester in two three-day matches. Border wanted both of his major pacemen to play in the second match, leaving the younger members of the side — Warne, Holdsworth and Julian — to play at The Oval.

As the start to a major series neared, Border would always grow increasingly edgy and, this time, the situation was worse, with Hughes still being a concern. What impact Warne would be able to have was also playing heavily on his mind. At least the batting was settled but an explosion was sure to come if anyone stepped out of line.

It came, sure enough, when slipshod work allowed the last-wicket pair of Neil Kendrick and Tony Murphy to add 30 and allow Surrey to scrape past the follow-on. Border had wanted to bowl a second time to get a second look at Julian and Reiffel and decide who would be the third paceman at Old Trafford. With rain threatening on the third day, the Australians may have missed their chance.

'You blokes are a bloody disgrace,' he roared when they entered the dressing-rooms at lunch, after dropping several catches.

'We're a week away from an Ashes series and you act like you don't give a stuff and couldn't care what happened. None of you deserve to wear the cap because you obviously don't care enough about it.

'When we go back out, no-one's wearing one and anyone with a jumper had better wear it inside out because you don't deserve to wear the coat of arms on that either.'

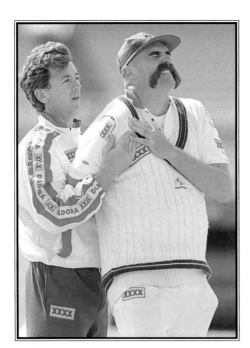

*Hughes with physio Errol Alcott, preparing for the first of the One-dayers.*

In chilly conditions, a jumper was essential but the force of Border's tirade had all the youngsters in the side greatly intimidated. Julian turned to his West Australian teammate Damien Martyn and asked if he thought Border was serious — should they actually wear their jumpers inside out?

'What if I go out there with it on inside out and he yells at me for being a dickhead?' Julian asked.

'I don't know. I'm not wearing mine, though. I don't care how cold it is,' Martyn replied.

Julian, Hayden, Slater, Martyn, Warne and Holdsworth would all go back on the field in just their

*The start of a one-sided psychological war — Graeme Hick falls to Hughes during the first Test.*

shirtsleeves and 12th man McDermott would be busy making six trips onto the ground early into the session when it became clear that Border would allow them to wear a jumper again.

Hughes went wicketless at Leicester on an under-prepared pitch and could boast only three first-class wickets on tour. Despite this, he felt confident about his recovery after several chances went to ground in the 97-run victory over the weak county side.

'I wasn't getting wickets but I finally felt like I was getting through the crease all right,' Hughes says.

'It rained for the entire two days of training before the Test but I just thought I could do all right because I was confident in my body again.'

In the prevailing damp conditions, Australia would prefer the pace of Julian to the spin of Tim May as their fourth bowler while England stacked their side with experience, including old campaigners Mike Gatting, Robin Smith, Phil Tufnell, Phil DeFreitas and Alec Stewart to complement their perceived big guns — Gooch, Atherton and Hick.

Gooch was delighted to win what seemed an important toss but England were brilliantly thwarted on the opening day by vice-captain Taylor. Taylor, who was dropped on 26 by Hick at slip, played one of the great under-rated innings to reach 124 and guide Australia to 5–242.

Off-spinner Peter Such, who was making his Test debut, had extracted sharp turn but Taylor batted for almost five hours for 12 boundaries and two sixes, just as his tenacious innings on the opening day of the 1989 rubber had set up that Test.

Taylor's opening partner, Slater (in his first Test), reached 58 but the quick loss of Boon and the Waugh twins soon showed how well Taylor was playing.

On the second morning, the Australian innings quickly subsided for 289 and Hughes would have the chance to show whether he was a contender or a pretender in this contest.

Atherton nicked Hughes through slips in the early stages of his innings and got an earful for his trouble. The opener knew then, that the Australians were switched on for the contest, compared to the way they had seemed to cruise, at times, throughout the One-dayers.

Atherton recalls: 'It was pretty obvious Merv made a conscious effort with me and Hicky to sledge us. I had really started playing consistently since about 1991 and felt a part of Test cricket, and pretty established with Graham Gooch at the top of the order.

'In the first Test, Hughes got straight into me right away and I knew the Australians were going to be making a determined effort to put me off my game. I nicked one early through the slip cordon and Merv stood there and gave it to me — "In four years, you've got no fucking better".

'I thought I would let him waste his breath.'

Atherton would grind his way to 19 in 100 minutes before Hughes had him caught behind by Healy. Hughes felt good. He had bowled a long spell, taken a top-order wicket and had forced each batsman to hurry a few shots. Late in his 13-over spell, Border brought Warne on at the Stretford end to partner him.

The leg-spinner spun his way into history with his first ball to Gatting, drawing an astonished response from everyone at the ground who saw that famous delivery — and no doubt in lounge-rooms across Australia.

One person, at square leg, wondered what all the fuss was about.

'When Warney came on, I was at deep backward square,' Hughes recalls.

'Gatt played at the ball and got knocked over and stood there carrying on. I came up from the deep and asked what the problem was. Heals told me it pitched off and hit off.

'I was going to sledge Gatt for hanging around but he was already too far away by the time I got there. Then I looked at the screen at mid-wicket and watched the replay. I thought, "Shit, good ball". I looked at Heals and said, "What are you talking about?" He said, "It pitched off the wicket and hit off-stump".

'You couldn't imagine what it must have done to their rooms. Gatting was THE player of spin and was there specifically to combat Warney.

'For him to go like that, and for the rest of the blokes in their rooms to see it, I was thinking, "How are they going to cope with that?" It was just unbelievable.'

In Hughes' opinion, Warne still hasn't got enough credit for what he did on that day. In just one ball, England were faced with a destroyer — and they had thought that the blond kid was just making up the numbers in the XI. For a second time, Warne had fooled a nation by hiding his best deliveries before a major game.

'I've seen the replay of that ball that many times and still can't understand how it happened,' Hughes says.

'The margin for error was so fine, for the ball to pitch where it did, miss everything Gatting had out for it, and still hit the stumps . . . If you tried to relive that, it would be like trying to retrace the magic bullet that got Kennedy.'

A bemused Smith, whose entire time at the crease during the series would be reminiscent of a rabbit staring into the headlights of an oncoming car, soon edged a catch to Taylor at slip while Gooch would smack a full toss to mid on, both from the bowling of Warne.

Australia had the psychological upper hand and would not relinquish it.

By the close, the home side had fallen to 8–202 and Hughes had added the scalps of Hick and Chris Lewis to his name, doubling his wicket tally for the tour in one day.

Hick struggled to 34 from 71 balls, hitting five boundaries, but never looked totally convincing. He eventually cut a catch to Border at point.

Hughes goaded him continually and, when he dismissed him, gave him a send-off as he departed. It worried ACB chairman Alan Crompton that Hughes would offer a send-off in the first Test he played after their pre-tour chat about the ubiquitous nature of television cameras.

Hick had been worked over physically by West Indies' Curtly Ambrose and Pakistan's Wasim Akram in his two previous home summers of Test cricket and now he had copped both a physical and verbal barrage from the Australians.

As the great hope of English cricket, he had still to fully display his talents but avers that the fault was his, not the approach of his opposition.

'Merv's style and nature was a definite one-off. I hadn't faced a bowler like him at all,' Hick says. His aggression was fair enough as far as I was concerned. The disappointing part for me was that only in the last Test did I finally realise I had to play my own game.

'I don't think it was the sledging that affected me, but just the fact that I let too many other factors distract me. I was thinking too much about the result of what may happen, rather than my game.'

With Hick still in single figures, he crunched a four through the cover region and received a volley from Hughes. Having only faced him briefly in Shield cricket in 1990–91, the batsman immediately thought he had the upper hand, not knowing the Victorian's personality.

'I often thought that a bowler who talked to me was distracted from his task but, with Merv, it was obviously an important part of his approach,' he says.

'He had a choice of three or four words, which I got to memorise very quickly and kept hearing them over and over again. Against that, some stuff out on the ground was actually quite funny and not at all abusive like many think.

'When the Australians came out with a lot of talk in that series, it wasn't anything new and it wasn't anything I wasn't expecting. He tried to be aggressive and he could be very intimidating at the first appearance, the way he steamed in at you.'

Even now, as Hick fights to establish his tenure in the England side, he says he does not mind the on-field exchanges between bowler and

*A famous moment in the first Test of 1993. Mike Gatting, back on his stumps expecting a bouncer, is bowled off his pads by the last ball of the fourth day ... a Hughes yorker.*

batsman. As long as it doesn't cross the line into vicious abuse or racist exchanges, he is happy to listen to whatever is said.

'I don't think sledging is a problem but obviously a lot of people have decided it should be taken out of the game. I think the game would miss that out in the middle.'

Australia secured a valuable lead of 79, with Hughes and Warne claiming four wickets apiece, and needed to bat solidly for the rest of the third day to ensure they did not waste their advantage.

The perfect man for such a situation was Boon.

The Tasmanian fell seven runs short of a maiden Test century in England but laid a sturdy foundation for Steve Waugh (78 not out) and Ian Healy (102 not out) to race Australia to 5–432 and an overall lead of 511 when Border closed the innings 80 minutes after lunch on the fourth day.

Border left his bowlers 127 overs to take 10 wickets with no real prospect of England scoring 512 for victory in just over four sessions. Hughes, having taken 4–59 from the first innings, would again be crucial.

After Warne had dispatched Atherton for 25, the experienced pairing of Gooch and Gatting had taken England to 1–133 when Hughes began the final over of the day. Gatting (23) was looking to stumps and no further.

He would try to leave everything and block anything on the stumps. When Hughes pitched short, it was a simple manoeuvre to sway out of danger. Hughes would make him wait for the final ball of the day, surely another bouncer.

Instead, Hughes pitched up on the pads and Gatting, surprised at a scoring opportunity, reacted late and the ball cannoned from his pads into the stumps. This success boosted the Australians going into the final day.

On the last day, Hughes would account for Hick for the second time in the match, this time caught off an edge to Healy, but Gooch stood magnificently in Australia's path.

The England captain, who endured such a miserable series in 1989, had lifted his own batting several notches since taking on the leadership and had batted for more than five hours for 133 by mid-afternoon. In almost three hours on the final day, Australia had taken just one wicket, that of Smith, and their chances of victory were quickly receding because of Gooch's obstinacy.

He had not given a chance and had struck 21 boundaries and two sixes in his 18th Test century. In the 79th over, with an old and battered ball, Hughes found some extra bounce from nowhere and, as Gooch tried to avoid the rearing short ball, it deflected towards the stumps.

Before the England captain had even realised what he was doing, he had knocked the ball away from the stumps with his glove. Hughes was certain he should be appealing for something — but for what?

'I still can't believe that wicket is not credited to the bowler. You do all the hard work, it's going to hit the stumps and he hits it away and then I don't get the wicket.' Hughes says.

'When it happened, I didn't know who to appeal to. I knew he'd done the wrong thing but I didn't know whether I was supposed to be looking at square leg or the bowler's end. As long as Gooch was at the crease, they were always a chance to save the game.'

With Gooch back in the pavilion, immediately ruled out 'handled the ball' by umpire Dickie Bird, each of the remaining batsmen could be chiselled out with a bit of time and effort. Not a single other England player would manage to bat for two hours in that innings, enabling Australia to wrap up victory with 10 overs to spare, winning by 179 runs.

Warne would be named man of the match for his 4–51 and 4–86, narrowly shading Hughes' return of 4–59 and 4–92. While Warne's second-day heroics had such a devastating effect on England in the long-term, Gooch felt the man-of-the-match judge had got it wrong.

'Merv's eight wickets in the first Test was the decisive performance of the entire series in my opinion,' Gooch says. 'We had high hopes for the series and, with McDermott going home early, a good start by us could have seen us do really well.

'As it was, Merv bowled his heart out on a flattie and got Australia home and their momentum went from there. He was difficult to play against and, as a captain, you would certainly want him in your side.

'He always wanted the ball and he did well, compared to other bowlers, in batsman-friendly conditions. He invariably got wickets when everyone else was struggling to find something in the wicket — and there was no better example of that than at Manchester in 1993.'

To back Gooch's assertion, new-ball partner McDermott went wicketless for the game while England's pace trio of Andy Caddick (1), Phil DeFreitas (2) and Chris Lewis (0) took just three wickets between them for the match.

When McDermott, Caddick, DeFreitas and Lewis manage match figures of 3–491 between them, Hughes' return of 8–151 is indeed sensational.

'Merv is one of those guys who once things happen, the more he wants to get involved,' Mike Gatting says. 'It snowballed for him and he was a bit like Ian Botham in many ways. Once he got on a roll, his confidence was hard to stop. He would bowl with injuries and somehow pick up wickets when things were going for him.

'Once Craig had gone home, Merv carried the pace attack on his own and just had Warne as the major support. With due respect to the other Australian bowlers, those two guys won an Ashes series and that's enormously disappointing for us.'

The Australians celebrated their victory long into the night at the Copthorne Hotel. Resurrecting the theme of the victorious 1989 tour, they trained hard, they played hard and, when they won, they celebrated hard.

*Surely this should have been credited to the bowler — England captain Graham Gooch prevents the ball from hitting his stumps by illegally pushing the ball away with his hand. He was given out 'handled the ball'.*

The itinerary of the 1993 Ashes tour was almost symmetrical, with two weeks between each Test filled by two county games, except the third and fourth Tests which had a three-week gap to accommodate a visit to Ireland.

Hughes would be given the first county game off against Warwickshire and play the match in Bristol against Gloucestershire as his preparation for the second Test, at Lord's. He continued his fine form with 4–27 in Gloucester's only innings and chalked off another first-class ground for his collection of venues where he had struck a six, lofting two balls over the fence in an entertaining unbeaten hand of 46.

During the game at Bristol, 'keeper Healy cracked a thumb but declared himself fit for Lord's. The only change would be the inclusion of spinner Tim May for Julian, while England would substitute Essex's Neil Foster for DeFreitas.

Hughes' knee had given him no serious trouble since Northampton but an ache was ever-present after a long day in the field. Even after a short stint of 15 overs against Gloucestershire, it was vital that he had time to rest himself before he bowled again. When Border won the toss at Lord's and decided to bat, Hughes would have until 11.55 on the third morning before he was required to bowl.

But for Mark Waugh being bowled between his legs on 99, the Australians would have become the first side in Test history to have the first four batsmen in the order post centuries after Taylor (111), Slater (152), Boon (164 not out), Waugh (99) and Border (77) tormented England on the way to a massive 4–632 declared.

Boon made up for the disappointment of missing a century in the first Test with a vengeance while Taylor notched his fourth century in England (all four scored on different grounds). Both innings were outstanding but paled in comparison with Slater's maiden century. Scored in less than five hours, Slater kissed the crest on his helmet when he reached three figures and Australia rejoiced in the arrival of a brilliant young batsman.

Unbeknown to the England side, while they were slogging away in the field on the second day, McDermott had to be rushed to hospital after complaining of stomach cramps and then collapsing in the Australian dressing-room.

In fact, the Queenslander would undergo emergency surgery to save his life after complications from an operation earlier in the year left him with a twisted bowel. His tour was over and Hughes was left as Australia's only experienced paceman. At the time, Border knew only that McDermott was unlikely to bowl again in the match and, as a consequence, put back his declaration from late on the second day to early on the third.

*Hughes with fellow fast man Craig McDermott at practice before the Lord's Test.*

When England would eventually bat, requiring 433 just to avoid the follow-on, only Atherton had any stomach for the fight after 13 hours of chasing leather in the field. His 80 offered the only significant resistance as England crashed to 9–193 by stumps. If Australia could somehow cobble together 11 more wickets in two days, despite the services of only three specialist bowlers, they could virtually claim the Ashes with a 2–0 lead.

Hughes' work on this third day was inspirational. With no slight intended on his makeshift new-ball partner, Mark Waugh, he had no fast bowling support.

Pounding the ball in at Gooch, Hughes softened up the England captain until one bouncer drove him to distraction and a top-edged hook, offering a catch to a diving May at fine leg.

The poorest fielder in the Australian squad held the catch sensationally and was so pumped up when he got to the celebratory huddle he had to ask who had been dismissed!

Hughes closed off the England innings on the fourth morning with his fourth wicket, finishing with 4–52 from 20 overs, and Border promptly enforced the follow-on. England would need a massive 427 to avoid an innings defeat but would at least show more fight in their second innings than the first, taking the match up to tea on the final day with a total of 365.

Hughes, as the sole fast bowler in the attack, would work through 31 overs for only 75 runs, maintaining the pressure at all times, and effecting the key run-out of Atherton.

Atherton, on 97, played a ball to deep square leg and, having run two, set off for the run that would have completed his second Ashes century. Hughes swooped and his throw to Healy caught the batsman stranded after he was sent back by Gatting and slipped mid-pitch.

Hick would make his way to 64 and, for the first time in four innings, would not be dismissed by Hughes. However, the Australians still felt the fast bowler had the England number five covered.

As Hick crunched the spin of May and Warne for his nine boundaries, Border would prop at silly point to chat to his former Queensland team-mate.

'Nice shot there, Hicky,' Border would say.

'You want to keep hitting them. You have to cash in now because the second new ball is due soon and you know who's coming back then.

'Big Merv will be back to see you, Hicky, and you know where they're going when he's bowling.'

Hick was dropped after the Test, as were Gatting, Lewis, Foster and Tufnell, as the English selectors put a broom through the line-up.

'Merv definitely won the battle with Hick and took him down,' Steve Waugh says.

'You could see in Hick's body language that every time Merv came on to bowl, he was thinking, "Here we go again, this guy is going to stick it up me and how am I going to play him".

'At Lord's, he backed away to play a cut shot in the first innings and nicked one and I think that was the final straw for the England selectors at the time. I think the white flag was up and Merv had won.

'He was the kind of guy that if he sniffed out a weakness, he would hone in and he wouldn't let up. He was relentless and it does take effect if you're copping a barrage every time he sees you.'

By the time the third Test was due to start at Nottingham, McDermott had returned home to the Gold Coast to recuperate. Strangely, the tour selectors would not call for a replacement and Hughes was now left with only the struggling Reiffel and the inexperienced Julian (one Test) and Holdsworth (no Tests) as support.

Reiffel had been pounded by Robin Smith in the second One-day, at Birmingham, in mid-May and, more than a month later, still did not look like forcing his way into the side. Julian would take McDermott's place for the third Test.

To continue his normal preparation for a Test, Hughes would miss the match against the Combined Universities and then played the game against Hampshire, taking 3–60 and 2–47. David Gower's hopes of a Test recall were dashed by Hughes in the first innings of that game at Southampton, caught cutting in the gully by Damien Martyn.

Smith, who had been under severe pressure to retain his Test place, would be given another opportunity to try to understand the spin wiles of Warne and May after belting a Warne-less attack for 191 in the three-dayer.

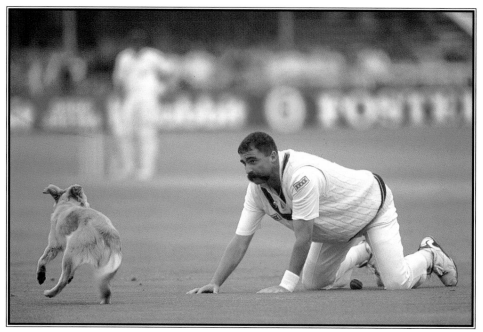

*Hughes at Trent Bridge, introducing himself to an intruder who interrupted proceedings on the opening day.*

The mistake Hughes would make at Southampton was that he bowled at full pace on the final day, rather than easing back a little as he had done before the first and second Tests. Australia were chasing a victory to maintain their shot at a cash prize for beating a certain number of county teams and the extra effort had not allowed Hughes the rest he needed.

Of more interest to Hughes was his unbeaten knock of 61, which was compiled from just 50 balls and included seven sixes, and representing the third first-class ground he had struck a six on during the tour.

'In the county games, I was basically batting just to hit sixes. Each time we got to a new ground, I'd start planning where I could hit a six if I got out there. Getting seven in one innings was a huge moment.'

In a bid to arrest a losing streak that had stretched now to seven Tests in succession, England included seven specialist batsmen in their line-up for Nottingham. The move had little effect as they still could not reach 350, being bowled out for 321 with Hughes taking 5–92.

His seventh five-wicket haul for Australia lifted him now to 194 wickets, within sight of becoming only the seventh Australian — after Dennis Lillee, Richie Benaud, Graham McKenzie, Ray Lindwall, Clarrie Grimmett and Jeff Thomson — to reach that lofty plateau.

In England's second innings, Hughes would feel his groin go on him in the lead-up to tea on the fourth day. At that point, he had taken 2–41 and England led by less than 200. Now, with him off the field, they could consider a possible declaration on the final day, and place Australia under some pressure.

'The thing that stuffed me up in the third Test was that I had to go at 100 per cent in the Hampshire game and then come up for the Test,' Hughes maintains.

'I just did too much in between and the body couldn't cope.'

Gooch would take full advantage of Hughes' absence, scoring his second century of the rubber and shepherding debutant Graham Thorpe to a century of his own as England climbed to 6–422 declared.

Of more concern to Hughes, and the Australian team management, was whether he would be fit for the fourth Test, at Headingley, in three weeks time. Thankfully, the lead-up to the Test at Leeds allowed for a trip to Ireland and an extra week for his recovery. Hughes would have been no chance of playing if there had only been two weeks up Alcott's sleeve but, even now, with the extra week, it would still be touch and go.

At tea on the last day of the third Test, Australia were tottering at 6–115 with just the bowlers to support Steve Waugh. Now, suddenly, Australia could go into the fourth Test with only a 2–1 lead. Whatever Alcott needed to do to get him right, it had to be done.

'When Merv got injured at Nottingham, it was a major task to ensure he would be ready for the next Test,' Alcott says. 'There was no-one else if he went down so we had to get him right and the only way to do that was for him to get away from the team and get fit, and not worry about everyone else. We went back to London for about nine days, because routine was important, and he worked hard to get himself right.'

A nervous Australian dressing-room sweated blood in the final session as Waugh (47 not out) and Julian (56 not out) defied England for 30.3 overs to ensure a draw and protect their 2–0 advantage.

*In the fourth Test, at Headingley, Hughes has Mark Latham caught behind in the opening over of England's reply to Australia's massive first innings total of 4 (declared) for 653.*

*Hughes becomes the seventh Australian to take 200 Test wickets —
Andy Caddick, lbw for a duck, during the final moments
of the fourth Test.*

Hughes rejoined the squad at Durham 10 days later, some six kilograms lighter and assured by Alcott he could get through a match. Driven hard, the fast bowler had worked assiduously at both his diet and his fitness while in London. Up until then, he had appeared not to have had too much success in keeping his appetite in check.

As recorded by Steve Waugh in his book of the tour, *Steve Waugh's Ashes Diary*, Hughes had one epic night at Planet Hollywood in the lead-up to the final Test where, according to Waugh, he consumed one plate of nachos, one mixed fajita, one chocolate mousse, six beers, one 'Terminator' cocktail, one 'Planet of the Apes' cocktail, three 'Beetlejuice' cocktails, two sambucas and six more beers.

While Alcott had managed to get the fast bowler fitter and lighter, there was no time for him to play in the final warm-up match at Durham to prove his fitness.

In faith on Alcott's word, Hughes would be picked for the crucial fourth Test, at Leeds. Hughes had no doubt he would be fit and would not let Australia down if Alcott said he would be right.

'Hooter is very good at what he does,' Hughes avers. 'There's been times I've been worried about injuries but he's eased my mind and he's never steered me wrong.

'He's told me when I've had to put up with pain, but couldn't make it any worse, and I've just followed what he said and he's been proved right. He alone has got me on the park when I didn't expect to play and Leeds was one of those games, just like in Adelaide in 1989–90.'

If Hughes had been a 30–70 proposition going into the fourth Test, it certainly didn't show on the field. Australia smacked a sorry England by a massive innings and 148 runs midway through the final day, prompting Gooch to resign his commission as captain.

Hughes' double of 3–47 and 3–79 included the wicket of opener Mark Lathwell (who had made his debut in the third Test), in the very first over of England's first innings, ensuring that their response to Australia's massive 4–653 was doomed to humiliating failure. On the final day, he joined the exclusive 200 Test wickets club with the wicket of Caddick.

If he was still going with all guns blazing on the field, it certainly wasn't the case in the rooms where, at the end of each day, his aching body would be covered in ice packs.

On the night Australia took an unbeatable 3–0 lead, Hughes' team-mates celebrated the retention of the Ashes long into the night, while he was in bed asleep by midnight.

The penny was now starting to drop in the camp as to how much his knee, and the rest of his body, was hurting.

'We had a pretty fair idea he was in some sort of trouble but Merv covered it pretty well,' Steve Waugh says. 'He didn't say what it was like but we all saw him, after games, covered in ice packs.

'He couldn't walk up stairs and he was in a lot of pain but we just knew he would front up for the next Test match, no matter what was happening, because of the kind of guy he was. Every ball, he would kick the ground or give his knee a bit of a touch-up so we knew he was in pain, but he just kept coming and coming.

*Australia have retained the Ashes after winning the
fourth Test by an innings and 148 runs.*

'He didn't use his brain at all because it was all heart and that cost him
in the long run. It put an end to his career in my opinion. He probably
should have stopped after that fourth Test and been Tommy Tourist but I
doubt he would have bought the idea anyway. I think he thought that,
"Every Test I miss is one I can never play again" and we were on a huge
winning roll and he wanted to be part of it.'

Border and Taylor, two of the selectors on tour, said they never
considered dropping Hughes because it would have been insulting to
him. If he was going to put his hand up to play, he was going to be picked,
no matter how bad he looked off the field and what he may be doing to
himself. It was his choice to play and he had earned the right to play.

'From my point of view,' Taylor says, 'it was never a choice to rest him
because I don't think Merv would ever have let that happen. I think he
really enjoyed the fact he was leading the Australian attack against the
Poms because he loved playing the Poms. He was having a great series
and if all of us tour selectors as a group had walked up and said we had

him booked on a flight home, he would have been really dirty. You have to take him on his word and he was still bowling well and at a good pace.

'As has always been the Australian way, if you have a slight niggle you just play through it. No-one thought it would be as bad as it was and would cost him the next half a season. I thought he might need a month off and would be right for the first Test at the end of November.'

The decision not to call for a replacement for McDermott had one obvious consequence when Julian broke down with a groin strain while training in the nets during the fourth Test. With only three fit specialist fast bowlers left in the party and one of those, Holdsworth, sadly out of form, Hughes was compelled to play in both matches between the fourth and fifth Tests.

The games against Lancashire and Glamorgan meant nothing to the fate of the Ashes but they did mean Hughes had no rest at all. His knee began to complain long and loudly every day and a limp began to develop in the field.

The lack of rest, according to Alcott, would be devastating for his long-term future in the game.

'The degeneration in his knee occurred from his bowling action, the amount of work he had to do and the weightload going through his knee. A time had to come where his knee wouldn't be able to stand it.

'If he had kept his weight down for all those years, he wouldn't have had the problems he had by that stage of the tour. When a bowler bowls, he is always doing long-term damage because of the nature of cricket but because of the lack of rest for a modern international cricketer, there is no time to rejuvenate and they get permanent problems.'

While he was struggling hopelessly by now for fitness, with a month still to go on tour, it did not affect his well-known exuberant personality.

As is traditional on each Test tour, the journalists who are following the Australian team host a drinks night for the squad and the 1993 affair was held in Neath during the match against Glamorgan.

Rain had fallen on the second day and play was not expected to be on time the following day, prompting all the journalists and most of the players to celebrate success on tour long into the night.

Hughes, who had finished the second day unbeaten on 25, had already struck two sixes and began skiting to Mark Waugh about how he was the better and bigger hitter. Waugh had inflicted substantial damage upon some modest county attacks on tour, including eight sixes in his 178 against Surrey and another eight in his unbeaten 152 on the first day against Glamorgan.

The conversation soon got rowdy and Hughes was challenged by the journos to put up on the next day or shut up, and a ridiculous group of bets was made:

10 pounds from Patrick Keane (AAP) for every six;

20 pounds from Malcolm Conn (the *Australian*) for every six;

One pound from Brett Walker (Channel Nine) for every run;

100 pounds from Jim Tucker (*Inside Edge*) if he ran out Allan Border;

50 pounds from Robert Craddock (News Ltd) if he could hit a car parked around the ground;

Five pounds from Ken Casellas (the *West Australian*) for each square cut for four;

Five pounds apiece from nine separate people if he faced up left-handed;

100 pounds from Allan Border if he could make a century.

The journos were so caught up in the emotion of the evening the only guarantee they got from Hughes was that he would pay each person 10 pounds if he didn't make another run and a whopping 100 pounds apiece if Border ran him out.

Resuming with Reiffel the next morning and Australia allegedly planning a declaration, he pushed on to make 71 and hit a further three sixes. He could not manage to run out Border but did pocket a healthy 136 pounds from a foolish group of blokes with sore heads.

As lunch and the declaration neared, Hughes patted back a full toss to the bowler and drew a blast from his team-mate Reiffel.

'He had all these bets going with the journos and was going to make millions of dollars for hitting sixes and fours,' Reiffel says.

'We were supposed to be setting up a declaration and Merv blocks a full toss back down the wicket.

'I went down and said, "You're batting for money here mate. You're not worried about the team at all".

'He said, "Full tosses are no good. I always get out to them. I try to slog them and end up hitting it straight to cover or back to the bowler".'

Reiffel retired to his end, still unimpressed with his team-mate.

The first ball of the very next over to Reiffel, from paceman Darren Thomas, was a full toss which he hit straight back to the bowler.

'Merv stood at the bowler's end and just pissed himself laughing while I walked off.'

It seemed the two Victorians were not the best of batting partners. Five months earlier, in the Test in Auckland, Reiffel had walked down the pitch to Hughes and told him not to walk across his stumps because Danny Morrison was bowling inswingers and could hit his leg stump.

Hughes told Reiffel he had never been bowled on leg stump in his Test career.

Promptly, Willie Watson bowled Reiffel leg stump with the first ball of his next over.

Hughes would not manage a wicket in the fifth Test, at Birmingham, but it hardly made a difference to an Australian side now playing at the peak of their form.

Reiffel would wreck England's first innings with 6–71 while May and Warne would share all 10 scalps in the second innings as Australia marched to an eight-wicket victory and a 4–0 lead.

On a turning wicket, May and Warne did the bulk of the bowling but Hughes would still keep an end tight when called on and contributed a vital 38 in the first innings of a stand of 107 with Healy, ensuring a first-innings lead.

Healy, who had played with injury himself in the second Test, says Test players only now are becoming receptive to the idea of missing One-day matches, but certainly not a five-day game.

'I think Merv was like all of us and his theory was, "play until you drop". He wasn't doing anything that most of us wouldn't have done and it's ultimately cost him.'

Hughes would miss one of the final two county matches before the sixth Test but, by then, the damage had been done.

A tired Australian side could not maintain their momentum for the last Test and the enthusiasm of a recalled Hick, Angus Fraser and Devon Malcolm carried England to a 161-run victory — their first in an Ashes Test for 18 matches.

Hick would make 80 and 36 against his nemesis Hughes, without being dismissed by him in either innings.

'The exciting part of playing against Merv was on the days when you had won the battle, like at The Oval,' Hick says. 'You felt like you had really achieved something because you knew he was busting a gut all the time. I felt really disappointed I didn't get a century at The Oval in 1993 but there was a lot of satisfaction to have done well against him. At the end of the day, he was the first to congratulate me from their side.'

If Graeme Hick could change just one moment of all his unhappy times in the middle against Merv Hughes from the 1993 series, it would come from that Oval Test match.

Ironically, it would not have been to ensure that he went on to a century in the first innings, but a moment on the last day as England pressed for victory.

'I bowled to Merv just before tea on the last day of that game,' Hick says. 'He nicked one and was given not out after we all went up for a huge

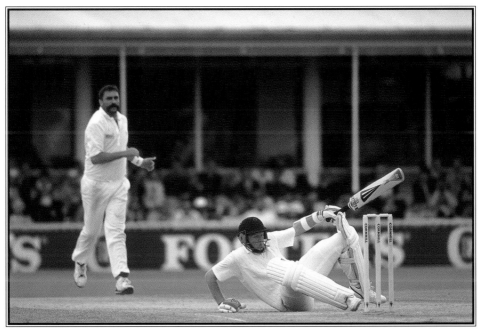

*Hughes puts English tailender Peter Such on his backside at Edgbaston.*

*Mark Waugh has just dismissed Robin Smith in the fifth Test, and Hughes (jumping in from the back) is keen to join his team-mates in the celebrations.*

appeal. After everything that had gone on during that summer, I desperately wanted to run down the wicket and give him a verbal but I didn't take the opportunity. A verbal isn't part of my game and I just didn't know how to deliver a really good one. I've regretted that quite a bit actually, because I wanted to say something to him — but I completely missed my chance. It would have been a good note to finish the summer.'

Through the sixth Test, Hughes carried an obvious limp and Atherton felt the fast bowler's pace had finally dropped markedly as his body cried enough. Still, Hughes found the strength to take six wickets and lift his tally for the series to 31 at 27.25. Only Terry Alderman (twice, in 1981 and 1989), Dennis Lillee (in 1981) and his team-mate Warne had taken more wickets than him for Australia in a series in England.

The wicket that would epitomise Merv Hughes in England in 1993 was that of Nasser Hussain, a batsman who scored seven first-class centuries that season for Essex, on the third day of that final Test.

Out on his feet with England at 2–180 and leading by almost 300, Hughes had Matthew Maynard caught by Reiffel for 9 to bring Hussain to the crease. Out of nowhere, he produced an evil throat ball that Hussain could only fend to Mark Waugh at slip, putting Hughes on a hat-trick.

When no other Australian bowler could find bounce in the track, he had procured a wicket out of nowhere. In the final Test of a long series, Border would work his fast bowler through more than 61 overs for the match. Hughes looked shocking, limping back to his mark, but kept assuring Border he could keep going.

'Even in the sixth Test, I thought I was getting along all right,' he says.

'I was bowling with Warney and I knew I didn't have to get through my overs quickly because we had Warne and May keeping us well ahead of the clock. I was just sauntering back and AB kept coming over and asking what was wrong. He said I looked ratshit and should stop bowling but I felt all right.'

In actual fact, he was ratshit.

After the English fans clapped him off the ground for the last time late on the fourth day, Hughes gathered yet another group of ice packs and contented himself with the thought he did not have to bowl again. He would have surgery and consider his rehabilitation for the start of the Australian summer.

Merv Hughes, in England in 1993, had given more than anyone had a right to expect.

# CHAPTER ELEVEN

# THE CLOSING CURTAIN

**M**erv Hughes underwent surgery on September 8, 1993 for what was hoped would be a routine clean-up of his right knee, to clear the floating debris that had caused his knee to lock during the England tour.

If the operation went well, he would be able to start training in mid-October and should be right in time for the opening Test of the summer against New Zealand in Perth — followed by Australia's first-ever series against an apartheid-free South African side.

His 208 Test wickets had placed him in an exclusive Australian club indeed, and he had also finished the series in England with 999 Test runs to his name for Australia. With just one more single, he would join Ray Lindwall and Richie Benaud as the only Australians to score 1000 runs and take more than 200 wickets.

However, Errol Alcott had suspected much greater problems could be lurking beneath what the scans of Hughes' troublesome knee had shown and flew down to Melbourne for the fast bowler's operation.

The expected swift clean-up of the joint quickly became a major procedure when it was revealed that Hughes had ground through his cartilage and had been bowling with bone rubbing against bone. The constant pounding without shock absorption had left the joint vulnerable to chipping and killed off an area of bone almost the size of a 50-cent piece.

When Hughes awoke, Alcott told him that he would have to stay off

*Opposite: Sue and Merv Hughes, at a tribute night at the Footscray Cricket Club in October 1993.*

the knee for at least six weeks, and any cricket at all before the New Year was unlikely.

With Australia scheduled to play five of their six Test matches for the summer by the first week of January, suddenly an entire international season appeared to have been stolen from his grasp. On top of that, the Australian squad to tour South Africa would be selected in mid-January and he could hardly expect to win a berth if he had not played any serious cricket in the weeks beforehand.

The closing curtain on his career was suddenly right in front of Merv Hughes' face.

'When I came out of the operation, the news was obviously pretty bad and it was a very tough blow to take at the time. Hooter was telling me the worst-case scenarios and the most-likely scenarios and I did have some thoughts that I might have played my last match for Australia. However, he also told me I could be playing by around Christmas if things went well so I had to take the most positive thing out of what he said and work on that.

'I looked at the Shield program and Victoria had a game against New South Wales in Sydney just before Christmas (December 18–21) where both teams would have all the Test players included. Immediately, I thought if I could get to that game and make an impression, the Australian selectors would look at me for later in the summer and maybe even the Boxing Day Test if I did sensationally. You have to be positive so that's what I was telling myself.'

Alcott reported the news of Hughes' operation to the national selectors, who were devastated by what they heard. The panel, already uncertain whether Craig McDermott would be able to come back from the serious surgery he had undergone in June, were now faced with virtually no experienced pacemen to call on.

'When Merv came home from England, the diagnosis from Errol was that he had done too much and just worn the knee out,' Sawle says.

'The selectors were told not to expect to have him available for the summer because he had paid the price for his effort in England.'

If McDermott was not to come up, Reiffel was the only incumbent left from the Ashes tour and, while he had starred in the last three Tests, he had still only played seven Tests in all. As soon as Hughes' surgery became public, speculation turned to a young New South Wales fast bowler, Glenn McGrath, and whether he could step up to international cricket ahead of his time. McGrath had yet to play a full first-class season but had finished the 1992–93 summer strongly and, while physically light, seemed extraordinarily tough and resilient.

But experience would still be in desperately short supply.

As it turned out, McDermott had pushed himself to the limits in his comeback and started the season on time with Queensland, playing their opening two Mercantile Mutual Cup matches before the start of the Sheffield Shield season.

A marathon spell of 41 overs in an innings against South Australia, for 4–111, was enough to confirm his fitness and a haul of 5–62 in the following encounter with Western Australia settled any lingering doubts over his form.

McDermott, Reiffel and the debutant McGrath would form the Australian pace attack for the opening Test against New Zealand in mid-November.

Meanwhile, Merv Hughes had surprised himself with the speed of his recovery and was able to again run on his knee. He was some three weeks ahead of schedule and could consider bowling again in the first week of December.

If he was able to bowl for any length of time, he decided he would make himself available for Victoria's match in Tasmania from December 10 to 13, the week before their scheduled game with New South Wales. The chance to play two Shield games before Christmas would offer a much better perspective for the national selectors. He would have to check his progress with Alcott but things were again looking positive.

Alcott did not doubt Hughes would drive himself hard in his comeback.

'Merv was the one for me who could do things that other people's bodies wouldn't allow them to do,' Alcott says. 'He could cop abuse, both physically and emotionally, but would bounce back and come back the next day. He would have surgery and come back and, because he was a tough man in that regard, you could never rule him out.'

*Hughes with Tim May (left) and Victorian team-mate Paul Reiffel during the '93 Ashes tour.*

Australia could not force a win against New Zealand in Perth but the loss of Martin Crowe, with a knee problem of his own, left the Kiwis threadbare for the second Test, in Hobart.

Unable to cope with the twin-spin attack of Shane Warne and Tim May, New Zealand were pummelled by a massive innings and 222 runs. Their cause was not helped by the late withdrawal of all-rounder Chris Cairns, even though his captain, Ken Rutherford, was prepared for him to play as a specialist batsman only.

Cairns' withdrawal would be noted by the Australians.

The final Test of the series, to be Allan Border's last at his adopted home ground in Brisbane, was played immediately following the conclusion of the Hobart Test, in the first week of December.

Alcott requested that Hughes come to Brisbane to train with the Australian side so he could monitor his progress and decide whether he could give Hughes the all-clear to return to first-class cricket for the match against Tasmania the following week.

Australia would soundly belt New Zealand again, this time by an innings and 96 runs, to claim the Trans-Tasman trophy 2–0 but the talking point would be Warne's on-field exchange with Cairns. The leg-spinner had come in for heavy criticism in New Zealand's first innings for giving Cairns a send-off.

In defence of Warne, Cairns had chipped him mercilessly when he arrived at the crease about how he was going to slog him out of the attack, just as he had done in Perth when he lofted a six down the ground. Warne got his man for 5, caught and bowled, and told him succinctly just who had won the battle.

Hughes bowled in the nets with his Australian team-mates but his knee swelled in the aftermath of his workout. Alcott felt he should not play against Tasmania and wait another week. Adhering to the physiotherapist's advice would, more than likely, end his chances of selection for the Boxing Day Test against South Africa.

'Once I was running, by December I had set myself for the Boxing Day Test because I would get two Shield games for Victoria,' Hughes says.

'It was a big disappointment when the knee puffed up but I couldn't go against what Errol had recommended because he had always steered me right. I just had to hope the New South Wales game would be enough to make an impression.'

Alcott could clearly see the amount of work Hughes had done in rehabilitating his knee but there was little evidence of any improved dietary habits. Hughes was as big as he had been when he finished the Ashes tour and Alcott kept reminding him that any problems with his knee would return more quickly the bigger he was.

Alcott could never understand how he had such discipline in one area of his life, with regard to working hard, and so little in another area, his diet — both of which contributed to his ability to stay at the top.

In hindsight, Alcott can offer some explanation: 'I've thought about it so much and I don't think he had a lot of self-esteem. Merv was a contradictory sort of person and maybe that was why he ate so much. There had to be a reason for it because he was just compulsive.

'I sometimes think he didn't rate himself alongside the likes of McDermott and Reid and some of his other bowling team-mates, and

*Although Hughes missed the entire international summer of cricket in Australia in 1993–94, while recovering from knee surgery, he still travelled to Brisbane to work with Errol Alcott (and be monitored by this interested observer) during the Australians' easy Test victory over New Zealand.*

would just keep bowling and bowling in a bid to prove himself. He was a great performer but he never thought he did much for Australia, which was a ridiculous thought.'

Victoria fell 41 runs short of forcing victory over Tasmania in their Shield game in early December but the two points for a first-innings lead had been enough to draw them level with South Australia in top place on the Shield ladder.

In Dean Jones' first year of his second stint as captain, following the retirement of Simon O'Donnell leading into the 1993–94 season, Victoria had already beaten Western Australia and New South Wales, thanks largely to Warne's 15 wickets in those two matches.

Reiffel, Tony Dodemaide and the young Simon Cook comprised the pace attack for the first three games while Damien Fleming had replaced Reiffel when he was away on national duty. Reiffel would certainly return to a full-strength Victorian team but Hughes also expected a place on the strength of his sterling efforts for both State and country, leaving Fleming, Cook and Dodemaide to contest the final position.

The Victorian selectors, who had not seen him bowl, asked Hughes to play in a trial game at the Albert Ground in Melbourne, in the days prior to the team's departure for Sydney on December 16.

He did so, getting through the run without any dramas but only bowling at three-quarter pace, because, he believed, there was no point going flat-out until he was in a match situation.

'I wasn't all that motivated to perform in that game and just wanted to stay on my feet and get through it,' Hughes says.

'The State selectors asked how I was feeling and I said, "Not too bad".

'They told me I didn't look too good out there and I said, "I just wanted to stay on my feet but I feel good".'

On his past record, and because he had given his word that he would not play unless he felt he could get through the game, Hughes expected to be chosen for the Victorian side. His anger could hardly be contained when he was told he would not be risked, but would be considered for Victoria's match against Queensland in early January.

The selection panel was split, with former team-mates Shaun Graf and John Scholes both feeling that Hughes should be included. His word and his record were good enough for them. Coach Les Stillman and chairman of selectors John Grant were not so sure and voted against Hughes. The decisive vote was with captain Dean Jones.

Jones voted no and, surprisingly, young all-rounder Ian Harvey was included in Hughes' stead. Hughes could not believe his former Australian team-mate, just four matches into his second stint as captain, had not taken his word.

'The selectors, in their wisdom, said they didn't want me in the side. That was probably one of my most disappointing times in cricket,' Hughes says.

'John Grant, Les Stillman and Dean Jones came to me on the balcony of the Albert Ground to tell me the decision after they had watched the game I was playing in.

'Les voted that it was a worry, John Grant said it was a worry, and they both looked at Deano and said, "Do you want him in your side?"

'He said, "No".

'I looked at Deano and I was stunned. After all the times we had played cricket together, he knew what I could do and I thought, "What more did I have to do to prove myself?"'

In Tony Dodemaide's opinion, that single decision to omit Hughes from the team to go to Sydney would be the catalyst for all the troubles that would plague Jones' captaincy two years down the track in the summer of 1995–96.

'Retrospectively, I think it was a tough call on Merv to leave him out,' Dodemaide says.

'New South Wales in Sydney is like a Test match and everyone wants to play that game. Merv was also trying to get back in the Australian side and it cut him pretty deeply.

'He probably could have got through the game, but not accepting his word is what would have really hurt him. He would never go off and play a Shield game for Victoria just because it was a good thing to do if there was the risk of breaking down.

'When the selectors started to question his ability, he really took it personally.'

A flabbergasted Hughes demanded answers from Jones.

'I was told, "They're a good team and we don't want you to get too many scars".

'I said, "Hang on, you were going to play me against Tasmania last week until the knee puffed up", but I was told no for New South Wales because they might take me apart.

'I said they could easily do that when I was fully fit and I had to try the knee at some point. "Is anyone ready to play first-class cricket, the first game they play after an injury?" is what I asked.'

Graf then re-affirmed his view that Hughes should be chosen but a 3–2 vote meant the die had been cast.

Hughes could forget about the home Tests against South Africa and his chances of touring the Republic would require a minor miracle. His only chances to impress now would be against Queensland in mid-January and South Australia at the end of the month.

'The most disappointing view of all was Deano's,' Hughes says. 'With the amount of cricket I had played with him, he knew my attitudes towards the game and what I would do to make sure I was right for a match.

'I felt really let down. There is one thing you don't do as a bowler and that's go into a four-day game, or a five-day game, with doubts about whether you can get through. If you are doubting whether you will hold up, you are wasting everyone's time by even playing.'

As it turned out, Harvey would bowl only three overs for the match in Sydney as Victoria fell an agonising one wicket short of completing an outright win, despite a further eight wickets for the game to Warne. New South Wales tailenders Adrian Tucker and McGrath held out to force a draw with no fast bowler of Hughes' ilk to ruffle their feathers in the closing stages of a dramatic game.

Rain ruined the Boxing Day Test at the MCG while South Africa pulled off a shock 5-run victory in Sydney when Australia could not successfully chase a target of 117 for victory.

Significantly, the behaviour of the Australian team again attracted much publicity, with Warne in particular being targeted for his on-field demeanour. He had given South Africa's Daryll Cullinan a send-off during the Sydney Test and would also have a run-in with the right-hand batsman during the One-day series. Again, in defence of Warne, the opposition player's role in the run-ins was not highlighted.

The baby-faced Cullinan made a first-ball duck in Melbourne and dropped four catches at slip but kept up a steady stream of advice to the Australian batsmen throughout the match. Eventually, Mark Waugh turned to him and told him he might like to shut up and try to hold a catch.

In Sydney, Cullinan chipped Warne and the bowler responded emphatically when he dismissed him twice for 9 and 2 in a match haul of 12–128.

The ACB had no jurisdiction over visiting players but the number of incidents occurring had drawn the attention of those in charge at Jolimont. Crompton, as ACB chairman, was now worried that Australia were starting to justify the tag of 'Ugly Australians'.

This concern was reflected generally across the 14 directors of the Australian Cricket Board. When the Board met in Adelaide in late January, it had decided there must be some action to curb the rising tide.

'The discussion about so-called "Ugly Australians" was emerging again at this time in early 1994,' Crompton says.

'This was a matter of concern to the Board. Player behaviour was on the agenda for the January meeting in Adelaide. A part of the reputation was deserved but I believe a greater part of it was undeserved.

'It was more a case of people jumping on the bandwagon and it seemed like the flavour of the month to be accusing the Australian team of poor sportsmanship. I thought that was unfair but I also felt that the Board should make its views clear on the standards of on-field behaviour expected of the players. We wanted people to have no reason to base these on-going accusations against us.'

After its Board meeting, before the start of the third Test, in Adelaide, Crompton would make a statement on behalf of the ACB.

The line was now drawn. The next player who stepped out of line, whoever and wherever that may be, could expect serious repercussions.

Though Merv Hughes was not even in the Australian team at the time, the message was to be sent to all first-class cricketers.

'Arising out of that meeting, the Board felt there were three types of behaviour which were totally unacceptable,' Crompton says.

'The first of these was pre-meditated and persistent sledging, second was dissent against umpiring and the third was send-offs. We on the Board know that Test cricket is a hard, tough, uncompromising game. We understand that this creates enormous pressure on the players. Notwithstanding that, there are these three areas that must not be crossed.'

Crompton said the Board did not have a problem with a few words said in the heat of the moment and, equally, a momentary expression of surprise or disappointment at a decision was also acceptable. Send-offs however, were considered quite unfair because the dismissed batsman had no opportunity to respond in kind.

At a press conference following the Board meeting, Crompton described send-offs as 'Cowardly, un-Australian and un-any other country you care to name'. Only this statement would receive a wide airing, and not the full text of his remarks.

While Australia were on the way to a victory in the World Series finals, Hughes finally took his place in the Victorian side for the game against Queensland and promptly claimed 5–70 in the first innings.

The national selectors would meet in the last week of January to pick the 15-man squad for South Africa, before Hughes' chance to play against South Australia, and he consequently gave himself virtually no chance of making the squad because of his lack of opportunities.

Reiffel and McGrath had alternated as McDermott's partner all summer but both seemed certain to make the squad for the Republic. Hughes could only aim for the fourth paceman's spot and would have to be chosen ahead of Western Australia's Brendon Julian and Jo Angel.

Julian had been inconsistent since the England tour but still had 25 first-class wickets at 31.56 to his name, compared to Hughes' five at 27.20, while Angel had even more impressive claims with 39 wickets at 17.77. Angel had taken four separate five-wicket bags, compared to Hughes' one, but all had been taken at the WACA and the perception was that Angel struggled away from his favourite Perth pitch.

The Australian selectors had to decide if Hughes' past record for Australia earned him the credits to be chosen for South Africa.

Victoria's selectors had decided earlier in the summer that all of Hughes' work for both Australia and Victoria was not enough to get him a game in a Shield match in Sydney but . . .

Hughes was picked to go to South Africa.

'I thought it was great that one bunch of selectors had a bit of faith in me,' Hughes says.

'Because McGrath and Reiffel were alternating, neither had had the chance to settle down and were under pressure every time they bowled. That helped me. I was clutching at straws to be picked but the selectors gave me a chance and I will always thank them for that.'

Sawle and the rest of a grateful national selection panel were happy to welcome Hughes back. His efforts in ensuring the Ashes stayed in Australia had not been forgotten.

'It's fair comment to say Merv had been picked for South Africa on what he had done for Australia in the past,' Sawle says.

'He had the credits there with what he had done on the England tour. All that was needed for the Australian selectors to pick him was for Merv to show his fitness in a couple of games and we would welcome him back.

'We picked him for South Africa once he got a five-wicket haul and hoped he would continue to improve in South Africa.

'We hadn't unearthed anyone in the meantime to fill the hole he had left because McGrath and Reiffel were only just emerging and neither one had consolidated a spot in the side.'

It was the earnest hope of the selection panel, and the wider cricket community, that Merv Hughes could still be a factor in international cricket for Australia.

# CHAPTER TWELVE

# ANYTHING BUT FRIENDLY

The first official Australian side to tour South Africa in almost a quarter of a century touched down at Jan Smuts Airport, Johannesburg, on a wet morning, February 6, in 1994, less than two months before the country's first all-race elections.

Kim Hughes' rebel band, which so decimated the strength of the Australian team during the summers of 1985–86 and 1986–87 but ironically allowed Merv Hughes the opportunity to make his Test debut, had visited the Republic almost a decade before. However, official on-field contact ceased in early 1970, after Ali Bacher's men closed out a 4–0 victory over a tired and outclassed side led by Bill Lawry.

The unpalatable prospect of anti-apartheid demonstrations during South Africa's proposed tour to Australia in 1971–72 prompted the cancellation of that series and a generation of some of the game's finest cricketers disappeared into a nether world of unfulfilled home summers in the Republic, occasional rebel tours and line scores from English county cricket.

When Allan Border's Australians arrived in South Africa, the general focus of the two cricket communities could not have been more different.

For many in the Australian party, South Africa was just another stop on the cricket circuit with most questions centred on whether they could do better than the disappointing 1–1 result garnered on home soil. The Australian team had been on the road continuously for some 17 months already since heading to Sri Lanka in August 1992, working their way

*Opposite: Hughes, with a new-found friend, in Soweto, February 1994.*

through tours of New Zealand and England (1993) between home summers, hosting the West Indies in 1992–93, and New Zealand and South Africa jointly in 1993–94. In just eight weeks time, there was the cherished prospect of some five months convalescing at home before visits to Sri Lanka (again) and Pakistan.

For South Africa, particularly those high up in the hierarchy of the game, the visit of a powerful country with such a proud cricketing history as Australia was a chance to firmly stake the place of Test cricket in the emerging new nation. United Cricket Board of South Africa President Krish Mackerdhuj led the way in declaring that this series, in his view, was the first between Australia and South Africa to be held on South African soil.

According to Mackerdhuj, the cricket played before the creation of a unified board was not representative of all South Africans.

'People tend to accept that we are just continuing from where we left off — with a big void in the middle of some 23 or 24 years,' Mackerdhuj told the *Australian's* columnist Mike Coward in early 1994. 'But that is not the case. What you are seeing is the new South Africa in cricket. It is not the old South Africa.

'We accept the talent of people who played — the Pollocks and Richards were geniuses of their time. But that was a different South Africa playing. It is not the old cricket that has been the agent of change. It is the new cricket dimension that has been the agent of change.'

Into a heady mix of politics and sport stepped the Australians, led by Allan Border, the most apolitical of all Australian sportspeople. Border's way had always been simply to play, and ignore everything else going on around him.

As the tourists settled into their three-week warm-up to the first Test, it was quickly apparent that politics would never be far away.

The Australians headed into Soweto to witness some of the work being done in the townships for black and coloured youngsters in a bid to mend a broken society but were also quickly exposed to the views of the white-minority hardliners who certainly did not want an end to the country they had known. All in the Australian party were stung by the ferocity of the right-wing views held by some and were equally disturbed by the attitude and approach of many white spectators in the early part of the tour.

Despite the best intentions of all those within the South African board, a generation away from international sport seemed to have bred a superiority complex among many average sports fans. Certainly, before the country was ostracised, it could justly claim to be the best in the world at both cricket and rugby union. While rugby union is certainly the foremost sport among the whites of South Africa, the cricketers of the Republic were treated as heroes upon reaching the semi-finals of the 1992 World Cup in their return to the world stage.

After a clinical, albeit dour, victory over India the previous summer, South Africa's supporters expected the Australians to be bested in similar fashion. The Australians soon had to become used to barbs and taunts from parochial fans, not only at net training and in matches where such banter was expected, but every time they ventured out in public. A constant diet of what on-field humiliations they could expect from the home side in the upcoming Test series, be it good-natured or much darker, soon began to weigh on the minds of the group.

Some would handle it much better than others.

The first playing duties of the tour sent the side to a festive warm-up in the lavish grounds maintained by diamond magnate Nicky Oppenheimer, before the eighth Australian party to South Africa got down to serious business with a four-day game against Northern Transvaal in Pretoria.

Unperturbed by the daily round-trip of two hours by coach, the Australians blitzed the provincial side by 249 runs with a full day to spare (despite several interruptions by rain). Openers Mark Taylor and Michael Slater managed a half-century apiece while Mark Waugh peeled off a superlative 134 from just 140 balls in the second innings, further frustrating whatever hopes Dean Jones may have had of a recall to the Test side.

Jones had not played a Test since being left out of the Australia XI for the series against the West Indies in 1992–93. However, a succession of exciting performances had earned a recall, first for the 1993–94 World Series in Australia, and now for the South African tour.

Jones top-scored with 85 in Australia's first dig but was denied the opportunity of a second hit and played just two more first-class knocks for

The Australian team that toured South Africa.
**Back row** (left to right): M.L. Hayden, S.K. Warne, S.R. Waugh,
T.B.A. May, M.J. Slater; **Middle row:** L.J. Trigar (Physiotherapist),
C.J. McDermott, G.D. McGrath, M.G. Hughes, P.R. Reiffel, D.M. Jones;
**Front row:** M.E. Waugh, M.A. Taylor (Vice-Captain), R.B. Simpson (Coach),
A.R. Border (Captain), Dr. C. Battersby (Manager), D.C. Boon, I.A. Healy.

the entire tour, in a meaningless game at Boland between the first and second Tests. When he was told, on the eve of the Johannesburg Test, that specialist opener Matthew Hayden would play ahead of him should Mark Waugh be unavailable to bat at number four, the Victorian captain felt deeply slighted. Before the end of the tour, the 52-Test veteran had decided he would quit international cricket, a decision made despite the best efforts of many of his team-mates to convince him otherwise; sadly, his retirement would prove to be premature.

While several questions were answered with regard to Australia's batting line-up, Allan Border and fellow tour selectors Taylor, Bob Simpson and David Boon were still puzzled as to the make-up of their pace attack.

Craig McDermott's position as spearhead was unquestioned but Glenn McGrath and Paul Reiffel had both been unable to consolidate a place during the summer in Australia. The pair had both played in the opening Test of the summer against New Zealand in Perth before swapping a new ball place over the next five matches — Reiffel playing thrice and McGrath twice with neither managing two Tests in succession.

The earnest hope of the Test selectors at home was that Hughes would return to partner McDermott while the less-experienced McGrath and Reiffel could jockey for the third paceman's position, should conditions warrant another seam bowler ahead of spinner Tim May.

Unfortunately, Hughes had returned to the Australian side considerably bigger than at the end of the Ashes tour and struggled through the game in Pretoria, returning 3–72 off 20 overs in the first innings and 2–30 off eight overs when the local side collapsed a second time. Hughes' first-up return was peppered with five wides and nine no-balls as he struggled for rhythm and his three first-innings scalps were hardly memorable — Steve Elworthy, Tertius Bosch and Chris Van Noordwyk — numbers eight, nine and 10 in the order!

'He was bigger again upon being picked for his return to the Australian side and I thought he had probably given up the battle to get under 100 kilos again,' Errol Alcott recalls.

'No-one could doubt him on the field but he needed to do more away from the field to ensure he was right to play. Merv's problem was his behaviour between matches. He just wasn't doing anywhere near enough to ensure he was ready to play international cricket.'

Alcott conveyed his doubts to the tour selectors and his recommendation on the best program for Hughes. Team management's concerns about their fast bowler, combined with the outstanding facilities available at Pretoria, convinced the Australians to return for centre-wicket practice on February 15 on the now-vacant fourth day.

However, in the delivery stride of just his second ball to Michael Slater, after an extended warm-up, Hughes felt a searing pain in his back and immediately feared the worst. Unable to continue and barely able to walk off the ground, his first thoughts were of being sent home.

Alcott diagnosed a muscle spasm, rather than a more serious disc problem, but wanted 24 hours to further assess the fast bowler's condition and his future in South Africa. The start to the first block of four

One-dayers, to begin in Johannesburg in four days time, was now out of the question. For Hughes, things could not have gone more badly. His tour probably never recovered.

Hughes and Alcott headed to the pool and the gym to work on his recovery while Australia went into the One-dayers against South Africa as the slightest of favourites after their hard-fought 2–1 victory from behind in the World Series finals in Australia.

South African vice-captain Hansie Cronje started the series in a blaze of glory and blitzed Australia for 112 and 97 in the first two matches, taking particular toll on Warne, with a total of six sixes in his two knocks. However, although Australia found themselves down 2–0 after two matches, not all the news was grim. Even allowing for Cronje's stellar back-to-back efforts in Johannesburg and Pretoria, Australia had got to within five runs in the first game and recovered to reach 209 in game two after being 4–34 at one point.

Much to Hughes' disappointment, McGrath and Reiffel were retained as McDermott's pace support for the next two One-dayers, which were shared, one win apiece. This left only the four-day match against Orange Free State in Bloemfontein for Hughes to impress before the first Test, in Johannesburg. Hughes' absence from One-day cricket had long offended him, but he bit his lip and resolved to throw himself into the game against Cronje's Free State side and lock up a Test place.

Centuries to the Waugh brothers in a stand of 232, occupying less than two and a half hours, blasted Australia to 8–450 and allowed Hughes the luxury of plenty of runs in reserve to test his comeback after his back problems. Stand-in captain Taylor was in no mood to push his man too hard and worked him in three six-over spells, broken by an adjournment each time, to ensure Hughes could test himself at his own pace.

Spinners Warne and May did the bulk of the work for eight wickets between them but Taylor was more enthusiastic after play about a return of 2–47 from the 18 overs sent down by Hughes. Both victims were top-order batsmen and Hughes was pleased his team-mates had been so supportive of his success when he wandered into the media box for a chat the next day.

'There have been a few changes in the side since the Ashes tour and I have to get used to being back,' he told the press corps.

'It was almost like I have to prove myself again.'

One journalist, though, was foolish enough to ask why Hughes had bowled his overs in spells of six, six, six.

'Because Mark Taylor worships the devil,' was the simple reply.

Hughes had stepped out of serious mode.

He was inspired as he watched Michael Slater flay 105 in the second innings with the help of five sixes. The talk among the Australian journalists soon turned to six-hitting and the memories of last year's Ashes tour, largely dominated in that area by Mark Waugh and Hughes. Sitting with his pads on as he waited to bat up the order, at number seven in front of both Waugh twins, Hughes calculated that his tally of grounds at which he had struck a six was now up to 28 or 29.

Upon the dismissal of Shane Warne for a breezy 34, Hughes lifted the first ball he faced, from spinner Kosie Venter, over long on, turned to the press box and signalled a cross, marking off another ground on his list and receiving a standing ovation from the Australians.

Provided he could get through the second innings and display some sort of pace and fire, he could just about pencil himself into the side for the first Test.

Taylor set the Free State an imposing 457, but forgot to tell Cronje that victory was out of the question. Riding his form wave that had already brought him 112 and 97 against the Australians (and would bring a Test-match century a week later), the heavy-handed number three smacked an unforgettable 251 from just 306 deliveries to bring his young side within 60 runs of a famous win. Hughes dispatched both openers, as well as another two wickets in the middle-order, but the fact that no other batsman could reach 40 made little difference to Cronje as he made a bold personal chase for glory.

Taylor gave Hughes the initial over after lunch on the final day and he lumbered in for his first ball, delivered it at three-quarter pace at best, and then doubled over clutching his back. With thoughts that their enforcer had again broken down, Taylor, Healy and the Waugh twins began charging up from the slip cordon to check the big man's health. As everyone approached, including a concerned Cronje, Hughes cocked one leg and dealt with the remains of whatever flatulence was brought on from lunch, and headed back to his mark for ball two.

Healy was barely able to glove the next delivery while Cronje just stood at his crease laughing. The moment is now a staple of the speaking circuit for at least six Australian players as their favourite Hughes story.

'I ran in and bowled the ball and then went "Oohhh", and bent over with my hands on my knees,' as he remembers.

'I looked up and Heals has his hands on his head while Tubby [Taylor] was just looking down and shaking his head. It showed they were still on tenterhooks about me. The slips cordon looked shattered and they all started to run towards me. Tubby got about five yards away and I let rip with a monster and just walked off. I bowled the next ball and I was hoping I wouldn't get an edge because they were all laughing.'

Hughes the personality was obviously unchanged and a long workout that yielded four wickets, albeit with some punishment from Cronje, was enough to convince the tour selectors he should partner McDermott with the new ball in the first Test.

'I felt they were coming out a lot better and I was just trying to prove I could bowl spells and tune-up for the first Test. I felt more comfortable and I felt I had rhythm and was hitting the crease. I started to relax for the first time on tour and I was in the same situation, I guess, as I was on the '93 tour of England.

'I was pretty confident I was going to play in Joburg and I think I would have been disappointed if I didn't play,' Hughes says.

Johannesburg has been the most successful city for South Africa in their uneven battles against Australia since their rivalry began with the visit of Joe Darling's side in 1902–03. Up until their visit to Australia in 1993–94, South Africa had won just 11 of 53 Test matches, against 29 losses, and seven of those victories had come in the last two rubbers of 1966–67 and 1970. A draw was often a moral triumph for the Republic in these early one-sided battles when considering that seven full series against Australia had seen them unable to complete a victory.

However, the story began to change from the time New Wanderers Stadium first hosted a Test match against Australia for the tour of Ian Craig's side in 1957–58. Previous internationals had been played at the original Wanderers Stadium. In five Tests spread over three rubbers, South Africa held a 2–1 advantage with Australia's only victory, by 10 wickets on Craig's tour, being engineered largely by a stunning match double of an even century and figures of 9–154 from Richie Benaud.

The portents for Australia were not good on match day when vice-captain Taylor was forced out by a virus, breaking his combination with Michael Slater, and resulting in Matthew Hayden being awarded his maiden Test cap. Aside from his Test average in the upper 40s, Taylor was an important on-field stabilising influence. The Australian tour party had already lost the services of physiotherapist Alcott several days earlier when he had to return home for personal reasons — a blow that would prove to be much more serious than it first appeared.

Since his appointment to the Australian team for their tour to the Caribbean in early 1984, Alcott had proved himself over a decade to be not only outstanding in his work at getting and keeping players on the park, but also vital in the role of unofficial counsellor and confidante to nearly every member of the side. The effect of his absence, particularly in light of the problems suffered by Warne in coping with South African crowds, has never been fully appreciated.

*Shane Warne in Johannesburg, first Test, 1994.*

South African captain Kepler Wessels won the toss but both sides seemed locked in the previous week's One-day mode over the first two days. The home side rushed to 251 and Australia replied with 248 — both innings were complete within 30 minutes of tea on the second day.

In his first Test match since August the previous year, Hughes had worked through 20 overs and finished with a pleasing 3–59, accounting for opener Gary Kirsten in his first spell and adding the wickets of Wessels and tailender Craig Matthews in the second and third sessions respectively. With the bat, his first single out of a tally of seven nudged him into the record books — having achieved the all-round feat of taking more than 200 Test wickets and scoring 1000 Test runs.

In the field, Hughes had been his usual self, employing every bit of body language and his usual pithiness if it would assist him in getting a wicket. Kirsten was the focus of much of his attention but the left-hander had fought well to contribute 47 in his side's first innings, a tally bettered only by middle-order batsman Jonty Rhodes' knock of 69.

However, down on the boundary, life was anything but friendly for the Australians. The walk to and from the playing field at the start and end of each session had to be made through a narrow aisle, running the gauntlet of the rowdier sections of the crowd. As Steve Waugh would later observe in his diary of the tour, the Australians appeared to start every session angry. Their focus was never entirely on the match and distractions were all about.

South Africa finished the second day at 0–42 and set about building a considerable lead when play resumed on the third morning, March 6. By stumps, Cronje had put South Africa most of the way towards their goal with a stellar century and the Australian team was being pilloried across two countries for their behaviour. By the scheduled lunch break, both Hughes and Warne had drawn the ire of match referee Donald Carr, and were each compelled to attend an ICC hearing after stumps.

South African batsman Andrew Hudson worked his way steadily towards a half-century and had already shown during the summer in Australia that any amount of chatter directed towards him had no impact on either his form or his resolve. As such, Hughes and a number of his team-mates focused most of their talk towards Kirsten in the belief he may crack and offer an out-of-character swipe.

Border did not employ Warne at all during the first 94 minutes of the morning session, preferring instead to try McDermott, Hughes, May and Mark Waugh in a bid to break an opening stand which had stretched to 76 by the 32nd over of the innings.

While Warne lingered in the outfield in front of a raucous crowd, waiting to bowl and fretting over the anger that had been consuming him for three days, Hughes was caught on camera offering his thoughts to Kirsten, who fell in the next over, swatting at May, for 35 just before the drinks break.

'I walked past at the end of the over and said to Gary Kirsten, "You're a weak little prick, why don't you play a shot?"' Hughes recalls his role in the day's events.

'He had been batting for a while and because they got that on camera, I got hauled in afterwards. Shep [Englishman David Shepherd], the umpire at the time, told me to keep it calm and I said, "Fine, it won't happen again".'

Hudson was joined by Cronje and most observers felt Border had to use Warne against the South African vice-captain before he was set. While Cronje had blitzed the star leg-spinner in the One-dayers and for Orange Free State, opinion was that the batsman would hardly be likely to chance similar risks, particularly with his sweep shot, in a Test match. Still, Warne cooled his fingers in the outfield for a further 12 overs while the pair raced on 47 in even time for the second wicket.

When the leg-spinner was finally called up to the crease, he responded by bowling Hudson in his first over and then giving him a fearful volley of abuse, rushing towards him as the South African departed the wicket. Warne had to be physically restrained by 'keeper Ian Healy as he lost complete control of his temper while Hudson, the most mild of men, turned back in shocked disbelief at the behaviour of his opponent. Post-match, Hudson was to borrow the parlance from another game and observe Australia had 'played the man, and lost'. A stern umpire Shepherd immediately ordered Border, in no uncertain terms, to bring his errant bowler into line but no report was made by either umpire.

Cronje went to lunch on 23 — the cheers for the South African batsmen quickly replaced by a chorus of boos from a packed Sunday crowd of 29,880 once the visitors reached the race. By tea, the South African vice-captain was within eight runs of a century and Carr, under his powers

*An angry Hughes at the Wanderers Ground during Australia's first Test in South Africa for nearly 25 years.*

as match referee to lay a report independent of the umpires, was calling for video replays of the incidents involving both Hughes and Warne.

Australian team manager Dr Cam Battersby was made aware of the potential for a report after calls from the Australian journalists within the press box, and began contemplating a defence. Dr Battersby had managed the Australian team that toured Sri Lanka in 1992, containing Warne, and the team to New Zealand in 1990, which Hughes was a part of, and had also been in South Africa within the previous 12 months in charge of an Australian Cricket Academy outfit. He had also been a frequent visitor to South Africa over the preceding 20 years and felt that he understood that country's sporting ethos.

Carr confirmed his reports of both players just before stumps and Battersby, Border and coach Bob Simpson were called to appear, along with both umpires and the bowling pair.

Hughes, just as he had done in his two previous ICC hearings in Australia in the summer of 1992–93, bluntly told the truth and owned up to why and what he had said to Kirsten, although Cronje gave evidence that he had not heard the fast bowler say anything untoward.

'The match referee asked me why I had said what I did,' Hughes remembers.

'I told him, "Kirsten was batting pretty well and looking pretty sound. If I can get an advantage over him in a mental battle and he gets out, I think that's a flaw in his game. That's the way I play. It's within the rules and that's something you can exploit".

'I was told I would have to change the way I play cricket and that I would come under a lot of scrutiny. I replied that I had always played that way and so be it.'

Both umpires Shepherd and Barry Lambson confirmed they had not felt the need to make a report as the fast bowler had stopped his sledging once asked; the fact Hughes was reported from the video still grates on the fast bowler now.

'The thing that most people forget is that neither umpire reported us,' Hughes says. 'We were booked by Donald Carr. The match referee asked the umpires about both incidents in the hearing and the umpires said, "We asked both players to settle down and had no further trouble from them after that".'

While Hughes may feel aggrieved, the ICC's charter does plainly state the match referee can lay a report independently of the umpires if he feels the game has been brought into disrepute and, particularly so in Warne's case, the umpires erred badly in not choosing to do so. Warne's outburst was completely over the top while Hughes had failed to recognise the changing tide over the last 18 months. Whether the message had been clearly stated to the members of the Australian team or not, the time was coming when poor behaviour was going to be stamped upon and this was not the occasion to try to bend the rules.

Carr told Battersby he would consider his decision and would phone him at the team's hotel once he had reached his verdict. Battersby felt the Australians had received a fair hearing and waited for news of the verdict, before ringing ACB chief executive officer Graham Halbish to report the day's events back to Melbourne.

'Donald rang me about half an hour after we got back to the Sandton Sun and told me the players had been fined 1000 Rand each [approximately $400 Australian or equivalent to 10 per cent of each player's match fee]. My reaction was to tell him the players were aware they could not comment to anyone and I hoped that this incident would not affect the good relationship we had had with the referee to this point,' Battersby said.

Carr's findings were greeted with universal disbelief within the press corps on both sides of the Indian Ocean, as the referee did have the power to fine a player up to 75 per cent of his match fee or even suspend an offender for up to three Test matches. Most expected Hughes to be facing a particularly stiff fine for a third offence while Warne's prospects looked bleak. Reports back to Australia to the major newspapers led with how the players' behaviour had blackened the name of the Australian cricket team, prompting a media storm at home after a summer in which 'niggly' incidents had been highlighted.

In contrast, the Australian party felt aggrieved. In their view, provocation had been a factor that was ignored by the media. Contact between journalists and the players was never the same for the remainder of the tour.

Mike Coward, cricket columnist with the *Australian* and the senior journalist on tour, felt the Australian team had wasted the opportunity to come to South Africa and make a major impact, to show how cricket was played in Australia, and relayed his views immediately to Battersby.

'Mike felt that in one Test match in Johannesburg, we had blown that totally out of the water,' Battersby said.

'I said I appreciated his view but that he had to understand it is the responsibility of the host country to ensure that the visiting team isn't subjected to the sort of provocation and abuse which our players were subjected to in Johannesburg.'

As one of the journalists on that tour, working for news agency Australian Associated Press at the time, I must admit my own reports on the two incidents carried little more than the facts of the hearings and their outcome. Partly because of the brief of working for AAP and the instructions to write as impartially as possible for all subscribers, and partly because I was unaware of how much of an issue sledging had become in Australia, I did not look deeply enough at what had happened during that day.

Rightly, the specialist newspaper reporters felt strongly that the image of Australian cricket had been done a grave disservice and I must admit to being out of touch with the public feeling back home. I didn't consider the opinion that many believed, that the two should perhaps even have been sent home, to be realistic.

ACB chairman Alan Crompton, who had counselled Hughes a year before after the tour of New Zealand and on the eve of the 1993 Ashes tour, following his run-in with Greatbatch in Auckland, had spoken out publicly of the Board's concerns about player behaviour after the Board's meeting in Adelaide less than five weeks beforehand. Along with his fellow directors, he was distressed to hear of the two reports and to watch replayed film of what had happened.

Crompton admired Hughes enormously for his work for Australia but he felt the fast bowler, as a role model for youngsters, did not work hard enough at the image he presented.

Of immediate importance was Australia's task of trying to save a match they had lost control of so completely during the third day. Wessels kept the enervated Australians in the field until the hour after lunch and pushed on to a neat figure of 9–450, setting the visitors an improbable 454 for victory or the more realistic task of holding out for nine hours and 133 overs to force a draw.

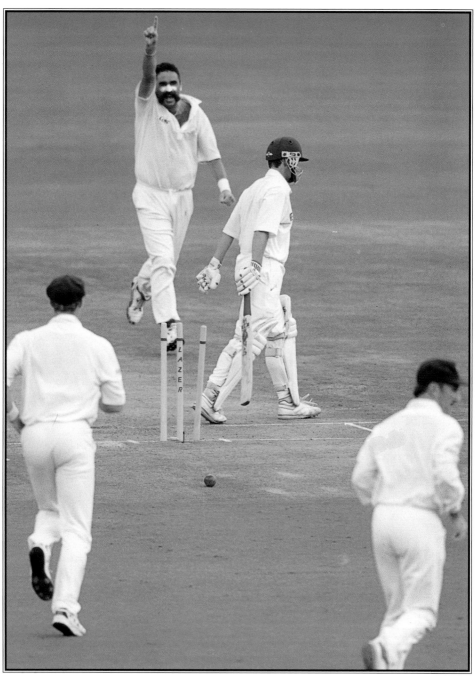

*Gary Kirsten, bowled by Hughes on the opening day of the first Test in Johannesburg.*

David Boon shepherded the score to 2–123 by stumps on the fourth day as Australians awoke to read of the third day's events, due to the time difference involved, causing further furore over team behaviour at home.

Boon resisted almost five hours in all for a determined 83, using up more time than the other five specialist batsmen in the side combined. Whether due to the surfeit of recent One-day cricket and resultant poor technique or the vagaries of a pitch now displaying variable bounce, Australia were haemorrhaging fatally at 6–194 by lunch on the final day. With more than three hours left to bat, the final pair, Hughes and May, came together.

Hughes, who once publicly stated in late 1986 that his dream was to score a Test run, determined he would not go down without a fight and elicited more than an hour of support from May, who had heroically brought Australia to within one run of victory against the West Indies in Adelaide just over 12 months before.

Allan Donald and Fanie De Villiers took the second new ball but the onset of light rain saw the players leave, with the Australians hoping that the weather might force a draw.

As the Australian pair headed up the race through the crowd, one spectator leaned over the divide and spat at the two batsmen, heaping invective upon Hughes as they passed. Hughes snapped.

'We were nine down and Tim May and myself had to bat for three hours to save the Test match. We were no chance and just hoping for rain.

'To this day, I can't tell you what he said to me.

'In 99 cases out of 100, you keep walking but that day I was frustrated and didn't feel like listening to it. I was annoyed with the way we'd been treated in South Africa. We would go out to dinner, to bars or to the ground and just everywhere we went we got volleys of abuse.

'I stopped, turned around and looked at him and thought, "Don't worry about it". I was thinking pretty clearly about it all. Maysie was coming up behind me and he gave him a spray too. I thought, "I've had a gutful of this shit and it stops here".

'I went back and hit well below the partition to scare him. As I was walking back, I could see his fingers over the top of the partition and I remember thinking, "I could break eight fingers here".

'I hit down and then leaned over the fence and said, "Mate, if you've got something to say, let's hear it". He looked at me and said "What?" I said again, "If you've got something to say, let's fucking hear it right now". He backed off and I said, "You're like every prick I've met here, you're as weak as piss".'

May had walked past Hughes as the confrontation occurred but went back for his team-mate when he sighted an Australian television crew filming the incident from the top of the race. Despite the fact the incident was captured on film and was playing repeatedly on Australian television within hours of the match finishing, few in the Australian rooms knew what had occurred.

'We were trying to save the game and we had been copping it for the entire match and I guess this guy spitting at him was the last straw for Merv,' May says.

'I didn't hear what was said because Merv was in front of me but I tapped him because I saw TV cameras at the top of the race. I thought, "This is trouble", and said, "Merv, keep going, there are cameras here".'

Upon the resumption of play half an hour later, with the clouds still low, man of the match Cronje had May caught at bat-pad to put South Africa ahead 1–0 in a series against Australia for the second time that summer. Hughes headed off dejected, unbeaten on 26 after almost two hours' resistance.

Battersby was told of the incident in the race but decided against filing a report to the ACB, feeling the bowler had been heavily provoked in a tense situation.

'Some idiot alongside the race made a comment to Merv about his mother and Merv took umbrage at this. I don't blame him,' Battersby maintains.

'He tried to frighten the character by belting at the post and there happened to be an Australian camera crew at the top of the race. I believed at the time, and still believe, that it was a total belt-up by the television companies. At the time it created barely a ripple in South Africa but there was an enormous fuss at home.'

An enormous fuss at home was an understatement and the Executive Committee of the Board happened to be meeting in Sydney as the Test concluded. ACB chief executive officer Graham Halbish rang Battersby in the early hours of the next morning to ask why he had not told the Board about the second Hughes incident, telling him the directors in Australia were extremely concerned about team behaviour in the light of the past few days and had placed an item on the agenda for their meeting.

'I told Graham it had hardly created a ripple here and didn't feel it was worthwhile,' Battersby said.

'He said it was huge news in Australia and the Board was meeting in Sydney and viewed it very seriously indeed. As far as I was concerned, the fines had been dealt with by the umpires and referee while the second incident was heavily provoked. In my view, if they wanted to censure Merv the second time around that was fine, but I believed justice had been done.'

For the ACB, the time had come to act, after what it saw as a build-up over the previous two years of a number of unsavoury incidents. Crompton, who was due to head to South Africa with Halbish just over a

*The infamous confrontation between Hughes and a South African spectator on the final day of the first Test. The other batsman is Tim May.*

week later, announced that the Board's Executive had fined both Warne and Hughes $4000 following their behaviour in the Johannesburg Test match, while Hughes had been issued with a $2000 suspended fine for his altercation with the spectator.

'The decision to implement the fines was very much a Board decision,' Crompton confirms. 'It was the Executive Committee of the Board that made the decision, which happened, coincidentally, to be meeting at the time. The decision reflected my personal view. The Board felt that we had to act and had to act strongly.'

'We considered the on-field incidents and the off-field incident to be quite separate and they were treated that way, and dealt with that way. The $4000 fines were not for those particular incidents in Johannesburg alone, but for a series of incidents over a two-year period causing the ACB to have a concern about player behaviour.

'Donald Carr dealt with the two players on the basis of what happened on the field on that day in Johannesburg, and the ACB had no argument with him in his role as ICC referee, but the ACB didn't take action simply on the basis of what happened that day.'

In the view of the ACB, with the chairman as its spokesman, the players had been given a final warning when Crompton spoke on behalf of the Board at its January meeting. Clearly, the next player, or players, who stepped out of line would face stern disciplinary action.

'It was a build-up and I had gone public on behalf of the Board in Adelaide to deliver a clear message to the players. The incidents in Johannesburg were the last straw in a series of incidents involving the same two players and other players over a lengthy period of time. We considered that the number of warnings in the lead-up was sufficient for all the players. I later became aware there wasn't much reaction in South Africa at the time but the reaction in Australia was extreme,' Crompton says.

When news of the fines reached the Australian team in Sun City, reaction was heated.

As expected, Hughes and Warne both felt they had been fined without the right of reply. Battersby was also at odds with the decision of his fellow directors.

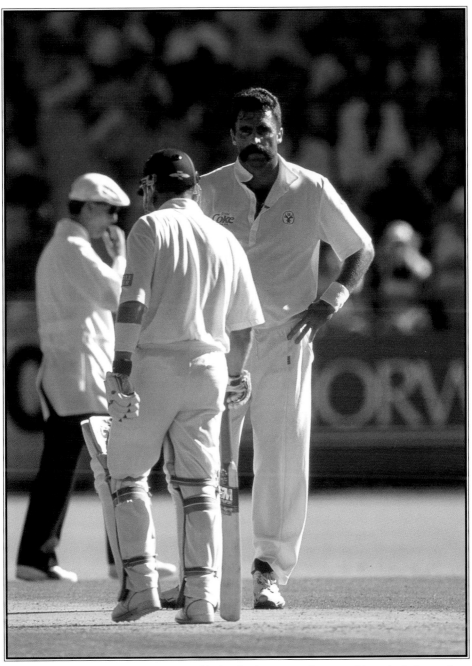

*Hughes, ever mindful of the reaction to his sledging of Gary Kirsten in the first Test, offers a half-hearted glare during the second Test, in Cape Town.*

'What I still feel is that, under the circumstances in South Africa, which I communicated to the Board at the time, it was an unduly heavy-handed penalty,' Battersby says.

'Given that, I have to acknowledge that in the long run the fines had the desired effect on Australian cricket because we haven't had a problem with discipline since then.

'I told Merv I didn't agree, but he had to understand the goalposts had changed as far as the Australian Cricket Board was concerned. We knocked it around for a few hours and decided we had to get on with the tour and try to get our wheels back on track.'

Border, a fierce defender of his players throughout his captaincy career, believes Warne and Hughes were criticised unfairly because the referee had not acted more strongly. In his view, a much harsher fine would have seen the matter end in Johannesburg but the leniency of the verdict kicked the story along.

'The Australian Cricket Board didn't handle that very well in my opinion. Why have an ICC referee if you are going to ignore him?' Border argues.

'Maybe he was a little bit light-on but we went in there and we argued a case. He came down with a ruling and whether it's too light or too harsh, that's the end of the story in my opinion.

'For the ACB to come in over the top, as a team, we were really dirty. The players stepped out of line but it wasn't their fault they were fined an amount that people didn't think was appropriate.'

Due to behind-the-scenes counselling, the ACB would not agree but, to this day, those who made that tour still firmly hold the belief that the direction from the ACB on what was expected in regard to improved behaviour was not made clearly enough.

Mark Taylor, then vice-captain and soon to be appointed as Australia's 39th leader with an avowed aim of cleaning up the side's act, remembers no firm edict coming from either Border or Simpson. The players had only heard of Crompton's comments in January through the newspapers.

'One of the problems we all had at the time was I don't think the players ever got told about it,' Taylor says.

'When we heard Alan Crompton's remarks, it was via a newspaper article, but what we really needed was the chairman to come into the rooms or tell Allan Border at the time to cut it out because it was going too far. The players had to be told what wasn't going to be tolerated but that never happened. All we saw was what was written in the newspaper — there was no direction from either the Board, the coach or the captain. If that had happened and then Merv and Warney had done what they did in South Africa and been fined, there wouldn't have been a problem.

'All in all, I think Merv was a bit unlucky for a number of reasons. It was a developing situation over a year and sooner or later the line was going to get drawn. It got drawn in South Africa. Merv had been doing what he had done for the last five or six years. People will argue he should have made a change but I think he would have made a change if he had been directed to. The incidents in South Africa were very unfortunate and I feel they could have been avoided.'

Be that as it may, since that time, no Australian player appeared before an ICC referee for a Test match offence in the three years up until February 1997. The only bookings that were made in that time came during a One-day series in Sri Lanka in 1996, when Taylor was injured and unable to tour. However, since then, Ian Healy was suspended for two One-day matches for throwing his bat after the third Test, in Pretoria, in April 1997.

Australia won the next Test match in Cape Town playing hard, tough cricket but behaving themselves.

Times had changed since 1993 when Hughes' in-your-face approach played a key role in Australia's successful defence of the Ashes. In my opinion, Hughes was unfortunate firstly to be booked and then to be fined as much as he was. However, once he was convicted of an offence, a poor disciplinary record told against him.

'From the way I played the game, what I did on the field in Johannesburg was no different from the way I played 50 other Test matches.

'Everyone was in an uproar over what happened with the spectator and that's fair enough. I was very disappointed everyone in the media said I tried to hit him. If anyone sees the replay, you can see that I didn't try to hit him because I hit about halfway down the partition.

'A lot of people ask me if I've had any regrets with my career. With the amount of trouble it caused for me, I wish I had hit that bloke.'

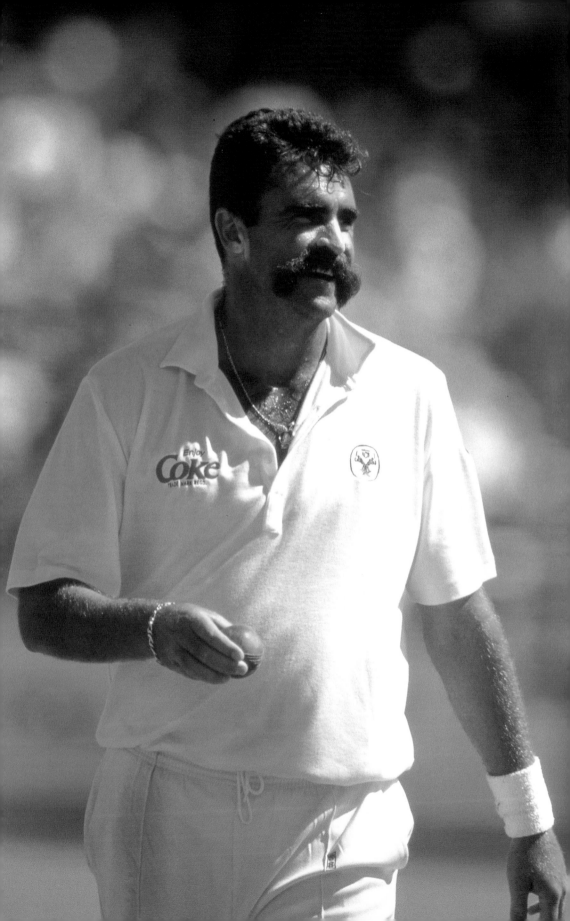

# CHAPTER THIRTEEN

# BURNT OUT?

**A**way in South Africa, Merv Hughes was inured to much of the controversy flying around in Australia in the wake of the first Test match in Johannesburg. However, at home, for Sue Hughes, who was four months pregnant with their first child, it was a nightmare.

Sue had found it difficult to cope with a lonely life as a cricketing widow when her husband was going through the best of times, as he was in England in 1993. Now, it was close to impossible.

'I never found it very easy in England when so many people would just come up and always want your time or some part of you,' Sue says. 'You have to be incredibly patient to be able to deal with that because you had limited time together anyway because the players were often away so much.

'When Merv was getting criticised in South Africa, it was a terrible time. When you never deal with the media, it's such an overwhelming thing to hear all this criticism and it was so stressful to go through.'

Sue had reluctantly agreed to have their wedding covered by a national women's magazine two years before but life in the limelight was certainly not her style. She could not wait for the tour to finish.

Defeat in the Test in Johannesburg was a heavy blow for the Australians, coming on top of a 3–1 deficit in the One-dayers. Australian touring teams, since the advent of World Series Cricket in 1977–78 had repeatedly shown a depressing inability to adapt to conditions away from home. A poor start, coupled with a lack of enjoyment for many players

*Opposite: Hughes in Cape Town, second Test against South Africa, 1994.*

because of their perceived siege situation with many local fans, meant the tour faced the very real prospect of descending to disastrous depths.

Once news broke of the Australian Cricket Board's decision to fine Merv Hughes and Shane Warne a further $4000 for bringing the game into disrepute with their ICC Code of Conduct convictions, the tour party closed ranks completely.

Repaired for three days of R and R to the luxurious resort of Sun City, which is as far away from the real world as nearly any place on earth could possibly be, the Australians met for a fiery session to resolve what action could be taken and to set their goals for the rest of the tour.

So aggrieved were some players with the events of the last few days that the idea of boycotting the upcoming tour match against provincial side Boland was tossed around. Luckily, for the image of Australian cricket — which had taken a beating over the last week and similarly when the same idea was aired after umpiring controversies on the 1988 tour of Pakistan — the suggestion was quickly argued away and never made public.

Warne had been crucial to Australia's successes against South Africa on home soil but the pressure of expectations in the Republic, coupled with some harsh treatment from Hansie Cronje, had clearly taken its toll on the 24-year-old. During the match against Boland, Warne confessed to feeling that he was 'burning up' every time he took to the field on tour. He knew he would snap at some point, but could see no way of stopping himself. He had quickly apologised to Andrew Hudson, the umpires and the South African team at large after the events of Johannesburg and was fortunate that help from his team-mates was close at hand.

Vice-captain Mark Taylor knew success would not be forthcoming in the Cape Town Test, just over a week away, unless Warne was comfortable within himself. Emphasising the leadership qualities that would soon see him elevated to the number one job, Taylor took it upon himself to counsel his young team-mate. Boycotts, which every member of team management deplored in this instance, would do no good and a response had to come on-field in the form of face-restoring success.

'The discussion we had about not playing the game in Boland was never that serious and everyone knew we had to get on with the tour,' Taylor says. 'Warney was crucial for us and I wanted a chat with him.'

Hughes had gone through his own purgatory, of course, after the events of Johannesburg but Taylor said he hadn't felt the need to take time out with the fast bowler.

'I sat down to speak to Warney because I saw a real difference in him compared to any other tour. I could see the pressure was getting to him and he was the centre of attention.

'Merv was unlucky because he had only done what he had done for the whole of his career. In my view, Merv was fine and there wasn't anything eating away at him like it was for Warney,' Taylor says.

Once he had begun to play consistently for Victoria and then Australia, Hughes had largely relied on his own abilities to dig himself out of a low and begin his preparation for the next game. Just as he had taught younger team-mates, Paul Reiffel and Damien Fleming, as they followed him into international cricket, Hughes was determined to find positive aspects of the Johannesburg Test and take them into the match at Cape Town.

A match haul of 4–145 from 45 overs may not have seemed that imposing but it did contain the wickets of top-order batsmen Gary Kirsten, Hansie Cronje and Kepler Wessels, while his dogged efforts with the bat had given Australia a faint hope of a draw.

'I was happy with the way I bowled in that second dig. A lot of people said I didn't bowl well but I was happy because I thought I was hitting the deck, without taking wickets. That can happen sometimes.'

Steve Waugh soon had confirmation that the ebullient Hughes personality was still in good order after accepting an invitation to see a film with the fast bowler.

Waugh, along with Tim May and Hughes, is among the group of Australian players noted for their addiction to movies as a way to kill time on tour. Waugh and May went to enormous lengths to obtain a copy of *Ferris Bueller's Day Off* while in Pakistan in 1988. The film struck a chord with the duo and, in ensuing Shield games over the next few years, each would try to make the other laugh at crucial times in play by repeating a favourite line. May and Waugh christened various other Shield cricketers across Australia as characters from the movie, according to similarity. May even left tickets marked 'F. Bueller' at the gate of every international match he played, in case Ferris ever decided to wag another day from school and wanted to catch some cricket. As for Hughes, more than one touring team has been driven up the wall by his penchant for repeating Doc Holliday's speeches from *Tombstone* ad nauseam or watching *Terminator 2* three times in a single night.

Hughes and Waugh loaded up with jaffas, soft drinks and lollies and decided to see *Robin Hood, Men in Tights*. Once in the cinema, they realised they comprised 50 per cent of the audience, joined only by an elderly couple seated several rows in front. In Waugh's opinion, Mel Brooks' standard of comedy films had slipped dramatically since the days of the 1974 classic *Blazing Saddles* and Hughes' boredom was soon something to behold.

'The film was one of the worst ever and there were just the four of us in the cinema,' Waugh says.

'Merv was starting to struggle from early on so he started pinging jaffas at the cinema screen and putting big dints into it. The oldies in front of us were getting cheesed off so he started throwing things at them. It wasn't a good move when they turned around and there were only two other people in the cinema to pick from as the culprit, one of whom was holding a huge bag of lollies.'

Steve Waugh in the Australians' dressing-room during the '94 South African tour.

In any case, the chance to blow off some steam had allowed Hughes to shrug off his unhappiness about the lack of contact from the ACB since he had been fined the extra $4000.

'Not at any stage did anyone from the ACB ring either Shane or myself, as far as I'm aware, to ask my side of the story,' Hughes complains.

'To get judged by the Australian Cricket Board in Melbourne, however far away it was, without the right of reply and without the right to defend myself, I thought was a bit rich. It was just bang, with a $4000 fine.'

To be fair to the ACB, chairman Alan Crompton and chief executive officer Graham Halbish arrived in South Africa the week before the Cape Town Test match, when the Australians were engaged in the match against Boland, and had sought a meeting with the team.

'Alan and Graham arrived during the game in Stellenbosch [against Boland] and their purpose was to meet with the team and explain the Board's actions,' Battersby recalls.

'After discussions between myself, Allan Border and Bob Simpson, we decided it wasn't the best time for the team to be distracted by these continued discussions before an important Test match. We were two days out of the Cape Town Test match and we really felt that, for those two days, we should be concentrating on cricket and not be involved in political discussions about what had happened to Warne and Hughes. For those reasons, there may have been a lack of communication with the two players concerned until the tour had been completed. However, we wanted to get on and concentrate on the Cape Town Test and win it.'

Historically, Australia boasted a successful record at picturesque Newlands at the foot of Table Mountain, with six consecutive wins from as many outings before their solitary loss at the hands of the all-conquering 1970 Springbok outfit. Vice-captain Mark Taylor and young fast bowler Glenn McGrath returned in place of Matthew Hayden and spinner Tim May while the home side went in unchanged, retaining a four-pronged pace attack.

South African captain Kepler Wessels won his second straight Test match toss and his intentions were made clear soon enough, bat Australia out of the match and protect a 1–0 series lead. Wessels will stand as one of the most unimaginative captains in Test match history and his tactics for this game were designed with nothing more in mind than insurance against defeat, no matter what the cost to his country's fledgling Test-match culture.

The home side laboured a ridiculous 144.1 overs and nearly 10 hours in all to compile 361, paying scant attention to the thoughts of the 27,000 or so spectators over the first two days. Andrew Hudson contributed 102 from 174 balls, cultured with 13 boundaries, but Peter Kirsten and Brian McMillan looked upon the idea of scoring as the last of their options.

Between them, Kirsten (70) and McMillan (74) batted for nine hours and faced some 403 deliveries with McMillan, particularly, looking all at sea against the spin of Warne.

Warne worked through a marathon 47 overs for 3–78 to convince all he was back on track while pacemen McGrath (3–65 from 26.1) and McDermott (2–80 from 27) never wilted at any stage, despite their workload. Hughes, on the other hand, had gone wicketless through 20 overs, conceding 80 runs, and rarely providing a threat to the South Africans. The big man had obviously toned down his normal on-field approach and the conscious effort of 'behaving' seemed to be affecting his form badly. He might have been well behaved, but he wasn't much use to captain Border.

'Because I had been fined, I knew I was really going to be under the pump and people would be looking at me,' Hughes says. 'I was more worried about how I was perceived on the ground with my demeanour than by actually bowling. It showed in the way I bowled.'

Australia fought their way to a valuable lead of 74, thanks to half-centuries from Taylor, Boon, Healy and Steve Waugh, but Hughes' Test match was rapidly becoming a nightmare from a personal point of view — out for a golden duck, trapped lbw by Craig Matthews.

For the first time in the 53 Tests that he had captained Hughes (over the past nine years), Border actually found himself questioning the worth of his fast bowler. Not because of his effort, which could never be questioned, but whether he could provide Australia with a wicket when they needed one.

'I think that whole tour for him came down to that incident in Johannesburg. I think that kicked Merv in the guts that much,' Border says.

While Border and most of his then team-mates felt Hughes was struggling because of the close eye placed upon him after the events of Johannesburg, coach Simpson and wicket-keeper Ian Healy were noted dissenters.

Through his four decades in cricket, Simpson has never been one to talk around a subject and, while it may be brutal to say, he felt international cricket had passed the fast bowler by during his lay-off for knee surgery after the Ashes tour.

'The wicket in Cape Town wasn't great but I don't think you can equate the psychological effect to what was happening, physically, to him,' Simpson says.

'It would be easy to say the psychological effect of his off-field troubles affected his form but I think that's wrong. That would be the easy way out, in my opinion. I think he just couldn't do it any more.

'The frustration of not being able to do what he wanted to do may well have led to the problems he had on the field and off the field in that series. We were worried about Merv going into the Johannesburg Test but we were relieved he got some wickets and we were hoping he would kick on from there. He never kicked on,' Simpson says bluntly.

Healy lays the blame for Hughes' demise from international cricket squarely at the feet of the man himself. As he has grown older in the Australian side, Healy has done more work, rather than less, so that he can keep pace with younger rivals and even improve further. Hughes should have done the same in his eyes.

'I looked at that tour and thought he was in trouble,' says Healy. 'He had no energy through the entire Cape Town Test match. That's the first time I could ever remember that. The Pretoria injury might have been bad luck but through that tour he would lie on his bed, rather than go to the gym. His energy level was so low.

'I think he had spent so much time getting his knee right, he didn't have anything left for the rest of his body. In the Cape Town match, watching him covered in ice every night and seeing his lethargy, I thought he was burnt out.'

Healy rates Hughes as the quickest of all the Australian bowlers he has kept to throughout his career, just shading the current spearhead McGrath, and was both angered and disappointed his inspirational team-mate could not extend his time at the top by disciplining himself better.

'I was one that said plenty to him about his weight over the years. He had been spoken to lots but just didn't respond. In my view, when someone does that, they have lost the willpower to get right. He was told he wouldn't last and that's exactly what happened. I was caring of him at first, and then disappointed to see the way he was in South Africa. Everything they had been telling him for two years came true,' he says.

Border gave Hughes just five overs in the second innings, which went wicketless, as Australia pushed relentlessly for a victory that would square the series. The South Africans did not begin their second innings until the hour after lunch on the fourth day but Border would not hear of the Test drifting to a draw.

At the close, South Africa had slipped to 6–100, of an eventual 164 all out. Steve Waugh and Warne shared eight wickets between them on a pitch playing tricks and Hughes rates Border's captaincy on this day as inspirational, crediting him almost entirely with Australia's victory against the odds by nine wickets.

Australia had shrugged off the troubles of Johannesburg magnificently to win in Cape Town with just 90 minutes to spare but Hughes had gone wicketless for the match and failed to score.

It was to be the last time he would play for Australia.

Cricketers never get to write their own epitaphs and Hughes' departure from the international scene is most undeserving for a player of his record and standing. However, Australia's Test performers are a pragmatic lot and few ever expect to be farewelled in grandiose style, such as was afforded to David Boon at the Adelaide Oval in early 1996.

When Greg Chappell and Dennis Lillee both departed the international scene to the cheers of thousands in the Sydney Test match against Pakistan in early 1984, their nine team-mates sat around in the dressing-rooms and wondered aloud about how their retirements would come about. Rod Marsh, who would join his two old comrades in retirement just over a month later, agreed with Allan Border that he wouldn't want a lot of fuss. Fast bowler Rodney Hogg was asked how he would like his last match for Australia to proceed and Border never forgot his answer.

'I'll just get dropped like most blokes do. You never get the fairytale you want,' Border quotes Hogg.

'Merv was a fantastic cricketer for Australia and he didn't deserve to go out on a duck and no wickets. If the incident at Johannesburg hadn't happened, I think it could have been a very different story. You always want to finish on a high note but it just doesn't happen that way for the vast majority of people.'

Hughes has a similar view.

'The way I look at it is, that the last Test match I played in, we won. I didn't contribute that much but that's not the important thing.

'I took no wickets and I made a duck after my mum and dad had come all the way over to watch me play. Mum thought I fielded very well. It was good she worked on the positives too.'

The deciding Test match in Durban was set down to start four days after Australia's momentous victory in Cape Town. The tour had been turned around and the party had high hopes of coming from behind to win the series and send off Border in grand style. The Australian captain had not confirmed to anyone he would be leaving international cricket but the suspicion was that he would retire quietly once the team got back home. While the lure of one last Ashes series at home, in 1994–95, was attractive, Border did not care to tour Pakistan for a fourth time in September 1994, and was not the kind of player to pick and choose when he was available for his country.

The Durban pitch had traditionally offered much assistance to the seamers, and Australia were certain to include three pacemen in their attack. The quandary, for the selection panel of Border, Taylor, Simpson and Boon, was the place of Hughes in the line-up.

Through the entirety of his career and especially so as captain, Border was loath to change a winning team but he had lost much confidence in his fast bowler during the Test in Cape Town. In the end, a unanimous vote, led by the captain, saw Paul Reiffel preferred to Hughes in the XI for the Durban encounter.

'Merv was probably the fall guy,' Border says. 'We had just won the Test match and I think Merv's attitude was good, but we were searching for that combination with the ball. We felt Mervyn hadn't looked great and I think his form just didn't warrant it at that point.'

While Border may have led the views of the selection panel, Simpson had always got the tough jobs when it came to telling a loyal servant he had been passed over. The coach was given the task of telling Hughes he would not play, just as he had been the one to inform Steve Waugh of his dumping in 1991, Geoff Marsh in early 1992 and Dean Jones in 1992.

'When you drop someone like Merv who had been such an enormous part of our success, it's a decision that you anguish over. It's a decision you never take lightly or take on just a hunch. It took a long while to reach that verdict and I remember it dominated most of our meeting,' Simpson recalls.

While obviously there was no thought he had played his last Test match for Australia at the time, Hughes was still cut deeply by his omission. His form had been poor in Cape Town but Hughes felt, since becoming a regular member of the side from 1989, he had never strung together consecutive poor performances. He felt his pride would not allow another display as bad as the second Test and this firm belief in himself, coupled with his own knowledge of Border's views on winning sides, left him bleeding badly.

To compound his disappointment, when Hughes rang home that night, he was told by his wife, Sue, that he would not be touring Sharjah at the completion of the South African trip. The national selectors had finalised their side but, due to a communication mix-up, Sue was told of his flight details back to Australia before Simpson had told Merv he had been dropped for the week-long One-day tournament.

The fast bowler was, by now, deeply depressed and headed out for the night to blow off steam with team-mate May. May had been dropped after the first Test and, with both being on the wrong side of 30, were questioning their futures with the national side — but both were committed to continuing their careers as long as possible. (May, however, would play only intermittently until his retirement in early 1996.)

'Maysie and I were talking about the future and where we saw ourselves going and I knew it was going to get hard. For my part, they had gone for Glenn McGrath and Paul Reiffel and that was a sign they were starting to bring along the younger players. Probably what disappointed me most of all was that it was such a crucial Test match. If we had won that game in Durban, we would have won the series. To be passed over for such a vital game was a very bad sign for me,' Hughes says.

It was obvious Border would not be around much longer as Australian captain and Hughes felt he wanted to know where he stood with vice-captain Taylor, the man the players assumed would get the job as the next Australian skipper. Conveniently, the pair roomed together in Durban and the big man was reassured to know he was still a part of the frame in Taylor's eyes, provided he could get himself fit.

Taylor had noticed a discernible drop in Hughes' pace and told him bluntly that if he could regain his fire, Hughes' personality was still welcome under his leadership if Taylor was awarded the number one job.

'I knew that if AB did retire, I was a chance of becoming captain so I told Merv that if I was the next captain, I wanted him as part of my team,' Taylor says.

'I said I was also sure the same would apply for Steve Waugh or Ian Healy if they became captain. I told him I didn't care about what a bloke looked like, but his performance was the key. Merv was definitely bowling slower as time was getting on. He had to find a way of either making that work for him, which was never Merv's way, or finding a way of getting his old pace back. If he could get his old pace back at 120 kg or 95 kg, I didn't mind, as long as he did it.'

When Taylor finally did get the top job some eight weeks later, he talked of a less overt Australian approach in the field in his inaugural press conference. Taylor's no-nonsense approach to on-field behaviour certainly helped him win the top job but he rejects any assertion that his appointment was the end of the road for M.G. Hughes.

'He's a bloke every captain would love to have and there was always room for Merv,' he says. 'He's not a fool and he's not a bloke who just throws it down with raw aggression. He knows exactly what he's doing and he's rarely out of control. I wish I had got to use him in a Test match.'

Out of the Test match and soon to be out of the touring team altogether once they headed to Sharjah, Hughes was desperate to play as many of the last four One-dayers on tour as possible, as much to reassure himself of his status as anything.

His fitness was obviously now paramount to his team-mates who were selecting the side and work had to be done. Victorian team-mate Dean Jones joined Hughes for a jog on the first day of the Test at Kingsmead but fortune had turned a dark eye on the fast bowler.

Having already hurt his back in the lead-up to the first block of One-dayers, Hughes was inconsolable after tearing a calf muscle during his run. Now there would be no chance to even impress in the nets and a horror visit to South Africa was as good as over.

Poor form can be worked through with hard work but injuries, especially when opportunity is rare, are devastating.

'I was enormously pissed off when I did my calf. Because you are not part of the team, you become part of the team that helps the team and it's your job to bowl whenever they need someone to bowl and to make sure everything goes smoothly for the 11 players trying to win the game,' Hughes says.

'Once I got injured, I couldn't do any of that and just felt useless. After I did the calf, I lost a lot of focus.'

Hughes flew home in early April, depressed about his omission from an Australian touring team and was faced with the very real prospect that his international career could be coming to a sudden end.

In May, Hughes and Warne were both called to appear before a full meeting of the ACB to have the reasoning behind their $4000 fines explained to them. It was the first contact Hughes had had

*Another side of touring — with David Boon (in sunglasses) and Tim May during a helicopter joy-ride above the sights of Cape Town.*

with the ACB Board, after team management had not allowed the meeting in South Africa between Crompton and Halbish and the players. It was at this meeting that Hughes learnt why he had been fined the same amount as his Victorian team-mate, even though Warne's offence of running at Hudson was much graver. While he could understand the reasoning behind the amount of the fine, the actual fine itself still rankled.

'We went to England in 1993 and everything I did was good, aggressive bowling,' he argues. 'We went to South Africa and it was suddenly bad sportsmanship. Where do you draw the line?

'I said if I was fined for calling Gary Kirsten a weak little prick, then yes I had done it and had to be fined.

*Allan Border, immediately after completing what proved to be his final innings in Test cricket.*

But I wanted to get my point across. I said, "I feel as if Shane Warne went right over the top but you [the ACB] couldn't fine him alone and you've given me $4000 as well".

'[Victorian director] Bob Merriman said, "No, you've been fined $4000 because it's your third offence. Shane got fined excessively because his outburst was a lot worse".

'That was all I needed to know. I had felt like I was being hauled over the coals because we couldn't take down the glamour boy of Australian cricket by himself. That wasn't having a go at Shane but I felt as though if I had done something like that, being so aggressive towards the dismissed batsmen and being held back by another player, I would have been suspended. When it was put into perspective by Bob Merriman, I could cop that.'

Hughes' closest cricket friend, Tony Dodemaide, provided a pillar of support but Dodemaide could see Hughes' focus shifting away from cricket, even if the man did not want to see it himself. The South African tour took a heavy toll on Hughes and it is Dodemaide's opinion that he never recovered.

'Merv was very low after that South Africa tour,' says Dodemaide. 'He took a long time to get over it and, in my view, his priorities were shifting a bit and he was starting to struggle for motivation by then.

'He felt that the Merv Hughes type of player was being phased out. It was no longer appropriate to play your cricket that way and, as you look back now, it was probably a changing of the guard.'

Hughes refuses to agree with his good friend and avers that he worked desperately hard during the winter of 1994 to be fit for the tour to Pakistan. The fact that he had never made a sub-continent tour drove him through countless road runs and he dropped some eight kilos, tipping the scales at just over 100 kg when the contracted Australian players gathered for a mid-year training camp in Adelaide. Once the tour of Pakistan was complete, the obvious attraction to every player there was a series against the Old Enemy and a third straight defence of the Ashes.

Team physiotherapist Errol Alcott may have headed home before the first Test match in South Africa was played but the nine-year veteran still had considerable input into the review of the players' fitness and attitude on that tour. When the squad for Pakistan was announced, both Hughes and Reiffel were passed over, in favour of Jo Angel and Damien Fleming, young bowlers who had finished the 1993–94 Sheffield Shield season in striking form.

Alcott had long warned of the day Hughes would regret not listening to his advice over the past few years and the day had come.

'I thought he was gone after South Africa.

'He and Paul Reiffel were both told after that tour to get with it or forget about it. Merv's problem was his behaviour between matches — he just wasn't doing anywhere enough to ensure he was ready to play international cricket. He worked really hard in the off-season, as did Pistol [Reiffel], but the decision had been made.'

Chairman of selectors Lawrie Sawle had been in the post in 1985 when the national panel had awarded Hughes his Test cap against India at Adelaide Oval. The taciturn Sawle had overseen Australia's rise back towards the top of the cricket tree and the team to tour Pakistan was to be the last he would pick before his retirement. Border retired before the West Indies were finally eclipsed in early 1995, and Sawle stepped down also, but he oversaw the decision of Merv Hughes, Ashes hero of less than 12 months before, being passed over in favour of youth.

'The writing was on the wall that Merv's days were numbered and we would have to unearth someone else in his place. The report we got back from South Africa was that there wasn't a lot of future in sending Merv on that tour to Pakistan,' Sawle says.

Alcott, like Healy, felt the Hughes career should have extended much further than it did.

'I reckon he cut short his career by three years. He should have been finishing up for Australia during the summer of 1995–96. When you look at the itinerary through that period and who we were playing, he would have had them on wood. He did himself an injustice and there's no doubt about it. I've told him that,' Alcott comments.

Hughes was in Townsville on a promotional trip for Tubemakers Australia when the squad was announced and, thankfully for him, was able to hide far from the media spotlight. Omission from the final Test match in Durban some months before had given him a clear signal of his sporting mortality at international level. Now, he had to concede his obituary had been written, lest he do something spectacular at the start of the 1994–95 season at home.

'When I didn't get picked for Sharjah, I was just hell-bent on making the Pakistan tour. I worked pretty hard to get myself right to go to Pakistan and when I missed out on that, it was like the arse fell out of my world.

'That was the end [of my career] for Australia when I didn't get picked for Pakistan. You still live in the hope you can get back but when I didn't make the team for that tour, I started to think, "this is it".'

For 1994–95, the challenge was to regain full fitness with Victoria and perhaps even force the national selectors to rescind the decision they had made.

# CHAPTER FOURTEEN

# A QUIETER SUMMER

The Australian cricket team stepped nervously into the post-Allan Border era in August 1994. Border had been a permanent fixture in the Australian XI for all bar one Test match since December 1978 (he was 12th man in the sixth Test, against England in February 1979) and had made a profound impact on the way his team played their cricket. Only David Boon of the then still-current Australian Test players had played a Test under another captain, and he had only played in the final game of Kim Hughes' tumultuous reign as skipper.

Australian team members under Border were hard in the field and expected to play the game as the captain did, with no quarter expected and absolutely none to be given. One-to-one personal skills weren't Border's strong point but he expected his players to treasure the Australian cap as much as he did. Respect was never automatic from Border, it was always earned.

Merv Hughes kept a low profile when the squad departed for Sri Lanka and busied himself with preparing for the start of Victoria's season in mid-October. In his personal life, however, there would be a massive change soon after the team's departure. Sue gave birth to a daughter, Madeline, after eight hours labour.

All people are changed in some way by parenthood and Merv Hughes was totally enamoured of the new person in his life. He had trained twice a day up until the birth but, once Madeline arrived, Sue noticed an immediate change.

*Opposite: Hughes dismisses Graham Gooch at the MCG, Australia A v England, World Series, 1994–95.*

'I think Merv's serious cricket finished the day Madeline was born,' she says. 'Right up until I was in the ninth month, he was getting up at six every morning to train, and training twice a day.

'As soon as Maddy arrived, he wanted to be around for everything and his training wasn't the same.

'It was quite beautiful to see him with a new baby and the change he went through but I think his cricket was never the same again.'

Dodemaide agrees with Sue Hughes: 'The arrival of his daughter was a big change, as you would expect, and his willingness to come back really hard seemed to be fading. We talked a hell of a lot around that time and he really found it hard to come to terms with the fines and everything else that had happened.'

Australia's 1994 tour to the sub-continent gave Glenn McGrath and Damien Fleming an opportunity to entrench themselves in the Australian side.

McGrath had been ordained by the incomparable Dennis Lillee as a potential 200-wicket bowler after just his first Test match and made further strides on the unforgiving Pakistani pitches. Despite a thigh injury that cost him a berth in the second Test, at Rawalpindi, the spindly New South Welshman bowled well in the two Tests he played and was equally impressive in the One-day series. He spearheaded Australia's win in the triangular series final over Pakistan in Lahore with a haul of 5–52 from his 10 overs.

Hughes' young protege Fleming also promised, on this Pakistan sojourn, to deliver Australia the swing bowler they had yearned for since the retirement of Terry Alderman in 1991. Like McGrath, Fleming had taken quickly to One-day cricket, bowling particularly well to Pakistan's dangerous opening pair of Aamir Sohail and Saeed Anwar, but found success in Test cricket much sooner than his downwind partner.

While McGrath started slowly in the Test arena (before his confirmation as a bowler of outstanding quality in the Caribbean in early 1995), Fleming was blessed with an unforgettable Test debut in Rawalpindi. Replacing the injured McGrath, the Victorian bowled impressively in the first innings for a haul of 4–75 and then walked into the history books with a second innings hat-trick on the last day.

First, veteran right-hander Aamir Malik chipped a catch to Michael Bevan to end a determined innings of 65 before Inzamam Ul Haq was trapped lbw first ball.

Fleming had to wait through the drinks break and an over from Jo Angel before he would get his crack at Pakistani captain Salim Malik, who had, by this stage, batted his side to a draw with an epic seven-hour knock of 237. As he prepared to bowl, Fleming jokingly called across to Justin Langer at mid off and declared, 'Salim doesn't know it yet, but he's about to become a part of history'.

The in-form batsman then tickled an edge to 'keeper Ian Healy and, from that point, the task for Merv Hughes to return to international cricket was made that much more difficult, with two considerably younger rivals now standing in his path.

While Australia unluckily lost their first Test series under Taylor 0–1, despite being in a position to win all three matches, Victoria started the domestic season in powerful fashion under the captaincy of Dean Jones, in the second year of his second stint as captain.

Western Australia and Tasmania were dispatched in the side's first two Mercantile Mutual Cup matches before New South Wales were blitzed by eight wickets in the opening Sheffield Shield encounter, at the Melbourne Cricket Ground.

Hughes was solid enough in the shortened games and felt well pleased with a match return of 5–103 in the Shield encounter, as Jones taunted a Blues side lacking the services of their Test stars. When on song, Jones has been an intimidating prospect for young bowlers throughout his career and racked up a match double of 94 and 103 not out. On the Sunday immediately following the Shield game, in a one-dayer between the two oldest States, Jones' spree continued with 76 as Victoria maintained their perfect record in that competition.

Unfortunately, the journey north to Brisbane to meet Queensland saw a return to traditional values — an early season belting for Victoria. Since time immemorial, either South Australia or Victoria would head to the Gabba for the first Shield game of the summer and return with their tail between their legs, defeat invariably coming in a little over three days. In 1994–95, South Australia had been pounded by an innings and 202 runs

*Sue and Merv Hughes' wedding day, May 1992.*

*Hughes with their daughter Madeline, at a Footscray v Fitzroy-Doncaster district game in 1996–97.*

while Victoria at least managed to force the Bulls to bat a second time, going down by five wickets.

Hughes returned a further four wickets to give him nine for the season at 26.55 while Reiffel's second consecutive five-wicket return saw both included in the Australian XI for the match against England in Hobart — the final chance to impress before selection of the first Test side. Fleming had damaged a shoulder late in the Pakistan tour and was still to play a game for Victoria since his return to Australia — opening the possibility of a vacancy in the Test side should he not make it through the Shield game against Tasmania that would run concurrently with the Australian XI match.

Hughes may have received a poor report card from the tour of South Africa earlier in the year but his papers had certainly never been marked 'never to appear again'. The Australian XI match, plus the introduction of an 'Australia A' side for the first time to join the World Series, offered the Test selectors the opportunity to look at Hughes if they felt it worthwhile.

The defence of the Ashes was enough to convince the panel they should at least check to see how the big man was going. Former team-mate and then Test-selector Geoff Marsh said the consensus was that Hughes would be an excellent reserve to have up their sleeve and could yet force his way into Test calculations if he regained his old fire.

'We wanted to let him know that we wanted him,' Marsh says. 'At the end of the day, it was going to come down to how much Merv wanted to get himself fit and sharp and ready to play.'

If the Test selectors were hoping to know how Hughes would fare against quality opposition, England did them a favour by naming eight of the XI who would play in the first Test, in Brisbane a week later, including perennial targets Graham Gooch and Mike Atherton.

Number three batsman Graeme Hick was rested after centuries in the lead-up matches against Western Australia and South Australia, but Hughes had the chance to work over four of the first five in the Test-match order — Atherton, Gooch, Alec Stewart and Graham Thorpe.

Atherton had been the thorn in Australia's side in 1993 but fell in Hughes' third over, edging a catch to Reiffel in the slip cordon. A haul of 4–51 from 17.4 overs played a key role in dismissing the tourists for 209,

*Damien Fleming, Australia's hat-trick hero of the 1994 Pakistan tour.*

forcing them to follow-on 177 behind, and had many observers predicting a recall of Hughes to the Test team which was expected to be announced at the end of the match. A day's rain put paid to hopes of victory but gave the big fast bowler a second chance to work over the England top-order and establish a psychological beachhead, should he be recalled.

Atherton atoned for his first innings failure with a second innings hand of 49 and noticed a crucial change in the Hughes approach. While the bouncer, the stare and the pace were still there in spades, gone was the trademark verbal barrage. Atherton had followed Hughes' dramas in South Africa from afar and then undergone his own inquisition later in the year with the infamous 'Dirt in Pocket' affair at Lord's, which resulted in the ICC's match referee fining the England skipper heavily. Atherton was convinced Hughes was not the same man after the fast bowler's run-in with officialdom.

'Merv was bowling to me for quite a long time but he didn't say a single word to me or Alec Stewart,' Atherton recalls. 'I had to ask him whether he couldn't pay his fine and the ACB had taken his tonsils out as punishment.

'From that time, I think cricket administrators all over the world made a conscious move to make the game appear to be a lot cleaner.

'Mark Taylor probably had to make his stamp on things after what happened to the Australians in South Africa. That was certainly how it seemed to an opposition player with a number of their guys so quiet that summer.

'Cricket these days has become rather dull with the way no-one is allowed to say anything to anyone else. Merv's swearing never worried me too much because it is a man's game. I always got on with him really well and the way Merv went about it always made sure I was concentrating and assured me that I was in a game that meant something.

'Merv was a hard man on the field and a really good bloke off it, which is probably the way to play,' the England captain says.

While Hughes had returned a steady four wickets from Hobart, compared to only two from Reiffel, Fleming had managed just 1–84 from 44 overs against Tasmania. Fleming had bowled steadily but lacked penetration, especially when compared to McGrath's form against Queensland. McGrath seemed certain to be named in the 12 and the groundswell of opinion was that Hughes would return ahead of Fleming. While the fast bowler was still big, his record against England was unquestioned and the value of Hughes' hold over Hick could not be under-estimated.

Reiffel expected to miss out but Hughes was again disappointed when the ground announcer at Bellerive Oval read out the Australian team late on the final day, jumping alphabetically from Damien Fleming to Craig McDermott.

Hughes had hoped desperately for a recall but, once he chewed the fat with Reiffel, soon saw things from Fleming's point of view. After all, the young swing bowler had done well on a difficult tour to Pakistan.

'I remember Pistol saying he didn't think he was ever a chance because, if he was in Damien Fleming's shoes, he would have been very disappointed if he had just come home from a tour and then been overlooked for the first Test.

'That Australian XI game was just for the Test selectors to see how I was going and it was a fair call.

'If I had gone to Pakistan and then been dropped for the first Test at home, I would have been pretty shellshocked. Once it was put in that perspective, I couldn't argue with the decision to leave me out of the side for Brisbane.'

Led by McDermott (8–143) and Shane Warne (11–110), Australia dominated the first Test, at the Gabba, to win midway through the fifth day by 184 runs. As it turned out, Fleming carried the drinks to allow a dual spin attack of Warne and Tim May but, with victory achieved so comprehensively, the Test XII had been set until at least the New Year.

England's reticence to play as many as eight matches in the traditional triangular series had prompted the ACB to suggest the inclusion of the Australia A side. Their governing body, the Test and County Cricket Board, jumped at a proposal that would allow their side to only play six One-dayers. However, the TCCB soon realised that, by playing two sides in the One-day competition against international opposition, Australia were benefiting enormously.

The two Australian One-day squads were named after the Brisbane Test and Hughes and West Australian Tom Moody were the only experienced players of note to be included in the Australia A squad.

Australia A, led by Damien Martyn and coached by Greg Chappell, was the side of the future and through the summer would provide Greg Blewett with his first chance to impress at international level, and Michael Bevan and Paul Reiffel to rebuild their careers after being dropped from the senior team.

Hughes relished the further opportunity provided to him by the Australia A concept, even if there was no prospect of playing in the back-to-back Tests over Boxing Day and New Year after Australia's successful opening gambit in Brisbane.

'I was surprised at getting picked there but that meant to me I was still being looked at by the selectors. The selectors had said they were only going to look at players who were going to represent Australia so I was very pleased by that. I took that as a positive and when I played for Australia A, those games were very important to me. I wanted to prove to myself and show other people that I could play One-day cricket.'

Coach Greg Chappell took Hughes aside and asked him candidly about what he hoped to get out of the summer — a few more games on the large stage thanks to Australia A or another genuine shot at the big time.

'I sat down with Merv before the first game for Australia A and asked him whether he wanted to train hard all the time and perhaps make himself available for Australia again, or whether he was having a nice farewell tour of the country in some One-dayers,' Chappell says.

'I said it was fine for him to be a clown because we loved his personality, but there would be a time when we had to be serious and I wanted him to prove something to me.'

Hughes did not let him down.

The selection panel had misgivings that Hughes may lead some of the younger players astray but he was totally committed to the cause and a key player in Australia A's surprise march to the World Series finals.

*Hughes with television identity Plucka Duck at the Dean Jones Testimonial game at the MCG in 1994–95.*

In his first four matches for Australia A, in December, Hughes returned figures of 2–21, 2–22, 3–33 and 2–22, using his head and bowling well with the new ball. Should anyone in the Test side stumble, Hughes was in form.

While the Australia A side were marching around the country, the senior side were less than thrilled about matching it with their juniors. Crowds at both Australia versus Australia A meetings were moved to barrack for the junior side, both in the hope of a good contest and because of the traditional Australian support for the underdog, which drew the ire of captain Taylor. Australia should have been bubbling along, 1–0 ahead in the contest for the Ashes, but vice-captain Ian Healy could sense a hole in the unit.

'That season, there was an obvious difference just on the bus and going to the ground each day,' Healy says. 'We were without Merv for the first time in a long time and we'd say, "Where's Merv?" Billy [McDermott] used to thrive on Merv's noise and his presence. When Billy was on his own, things weren't the same with him and he was aware of what Merv was putting in.

'In our team, we have never replaced him since but McGrath is getting close to it now as a Merv-type character at the centre of the unit.'

After the first block of One-day matches, Victoria headed to Perth to meet Western Australia in a Shield game to give all the Test players a first-class encounter before the Boxing Day Test.

In his 11th over of that match, Hughes felt pain in his right groin and took no further part in the match, ruling out whatever slim chance he may have had for Tests two and three at the MCG and the SCG respectively.

He was fit again by mid-January, and able to play for Australia A in the second block of One-dayers. The decisive match for the young side was considered to be their January 12 encounter with England in Sydney — if victory could be garnered by at least 25 runs, England would be tipped out of the World Series finals.

This they achieved, but for Hughes there was an awful downside to the contest. In the effort of bowling his eighth over, his right hamstring gave way. Not only would Merv Hughes not play for Australia A again that summer, wrecking whatever hopes he still harboured of higher honours, he would, in fact, never play for Victoria again either. At that point, the Test selectors lost faith and those in Victoria were beginning to wonder whether their man could be in trouble.

Marsh had waited all summer in the hope that Hughes may blast through a side and prove he was still 'Merv Hughes, ENFORCER'. However, two strained muscles in less than a month convinced him that the body of Merv Hughes was crying "enough".

'His fitness became a problem after the first Test,' Marsh says. He got injured after Christmas and I think he sort of lost the desire to get himself as fit as he could. I think he just lost the edge and couldn't quite get himself fit enough.

'I'm sure he felt he could handle it at the time but with the increasing amount of cricket we were playing, it was always going to be a problem and his groins and his legs started to say it was hard work.'

Injury on the eve of the One-day finals, with the team for Australia's eagerly anticipated tour of the Caribbean about to be chosen, convinced Hughes his Australian days were over. No bowler comes back at the age of 33 after more than 12 months out of the national side.

'The first part of the summer went really well. After Christmas, I was trying to get right for the Australia A finals and it was just frustrating that I couldn't get on the park,' he says.

'I was finding it hard to get through games and that was a bad sign. I was thinking, "This could be it" as far as Australia was concerned. Even then, I was hoping to go to England in 1997 but realistically I had been 12 months out of the Australian side and suffering with a spate of injuries, so my hopes were gone by then.'

Merv Hughes' last effort for the Australian Test side had been in Cape Town in a winning Test match nine months beforehand and his last Test scalp had been the wicket of Hansie Cronje in the tumultuous Johannesburg encounter. As befitted his career for Australia, the final wicket of 212 was that of a batsman well set on 122.

When no other bowler could get a breakthrough, Merv Hughes provided one.

The Australian selectors had finished a long way in front after their punt, nine years before, on a raw Victorian bowler who had genuine pace. During the winter of 1995, former chairman of selectors Lawrie Sawle would mail Hughes a letter congratulating him on all he'd done for his country during his career.

The Hughes focus now shifted towards his State side, sitting atop the ladder in the Mercantile Mutual Cup competition with a perfect record of three wins from three starts and third on the Shield ladder, two points behind equal leaders South Australia and Queensland.

Throughout his career, Hughes had never collected a trophy as part of a Victorian team. Their only Sheffield Shield title during the past 15 years had come in 1990–91 while he was away in the West Indies and the last domestic one-day championship was won way back in 1979–80.

Victoria were due to meet New South Wales in Sydney during the last week in January, while the Australian team were engaged in the fourth Test, against England, in Adelaide. In the nets in the lead-up to the Shield encounter, Hughes felt some tightness in his hamstring again and did not want to run the risk of leaving the side a bowler short, as had happened against Western Australia before Christmas. As a consequence, he withdrew and was replaced by Simon Cook.

'My hamstring was a little sore and I wasn't sure in the lead-up to the game. I trained the next day and it just wasn't right so I pulled out.'

Despite his absence, thanks to an unbeaten 154 from Jones in the second innings and five wickets apiece for the game to Reiffel and Cook, Victoria belted the Blues by 254 runs to head to top spot on the Shield table.

A muscle injury had accounted for Hughes for the second time in a month and, despite his record, there was unhappiness from captain Jones and coach Les Stillman about how the fast bowler was travelling.

A strong start to the summer counted for little in their eyes at the business end of the season.

Jones, who a year before had cast the deciding vote not to take his close mate to Sydney for a pre-Christmas game when Hughes declared he was right, now decided Victoria would go through the rest of the year without the fast bowler. If that would end Hughes' career, so be it.

'He wasn't getting the figures and he wanted to get back in the Australian team, but every time he tried something he would break down again,' Jones says. 'I felt he had lost the spark. I had to make the tough decision, as I did with a few other players. That's the way cricket is sometimes.

'My job, as captain, unfortunately, is one where I have to finish some guys' careers. At the same time, I make them as well.

*The former Test stalwart clearly enjoyed his time as the 'senior' professional in the Australian A side.*

'This guy was a mate and that was such a tough thing. I had to say, "Sorry Merv, we don't think you're right".'

A series of niggling muscle strains over the next five weeks ensured Hughes did not play another match that summer, missing Victoria's eventual victory in the Mercantile Mutual Cup competition. In the Shield, Victoria narrowly missed the final, finishing third behind eventual champions Queensland and runners-up South Australia.

With two games to play, Victoria sat level with South Australia in second spot but missed out on six crucial points against Tasmania when set an impossible target of 362 for victory in less than a day. South Australia won both of their last two matches outright to reach the final but, ultimately, would be responsible for ending the most famous drought in Australian sport, crashing to a massive innings and 101-run defeat in the final at the Gabba.

Hughes battled hard to return to the State side but was continually frustrated by hamstring and calf problems and was not selected for the initial XII for any of the final four first-class matches or three one-dayers. As far as Hughes was concerned though, he was still a first-choice bowler for his State, when fit, and was deserving of a place in the side if he declared himself ready. The view of Jones and Stillman was markedly different. Unfortunately, Hughes would not find out how Jones and Stillman were thinking with regard to his future until much later.

Jones, for all his quirks, has taken more hard knocks than most cricketers and yet always bounces back, ready for more. Few, if any of his Australian team-mates, have ever felt confident to say they always knew what he was thinking as his mood swung between the highs and lows he was experiencing on the field.

Jones and Stillman had clashed famously under Simon O'Donnell's captaincy when Stillman first took the Victorian job but the pair had mended their differences when Jones assumed the leadership of the State side. Jones wanted to get on with the job of leading the side and his captaincy style was very much the Jones way. He could be abrasive and would run over those who didn't fit the Jones plan.

The trouble for Jones was that some were less than happy to get run over along the way, including Merv Hughes.

'Les and I had had a run-in a few years back and I could understand if other blokes had had a run-in with him,' Jones says.

'At the same time, we had a job to do to try and get everyone together. Sometimes, you just have to wear the abuse from the captain or the coach and get on with the job.'

Interestingly, Stillman says Hughes should not be remembered as a Victorian bowler, because of the breadth of his achievements for Australia.

'Merv's an Australian bowler, even though he's very much a Victorian, and I remember him as an Australian bowler,' Stillman says. 'That doesn't detract from nearly 300 hard-earned wickets for Victoria but he was well over and above that level of Shield bowler.

'I think he should be best remembered as an Australian fast bowler, not for whatever he did for Victoria. He's part of Australian cricket folklore and that's fantastic for him.'

Stillman does offer a rider, though.

'I think the saddest thing, and I hope he feels it acutely, is that he never played in a winning Victorian Shield or one-day side.

'I think the percentage of games won over the Hughes era would be disappointing to someone as competitive as him. I'm not saying it was his fault but I think it would disappoint him.'

In that regard, Stillman's comments are enormously unfair. Victoria won a Sheffield Shield in 1990–91, beating New South Wales in the final, but Hughes was away in the West Indies with the Test side. The aim of the Shield competition is, primarily, to produce players for the national side and Hughes had progressed to a higher level. The fact that Victoria happened to be successful while he is away should, in no way, be held against him with regard to his performances for his State.

If the Test players had been home in the latter half of the 1990–91 season, who is to say that a Victorian side, boosted by the inclusion of West Indian tourists Hughes and Jones, would have been able to hold off a New South Wales outfit able to call on their internationals Mark Taylor, Mark Waugh, Steve Waugh, Greg Matthews and Mike Whitney.

In Merv Hughes' mind, the end to 1994–95 had been enormously disappointing after promising so much. The triumphs of the national side had ended any serious chance of his return to international cricket, while injuries in the latter part of the season had robbed him of some much-deserved success with the State side.

On March 5, a very green Victorian side gathered around captain Jones to pose with the Mercantile Mutual trophy, having eclipsed South Australia by four wickets in the final at the MCG with more than five overs to spare. Surrounding Jones were team-mates Matthew Elliott, Brad Hodge, Ian Harvey, Darren Berry, Ian Wrigglesworth, Jason Bakker, Troy Corbett, Rohan Larkin, David Saker and Brad Williams.

Aside from Berry, who had debuted with South Australia in 1989–90, only Matthew Elliott, in just his third year for Victoria, had played more than two seasons of first-class cricket.

Hughes, of course, was unavailable due to injury, and Jones and Stillman had ignored several experienced hands such as Tony Dodemaide and Warren Ayres. Their punt on youth had paid off. The pair thought they had seen the future.

By the middle of next season, with Hughes now finally discovering he was on the outer, Berry would also be gone from a team of youngsters. And the Victorian cricket side would be in turmoil.

# CHAPTER FIFTEEN

# IT'S NOT PERSONAL, IT'S BUSINESS

V ictoria concluded the 1994–95 summer with the first trophy in their cabinet in a decade and a half from the one-day arena and a pleasing result from the first-class season. Looking at their winter training squad, there was much to be confident about in the lead-up to 1995–96.

Dean Jones, now having reneged on his April 1994 decision to retire from international cricket, had certainly been the standout batsman in domestic cricket in 1994–95, even if he did not get the chance to display his wares for Australia again. Jones had also been the Shield's Player of the Year in 1993–94 and he had two excellent proteges, Matthew Elliott and Brad Hodge. Hodge had made almost 1000 first-class runs as a teenager in his debut season of 1993–94, while Elliott, a latter-day Bill Lawry, built tall, angular and left-handed, had been scoring heavily at the top of the order at the MCG, then the most difficult pitch in the country. Observers felt that Jones had two players of enormous potential to school in the art of batting at the highest level; one who looked certain to play for Australia (Elliott) and one who fell into the large bracket of Shield players that may play for Australia (Hodge).

Behind the stumps, Darren Berry was rated as having the best hands in Australia, even if his batting was only serviceable, while his understudy Peter Roach had won high reviews from the incomparable Rod Marsh after his stint at the Cricket Academy in Adelaide.

*Opposite: Hughes in late 1994, at Australia A training.*

In the bowling ranks, Victoria could boast an embarrassment of riches. At full strength, they could call on an individual already rated as the world's best slow bowler and well on his way to vying for the status of the best leg-spinner in the game's history — Shane Warne. While Warne was a once-in-a-generation bowler, there were fellow internationals — Paul Reiffel and Damien Fleming — who could argue new ball duties with recent internationals Merv Hughes and Tony Dodemaide. Hughes (1994) and Dodemaide (1993) had both represented Australia within the past 18 months and both had offered more than a decade of sterling service to their State.

Victoria also had an impressive crop of players learning the game, including pace bowlers Brad Williams, David Saker, Troy Corbett and Ian Hewett, and all-rounder Ian Harvey. Simon Cook would have been among that group too, but had assessed the depth in the squad and headed north to New South Wales, where he immediately broke into a full-strength Blues team able to call on eight current or past Test players in their first line-up of the summer. Williams offered Victoria sheer pace unmatched by anyone in the country, Saker an aggressive outlook and niggardly line, while Corbett and Hewett were that cherished breed of left-armers able to bowl sharpishly and bring the ball back into the right-hander, as well as slanting it across the batsman.

The future for Victoria looked rosy indeed.

While Hughes' hamstring injury and other niggling problems had ended his 1994–95 season, when fit, he had been on the fringes of national selection. Hughes believed he had to regain his fitness over the winter and would then be an automatic selection for Victoria again. His record since 1981–82 for the Vics over 76 Shield matches was an impressive 267 wickets at 30.59, 14th on the all-time list in Shield cricket. His days of playing for Australia might be gone but the goal now was to overhaul Alan Connolly (297 wickets from 71 games) as the leading Victorian bowler in the history of Shield cricket.

'My winter in 1995 was fairly busy with a lot of PR work and a lot of travelling, but I still trained pretty hard,' Hughes says.

'I was still keen and enthusiastic about getting into the side but the vibes I got going into the summer were that maybe I wasn't going to play. I was too old and I was being measured up against the young blokes in the side.

It didn't seem to be a matter of losing 15 kilograms but rather losing five years, and you can't do that.'

The harsh reality was, in the eyes of Jones and coach Les Stillman, that Hughes was now a reserve bowler at best. He may well have played for Australia A the previous season but, as far as the Victorian selectors were concerned, that didn't seem to count for much. His size was to count against him immediately, even though Hughes felt his stamina was not in question. Stillman said the prevailing view was that Hughes would be a handy back-up once the season began and international commitments began to cut into the depth of the side.

'We felt he wasn't going to start off the season because we had a surplus of bowlers,' Stillman says. 'We felt he would be better served, given his condition, if he was going to make the commitment, to work towards joining the side later in the season when the Flemings and the Reiffels were away on national duty.'

Even now, Hughes still fumes whenever his weight is thrown at him as a reason for his demise but, his first captain, John Scholes, had always advised him that this would be the case. Hughes respects Scholes like no other man in cricket for his straight-down-the-line approach. The veteran Scholes, who was still playing grade cricket as he neared 50, continually counselled the fast bowler that his size would make him an easy target.

'I can remember Bob Simpson giving him a hard time in 1992 about his weight and his reaction was that while I'm getting wickets it's not a problem,' Scholes remembers. 'I told him that when you stop getting wickets it will become an issue. I guess with the State squad here it had always been an issue but while he got wickets, he was never going to be challenged about it. When you get older, the legs don't carry the weight as well and, from the time he got to about 32, it started to take a toll on him.'

Hughes felt he was still working hard at his cricket but that view was obviously not shared by the Victorian State selection panel, who felt that first-class cricket was no longer Hughes' top priority. To an outsider, it seems amazing that his place in the first choice XI would be in question coming off a season where he had played representative cricket. Hughes was around the 115 kg mark at this time, a good eight to 10 kilograms over what he had weighed when he last played for Australia, but had showed he was bowling 'smarter' as he was getting older.

The view from within the ranks would also hurt Hughes. Both Reiffel and Dodemaide, two of his best mates in cricket, felt his focus was starting to fade. While they could see he was still doing the work, there was no longer the burning desire to take on the extra load that had characterised Merv Hughes at his peak.

Dodemaide feels Hughes reached the peak of his mountain in 1993 with his 200th Test wicket on the Ashes tour, and was never able to motivate himself entirely to climb as high again.

'The 1993 Ashes tour was definitely the jewel in his career,' Dodemaide says. 'It is something that everyone will always remember because it was a shocking injury to keep bowling with, but he carried it through. However, I don't think the knee finished his career.

'Even though it was a huge hurdle to get over, I noticed a change in Merv after 1993. He will probably bag me for this but I think he started to drift away from cricket a bit after that. He had been very successful over a four-year period and I think the 200 wickets was a big thing for him. He had proved a few people wrong, particularly Ian Chappell and a few other ex-players. He idolised Ian Chappell and he desperately wanted to prove to a bloke like him that he belonged in Test cricket.

'I think he started not to do as much at training and started to do a lot of other promotional work that was cutting into his time. He had other things in his life, like his marriage and then the birth of his daughter. I think his focus changed and he wasn't doing enough to stay ahead of the pack like he always had.

'To get to the start of a first-class season, it's becoming harder and harder because the amount of training required has increased exponentially. I think the success he had on that Ashes tour, and what it meant to Australian cricket at the time, was really a crown for him. I think he started to drop off after that; that accelerated his decline and reduced the amount of effective playing time he had left.'

Hughes' breakdown in the match against Western Australia and his withdrawal from the game against New South Wales during the summer

*The young Victorian side, captained by Dean Jones (at front, centre) and without Hughes, after winning the 1994–95 Mercantile Mutual Cup final.*

of 1994–95 seemed to be playing heavily on the minds of the selection panel as the start to 1995–96 drew near.

Victoria were due to open their season exceptionally early on October 8, playing the first Mercantile Mutual Cup match of the season against Queensland in Brisbane. Grade cricket in Melbourne is often lucky to be played at all until late October due to a combination of weather and the recovery of grounds after the football season. It had been decided that if Victoria were to have any chance of success in their opening encounter for the season, a frontline squad of 15 would head to Darwin for eight days in mid-September for a training camp. Obviously, those who missed out on the training camp were no chance of playing in the first one-dayer, or the opening Shield game in Brisbane later that month, due to the lack of cricket in Melbourne.

The importance of being in the squad for Darwin was paramount to Hughes and he sat down with Jones and Stillman during State squad training, just before selection, to talk through his goals and ideas for the coming season. The trio talked for more than an hour in the Victorian dressing-rooms at the MCG on Sunday August 27.

'It was going to be a big test over five days for me. If I had to bowl in every game, then so be it, but I wanted to prove my fitness,' says Hughes. 'I wanted to prove to myself I could get through a workload and whether I could stand up to the pressure or not. It would set the foundation for the season ahead. That was on the Sunday. On the Monday, they selected the side and were announcing it later in the week.'

Hughes left the MCG with the impression he would be going to Darwin and that it would be up to him to get through the games up there. As he saw it, if he made it through the work asked of him in Darwin, he was in the picture. If he didn't, his career was in trouble.

Jones and Stillman tell a different story.

For Jones, there hadn't been anywhere near enough work done by Hughes during the winter for his liking. Hughes' breakdown in one match last summer still played heavily on his mind and the fact that the bowler was still the same size indicated that Hughes wasn't committed to playing first-class cricket as far as he was concerned.

'The selectors weren't happy with his efforts up until the squad for Darwin was picked,' Jones declares. 'I had had a number of meetings with Merv before then. The selectors weren't going to waste money and time on Merv if he wasn't going to put in some sort of effort before then.

'He wasn't fit enough to go on that trip and the selectors were saying that he just couldn't expect to be picked on six days work, particularly for up in Darwin where it would be hard. No matter what he said, the selectors believed he would not get through the days because he had done so little work. It was a hard one. I was a selector but it's tough when you're dealing with your mates, their careers and their livelihoods.

'Unfortunately, sometimes they take it badly but you have to make a decision and that's part of your job. Past credits do count but each year is different. If he had put in a very good winter and pre-season, he would have been going but he didn't do that. He had lost the edge and when you lose the edge in any sport, you're gone.'

Jones' summation of his close friend was brutal. It was black and white, with absolutely no grey for longevity, record, reputation or friendship.

As for Stillman, his criticism was not as trenchant. His main concern was that Hughes would break down in Darwin because he wasn't fit enough and would ruin any chance of a start to his first-class season in November-December.

'It was spoken about when we were picking the side that, given the level of his fitness, there was an even greater chance he would break down in Darwin,' he says. 'Merv is a full-on guy and we knew that once he had the ball up there he would go flat out and pick up an injury. He would say he was more sensible than that but we all know that Merv would start running in and bowling as fast as he could.

'He really hadn't done the work and had had a lot of other things on in his personal life. In the past couple of years, he had had a lot of sponsorship work and had missed an enormous amount of pre-season.

'We felt he should just work on his fitness through October and November. There would then be an opportunity for him and he would have had a longer time to get ready for the season.'

With coach and captain not in his corner, M.G. Hughes was missing from the squad named to travel to Darwin on that Friday, September 1, ruling out any hope of him joining the Victorian side for the start of the season.

As an outsider, it is still hard to believe his name could be missing from Victoria's first 15 for that Darwin camp. Given his long service to his State, one would think he deserved the opportunity to go to Darwin and at least try to get through the week. If he failed, there could be no question that the selectors would have no option but to ignore him and, if he succeeded, he was an experienced bowler with much still to offer, both as a performer and a teacher.

Obviously though, the decision had been made and had to be lived with. However, neither Jones nor Stillman rang Hughes to tell him he had not been chosen. Even if it could be argued that Hughes should not have been taken to Darwin, it remains unforgivable that neither captain nor coach would tell the most senior bowler in the squad he had been dropped.

Hughes was away in Brisbane when he learned of his omission.

'I had to go to Brisbane and I got a phone call from John Grant [another selector] telling me I wasn't in the squad,' he recalls.

'I got off the phone, kicked the chair in the room and thought, "What the fuck is going on?" I was fuming.

'I got home Saturday morning and was still fuming about it when I got to the Junction Oval for State training. I jogged a lap and ran into Les Stillman and said, "Thanks for the fucking phone call". He said Granty should have rung me.'

Hughes gave Stillman a short, sharp burst, asking why neither he nor Jones had rung him and why Grant knew nothing about the conversation the trio had had at the MCG the previous Sunday. He wanted to know if the other selectors knew of his request to go to Darwin to find out whether he was fit enough to start the season with the rest of the team.

Stillman floored him by telling him he was not in consideration for the Victorian side for the early part of the summer. The rumblings that had been passed on via word of mouth to Hughes had finally been confirmed to his face.

'Les said the selectors were picking from this team to go to Brisbane for the first one-dayer and I asked, "So this means I'm not going to be considered for Brisbane either?"

'He said that was basically right. I asked why and he said it was based on my performance and my injuries.'

Hughes repeated his assertion that he deserved to be given the opportunity to prove he was capable of standing up to the workload, rather than being left in limbo. It was then that Victoria's soon-to-be-enacted youth policy for the summer was laid out to him.

'Les said they had to go with the blokes who played last year because they won the Mercantile Mutual Cup,' he remembers.

'I said I had played the first four games of the Mercantile Mutual and the young kids were only playing at the end because I was injured. I asked how many blokes of this squad had been part of the international season, which I was with Australia A, which is what we are supposed to be aiming for.

'I got told, "It's not what you do at that level that counts, it's what you do for Victoria". I looked at him and told him, "You're a waste of space". I've never forgotten that.'

Hughes and Stillman were never close in the first part of Stillman's six years as Victorian coach, but they were certainly not sworn enemies. As a regular international player, Hughes did not have a great deal to do with his State coach between 1990–93, only crossing his path during irregular State duty.

The fast bowler had heard about communication problems a number of his team-mates had with the coach but had been reasonably ambivalent in his opinions about Stillman. Reiffel had felt decidedly uneasy during the summer of 1991–92 after a campaign to see him axed from the State side gathered momentum just as Australia were considering him for an international debut. Warne, then a young spinner at the start of the same season, had considered re-locating north to New South Wales, at the suggestion of Steve Waugh, after being told by Stillman there was no place in Australian cricket for slow bowlers. Thankfully, Warne persisted in perfecting the art of leg-spin.

'I had been told a few guys had problems with Les but my eyes weren't opened for a couple of years,' is all Hughes says.

Hughes seethed through Victorian training that mid-September morning and fronted both coach and captain at the conclusion of the session, repeating his anger at being overlooked. He told the pair he felt they would be throwing a group of young kids in at the deep end. In the early part of the season, the youngsters would be up against full-strength sides and Victoria would not be competitive, writing off any hope the side had of making a strong start.

Hughes believed that, once a poor start to the year was in motion and the young players were struggling, the likes of Warren Ayres, Tony Dodemaide and himself would be called into action late in the summer to try to restore some respectability. In his view, the young players had to be blooded through the summer, rather than injected as a group at the start of the season.

After showering, and still burning with anger, Hughes called Jones aside in the dressing-rooms.

'I fronted Deano and said, "I'm going to say a lot of things this summer. I'm going to have a bit to say about selection and things like that. We've been mates for a long time and I want you to know it's not personal, it's business. I don't want this to affect our friendship". He said okay.'

The Victorians flew out to Darwin and returned on Grand Final day, to play an internal one-day trial match at Frankston on Sunday October 1. Hughes and Jones were to be on opposite sides for that match.

# CHAPTER SIXTEEN

# WHAT'S THE USE OF THE FRIENDSHIP?

**A**player good enough to wear the baggy green cap for Australia is automatically both talented beyond the norm and tremendously dedicated. Whether an aspiring cricketer begins his journey to the Test side on a suburban ground or a country backlot, he will not progress to the highest level without a significant amount of both talent and commitment.

However, the personalities that have represented Australia during the 120 years of Test cricket cannot be encapsulated so easily. All types, all sizes and all kinds of men have made it to the highest level: driven champions such as Bill O'Reilly, laid-back naturals such as Doug Walters, sweat-soaked toilers who used every ounce of talent such as Geoff Marsh, to the sad and lonely such as legendary 1890s all-rounder Albert Trott, who took his own life after a stellar career.

To sum up Dean Jones would be among the hardest tasks of any cricket historian. To his team-mates in the Australian side between 1984 and 1994, he was 'Deano' or more often 'Legend', the nickname he had supposedly bestowed upon himself early in his career. It can be argued that there has been no finer One-day batsman since the shortened version of the game became an accepted part of the international circuit. A technically fine player, he could improvise as an innings progressed and no-one could match him as a runner between wickets. In the field, he was fast, could catch well and had a strong, reliable arm. The prototype One-day cricketer.

*Opposite: Hughes and Dean Jones in happier times — following their famous ninth-wicket partnership against the Windies in Adelaide in 1988–89.*

But to focus on his One-day achievements annoyed Jones immensely, for he yearned to be regarded as a Test player of class and quality. His knock of 210 in Madras in 1986 will probably never receive its due recognition because the innings was seen by so few Australians. It was played far out of sight on the sub-continent and, unlike other outstanding batting performances such as Steve Waugh's epic knock of 200 in Jamaica in 1995, it was not telecast into Australian homes. However, Jones' innings remains unchallenged as the greatest performance by an Australian for all those who saw him play at Chepauk Stadium over those two days. It must never be forgotten either, that Jones averaged more than 46 over his 52 Tests and scored 11 Test centuries. Towards the end of his career, he was roundly criticised for not scoring enough runs in decisive Test matches, but he remained an everlasting favourite of all the crowds he played before.

As a person, he seemed to be many different people all trying to get out at different times. I worked as a journalist on six Australian tours that Jones was a part of and he was always popular because he was enormously interesting to write about, and was never short of a quote when the tapes were turned on. He could be the warmest of interview subjects yet would also impose media bans on himself from time to time for reasons only he knew, before bursting forth again with another theory on the game. He could occasionally be difficult but that is to be expected from all elite sportspeople; I knew of no Australian cricket journalist who did not regard him warmly, for all his foibles.

If he seemed confusing to an outsider, it appears (after researching this book) to have been no less the case for his team-mates. No player could give an opinion of Jones without a large number of contradictions and Bob Simpson provided such a summation when he looked back on his decade as Australian coach.

'Frustrating, exciting, reliable, unreliable, unpredictable, selfish, unselfish, a mug lair, a team player,' Simpson wrote in his 1996 book, *The Reasons Why*.

'How many other ways are there of describing one man? And which is the real Dean Jones? I sometimes wonder if we will ever know and perhaps that is the real charm of the bloke.

'Deano polarised opinions, people tended to either love him or hate him. At one moment, he was generous, kind, the first person to offer help to anyone in trouble; at another he was arrogant, mischievously opinionated, prone to flashiness, the flashier the better. The whole man came through into his cricket and that is why he was such an exciting player. In the end, he was just Deano being himself, a mixture of so many traits and qualities.'

On Sunday October 1, 1995, Jones was in a mood that would brook no mucking about. Victoria were to open their Mercantile Mutual Cup campaign in a week's time in Brisbane, and a trial match at Frankston would be the last match practice for those heading north. Jones captained a side including Shane Warne, Damien Fleming and Paul Reiffel, while Tony Dodemaide's XI contained an impressive bowling line-up that included Merv Hughes, Brad Williams and David Saker.

Jones approached the encounter with the utmost seriousness, viewing it as an important hit out despite the moist pitch and overcast conditions. However, the mood in the other camp was decidedly more relaxed.

Dodemaide had told his troops they would be trying, but no-one was to bust a gut as it was still a trial match and it would be silly to risk injury before the season.

'We were a little bit more relaxed about the game than Deano, he was very fussy about getting everyone up and out of the rooms and ready for the game. He was very agitated. I told our guys we would be trying for this game but obviously we were just easing into the season,' Dodemaide recalls.

Hughes arrived with Dodemaide between 20 and 30 minutes before the scheduled start, prompting an explosion from the Victorian captain. When the match started and Jones' side was batting, he was ropeable. When riled, or when he is trying to ruffle an inexperienced opponent, the Jones tongue can be as sharp as any in the game.

'Merv was very, very late for that trial match,' Jones says. 'That, to me, after not being picked for Darwin, again showed a lack of respect for his team-mates. There was no excuse given for why he turned up late. He was still overweight after we'd been away and I was upset with him, as were the other selectors who knew about it.'

Dodemaide gave Williams the new ball downwind while Hughes worked uphill into the breeze. Jones opened the innings.

As soon as he took strike to Hughes in the second over of the day, Jones charged the bowler and tried to lift him over the top. Despite the wet conditions and a moving ball, Jones was batting against Hughes like a man in the final overs of a One-day innings on a perfect pitch. Those at the ground felt Jones was trying to prove a point at Hughes' expense.

Words were exchanged.

The confrontation got nasty and very personal very quickly.

Jones again charged Hughes and was beaten by the movement off the wicket, with the ball going through to the 'keeper.

'Are there a few people here to watch you, Deano? Is that why you are playing the big shots?' Hughes called down the wicket.

When Jones charged again in Hughes' third over, the bowler chipped him again.

'Listen dildo, why don't you try to get some batting practice?'

'Why don't you learn to fucking bowl,' came the reply.

To the next delivery, Jones advanced again, turned it into a half volley and the ball was creamed down the ground for four.

'That's why you're number one, Deano, I can't compete with you.'

Hughes felt he had Jones riled, which was certainly true, and he was now determined to keep niggling him in the hope that he may get out playing an over-adventurous shot.

'I work on the theory with Deano that if you get under his skin, he gets very emotional and can get out. In a one-on-one battle with Deano in that situation, I would back myself in most instances,' Hughes says.

Hughes found an edge with the third ball of his over but the nick fell short of Dodemaide at first slip, bouncing clearly in front of the slip cordon.

'Geez, I wish I could bowl quick.'

'Don't we all,' came the reply.

That got the bowler's attention.

'I beg your pardon?'

'I fucking wish you bowled quick like you used to.'

'Listen, dildo, why don't you worry about your batting and I'll worry about my bowling.'

'You've got a lot to worry about, too.'

Jones charged again for the fourth ball but did not get hold of his drive, spooning a catch to Saker at mid on. Hughes gave him a fearful departing spray.

'I yelled out, "Well played, dildo", and gave him the biggest send-off of all time. From that particular day our relationship changed a lot.'

Hughes celebrated his wicket but he was burning inside. As Jones neared the pavilion, the bowler was still enraged by the confrontation that had gone on, feeling the captain had deliberately set out to make an example of him.

'It was as though he was out to prove, on that day, that I wasn't up to playing at that level and to justify that I shouldn't have been picked to go to Darwin. It was frustrating to me that someone I had played so much cricket with was doing this and saying these things.

'I still respect Deano as a player, because he's a fantastic player, but I thought he was trying to take me down. He was forever saying that if you have a crack at someone, and they take it personally, they are thin-skinned. I thought he was thin-skinned here because I beat him on the day.'

Jones fervently denies he was trying to make Hughes look foolish, declaring that his tactic of running down the wicket was a ploy he often used in the initial stages of One-day games and was done here purely to break up the bowler's line. Even though it was done to most of the balls he faced from Hughes, Jones said the tactic was legitimate. As such, Hughes chipping him was grossly disrespectful in his eyes.

'He was sledging me and treating me with contempt,' Jones says. 'I ran down the wicket a few times but that's the kind of thing I do. I didn't do it too much in Brisbane a week later because the circumstances didn't allow it, but I wasn't out to teach anyone a lesson or anything.

'Merv sprayed me and asked why I was going to bat like a dildo. He gave me a big burst and I didn't think I deserved it because he wasn't giving me respect as captain. If he was angry or upset with me or whatever after Darwin, he should have been around long enough not to have a go back.'

As Jones and Hughes were going head to head over the course of a couple of overs, there was total silence from the rest of the players on the field. No-one could believe what was happening.

*Jones in 1995–96, his final season as Victoria's captain.*

Berry, who was preparing for his seventh first-class season, recalls the incident:

'As someone who had been around for a while, to see that was just so disappointing. We all knew what Dean Jones and Merv Hughes had been through together for Australia and for Victoria.

'I think for all the others in the squad to see that, especially the young kids, it was so disappointing. Here was someone we loved and respected in Merv and someone that everyone admired for what he had achieved in cricket in Jonesy, and they were really going at it. It wasn't friendly banter, it was genuine bad feeling. I was upset to watch it.'

Hughes cherishes respect from his peers above all else and the confrontation distressed him greatly. Once he had lost faith in the team's management, what hope could there be for the squad? From that Sunday, Victorian morale was poor for the entire 1995–96 season.

Almost 18 months on, Stillman can now see clearly that his last season in the Victorian job was doomed to be unsuccessful and, in all likelihood, extremely unhappy.

'Because Merv and Dean had played a lot of cricket together and, with Shane Warne, were the highest-profile Victorian players of the last 20 years, a confrontation between them was always going to cut deep,' Stillman confirms.

'One was the captain and the other was bigger than big and had a lot of support throughout the squad. When you had two players like that in conflict, it creates a lot of tension.'

Dodemaide, who understands both sides of the picture when most cannot, says neither Hughes nor Jones is blameless, although neither is entirely responsible for what occurred. But the Victorian cricket side paid a heavy price for the run-in.

'My impression was that Deano and Les were pretty agitated with Merv's fitness levels,' Dodemaide says. 'I think they felt his commitment wasn't up there and they were going to make an example of him.

'Merv was just bowling seam-up stuff which, on that wicket, was pretty appropriate really. I don't think you would be expecting Merv to be steaming straight in off the long run but perhaps Deano and Les were.

'Both players thought there was a real lack of respect for each other during their exchanges. I think Merv was affronted by what Deano was doing and Deano couldn't cope with Merv spraying him. Both were wrong up to a point. Merv was very much a senior player then and a barometer of how the rest of the team were feeling. Everyone was still looking to Merv for a position within the team and whenever we were low, we would look to him as the guy who would lift us up. By getting into Merv, rightly or wrongly for whatever reason, Deano and Les were really making a big stand. Merv thought that was really inappropriate. It gave him the shits and once he got the shits, he started to disbelieve in what they were doing.

'It was a very significant moment in the season. It probably never occurred to Deano what effect it had on the other guys. The other guys really picked up on it. For someone who was as respected as Merv to be having problems with team management, where did the rest of the guys stand?

'If Merv had got really fit and started the season bowling well, it wouldn't have happened. Even if he wasn't bowling fast, but was fit and using his skills, it could have been avoided. That's ideally what we would have liked and perhaps what Les and Deano were looking for. If it was a bid to try to crank him up, it backfired.'

At the end of the day, the Victorian side to play in Brisbane in a week's time was announced. As expected, those who had gone to Darwin comprised the XII with Hughes among those who were omitted. The pace attack would comprise Reiffel, Fleming and the newcomer Williams.

The full State squad would train at the Junction Oval on Tuesday and Wednesday before the team left for Brisbane on the Thursday morning. On the Sunday night, the Hughes–Jones relationship was teetering on the edge of a precipice. Within three days, it had plunged into the abyss.

Hughes went to practice on the Tuesday, determined to bowl at Jones again and to show him that he was putting in at training. Never having been too subtle in this department, there would also be a fair bit of niggle for the captain when the opportunity arose.

'I bowled to him and first ball I beat him. To warm myself up, I said, "It's a two-piecer Deano, that's the only reason I'm swinging it".'

'So you should be swinging it, you're bowling 50 miles an hour slower than last year.'

The captain was still in no mood for the Hughes levity and the training session was conducted with tension in the air. Jones chipped the fast bowler several times during fielding drills, much to the displeasure of Hughes.

Hughes does not like to be told he is not putting in, and decided to front Stillman after one fielding drill. He asked if the coach thought he was not trying. Stillman replied, 'I think you're trying'.

'Then tell your dildo captain to keep his fucking mouth shut.'

Hughes went home seething.

'From the point when I chipped him, everything I did, he was having a go at me,' Hughes says.

'In the fielding, he was into me, trying to put me down in front of the other blokes. At this stage, I was thinking things were fucked. You take criticism on board but you can only take so much if you feel it's not warranted at all.'

If he was unhappy on Tuesday night, Hughes was livid on Wednesday morning. Reading the *Herald-Sun*, Hughes came across a backgrounded story without quotes by senior journalist Ron Reed detailing the fast bowler's current weight problems and the battle he was expected to lose in returning to first-class cricket.

The story said Hughes had broken down twice in Shield games the previous season and could no longer be guaranteed to get through a four-day match. The story continued, stating that in those two matches in which Hughes had broken down, Victoria had missed out on a possible 12 points, costing the side a place in the Shield final. The inference was obvious — Hughes' lack of attention to his fitness in 1994–95 had cost the State dearly and would similarly cost the player dearly this summer.

'I was pretty down after missing out on Darwin and I was still thinking about what was going on with Deano,' Hughes says.

'I pick up the *Herald-Sun* and read a long article by Ron Reed about how I had broken down in two games the year before, both in the second innings, and how those games had cost us a place in the Shield final.

'I rang Ron, wanting to know where he got his information from.

'I said, "Listen Ron, I'm trying to get back in the State side and I read this. It shouldn't have been in the sports pages, it should have been an obituary. You've just killed me".

'I said I had to know because it was wrong and I wanted to know who to front about it. I told him I broke down in the first innings in Perth but we got six points. Later in the season, we went to Sydney and I pulled out before the game. Simon Cook replaced me and we got six points from that game.

'I asked, "How many more fucking points than 12 are we supposed to get from the two games?"

'I said it could only come from two people, either Les Stillman or Dean Jones, and I had to know.'

Reed would not say who his source was, but did tell Hughes that he had not spoken to Stillman after training the previous night. That was enough for Hughes to be convinced that Jones was the source and he would front him at training that night.

Jones denies being the culprit.

'I don't think the stuff came from me. There may also have been a selector very irate with his efforts.

*Young quick Brad Williams, seen by many as the fast man most likely to succeed Hughes in the Victorian team.*

'Just because you've done a lot of work in the past, it doesn't mean you're going to get picked in the future,' Jones says of the tumultuous build-up to the 1995–96 season.

'We weren't happy with our efforts in the Victorian cricket team and we weren't going to be complacent. We weren't going to pick guys who weren't putting in the efforts or turning up on time. I thought he was treating the cap with a little bit of disrespect.

'It's the first time I could ever say it, but he wasn't really putting in for his State side in a pre-season. We were trying to crank him up and get him going. I was getting irate in that I knew he was on the chopping block but he didn't seem to be doing a lot about it.'

On the Wednesday, when Hughes arrived early at the Junction Oval for practice, the rooms were virtually deserted. Jones was changing in a corner while opener Matthew Elliott was on the other side of the room. In the trainer's room, regular State room attendant Greg Jarvis was giving Paul Reiffel a rubdown.

Hughes went straight over to Jones, pausing only to drop his coffin on the floor.

'Listen Deano, if you are going to give information to the press, I would be appreciative if it was true and not something that was just to help your cause.'

'You get your fucking facts right before you come to me,' Jones replied.

As Hughes tells it, he told his captain he had spoken to Ron Reed that morning and the conversation changed abruptly.

'His face just dropped and then he said, "What was that shit about on Sunday?",' Hughes recounts.

'I asked, "What shit?"

'That shit you were going on with about me.'

'If you bat like a dildo, you are going to get treated like a dildo. You were batting like a dildo.'

'I deserve your respect.'

'You deserve shit if you carry on like that. You certainly don't deserve respect, you have to earn respect.'

'Listen, I've done more in this game than you'll ever think about doing,' said Jones.

'You're talking to me now, Deano. You're not talking to one of the kids.'

'How can I pick you in my side if you're not fit?' asked Jones.

'I haven't been fit for 10 years according to everyone who knows about these things.'

'You can't even do 10 in the beep test. How are you supposed to go in a game?'

'I'll get you one of the kids who can do 15 in the beep test but he won't get you any first-class wickets,' answered Hughes.

From that point, the argument developed into a lengthy and fiery swearing match as other team-mates began to arrive for practice.

Vice-captain Warne arrived as the pair were going hammer and tongs, he was worried there would be punches thrown. Finally, Jones took his leave and headed across to the nets while Hughes turned away to change.

'That was the last time we spoke for three months. Blokes asked what was going on and I said, "It's not my problem". I believe it all stemmed from Dean Jones being thin-skinned about something that happened on-field,' Hughes says.

While only three other people had been in the rooms when the pair began arguing, with several more arriving during the confrontation, word spread like wildfire. The last full State squad training session before the team's opening match of the season was a sombre affair. Morale had hit a low when everyone should have been bubbling about the season ahead.

When the State squad would meet for full training during October, November and December, Jones would not speak to Hughes at any stage and would not even acknowledge his presence at the occasional social functions where they crossed paths.

At the Victorian Cricket Association's Centenary Dinner, the feud became public knowledge to many of the pair's former team-mates when Jones greeted the likes of Jamie Siddons, Michael Dimattina and former opening batsman Gary Watts and pointedly ignored Hughes, who was seated at the same table.

Siddons, who had left to captain South Australia immediately after Victoria's last Shield title in 1990–91 but remains a close friend to many of his contemporaries, was deeply upset to hear of the problems within the side. Since Hughes had begun to struggle with his fitness, the South Australian skipper had agonised over what opinion he should provide to his friend about his future, before telling him to continue if that was what he wanted to do.

'I'd had a lot of thoughts about Merv, because I was really upset for him when I saw him struggling to bowl well and not getting picked for teams,' Siddons says.

'It's probably a little bit sad he didn't retire when he was on top but that's the way he wanted to do it and he loves playing cricket. He kept dreaming he might come back one day and the knee wouldn't be sore.

'Deep down he knew it was finished but he still loved to play, so I told him that was fair enough. I told him he was still going to remembered as a great fast bowler and people will soon forget this period when he struggled.'

In following weeks at State training at the Junction Oval, Jones would turn his back on Hughes, his friend of 18 years, in the dressing-rooms and would not answer when he was addressed, leaving the room or ignoring the question.

Jones does not deny any of the behaviour Hughes charges him with during his 14-week freeze-out of the State's most successful Test bowler.

'I didn't think he was any value in the squad at the time because he was a bloody nuisance to be honest,' Jones says. 'He was doing a lot of other things and he just wasn't focused on wanting to play for Victoria.

'I was thinking if anyone is like that, they're a waste of time and I just don't want to speak to them. If you don't want to play for Victoria and work your tits off, you shouldn't be there.

'If Merv was focused and working hard, he still had at least one real good season to finish off for Victoria. I think his days of playing for Australia were gone but I wasted a lot of time trying to get him right so the selectors wouldn't burn him.

'I thought he was letting himself down in front of his peers but I never sledged him in the papers at any stage, and just kept it in-squad.'

It was plain to the rest of the squad that the captain had no time for the State's most popular figure, and this only heightened Hughes' sense of isolation from the group. Since his triumph on the 1993 Ashes tour, Merv Hughes had played just six Sheffield Shield matches and two Mercantile Mutual Cup games for Victoria. His career was over and an important friendship was in critical condition.

Hughes was chosen for a State second XI match against South Australia in early November but broke down with a hamstring strain during the first innings. In early December, when he was playing for Footscray again, four State selectors — Stillman, Neil Buzzard, John Grant and Geoff Tamblyn — headed out to Northcote on a Sunday morning to watch him bowl.

Unbeknown to them, he had strained his left groin with the second-last ball of the previous night's play and stood at slip all day.

'I was given the opportunity to find out if I could get through four days or not and I couldn't do it. Having the selectors there showed me they were still keen but I just couldn't stay on my feet. Victoria were struggling but I couldn't stay fit to get back in there,' says Hughes.

'If I had been fit, I would have played. I didn't give myself any chance and I must admit I had lost a lot of interest after the run-in with Deano.'

The fact that Hughes did not tell the State selectors he would not be bowling at Northcote, when they went out to watch him, angered Stillman in particular and confirmed the view that Hughes was no longer in contention for first-class cricket.

'A lot of people had lost confidence in his ability to stand up and he was showing that by simply not being able to bowl,' Stillman says. 'When four selectors go out to Northcote to watch him and we realise he's only bowled a couple of overs the night before and broken down again, there comes a point when you lose faith.

'Despite Merv having an enormous amount of credits, the general feeling was that those credits had been used up because he was breaking down. He wasn't only breaking down for Australia and Australia A, but for Victoria and even in district cricket. If you are breaking down in district cricket, it's a terrible sign. Everything that happened to Merv evolved from nothing else but the fact the selectors had lost confidence in his fitness. He was desperately trying to say I am fit but never really showed it.'

While Hughes was slowly fading from the first-class scene, the Victorian side were struggling badly by mid-December. After three Shield games, they had posted just two points and been beaten outright twice.

Wicket-keeper Berry hurt his back during the Shield game in Adelaide over November 30–December 3, forcing Jones to deputise behind the stumps as the South Australians stormed to an emphatic six-wicket victory.

At his post-match press conference, Jones declared the side would be competitive if Victoria could find another batsman, an all-rounder and a spin bowler. His support base, already fragile within the team due to the conflict with Hughes, eroded completely with his public statements.

After the game in Adelaide, a team meeting was called, at which Hughes was not present.

*Long-time Victorian 'keeper Darren Berry (left),
who was controversially dumped from the Vics'
side during the 1995–96 season.*

Jones' comments about the weaknesses in the line-up had caused much consternation within the ranks and it was felt the issue should be talked through. Some home truths were told on both sides of the fence, directed at Jones from his team and at the players from Jones. The fact a meeting was called did hurt the captain greatly, though.

It remains a point of contention still with Dean Jones as to who organised the meeting; whether it was an initiative of coach Les Stillman or was player-driven. The view of the squad, at odds with Jones, was that it was initiated by Stillman.

Berry's back problem forced him to withdraw from Victoria's next Shield game against Tasmania at the MCG, and he was replaced by Peter Roach, who did well enough on his debut, remaining unbeaten on 62 and 10 in his two knocks. However, the Victorians fell to their third consecutive defeat and outright bottom of the table after Tasmania powered to 6–313 in a sensational last-day chase.

Berry declared himself fit for Victoria's New Year meeting with Western Australia in Perth but was not chosen. The team, released on Christmas Eve, included Roach ahead of the seven-year veteran and caused a media storm. Berry would not play for Victoria again for the season.

Warne and Reiffel, who were preparing for the Boxing Day Test, could not believe Berry had been passed over. Hughes was outraged, feeling personalities and not form had led to the wicket-keeper's demise.

When rung by Malcolm Conn of the *Australian* for a comment on Berry's omission, Hughes let fly on the record for the first time.

'People in authority in Victorian cricket, instead of accepting responsibility, are too quick to point the finger at others,' Hughes told Conn.

'That's got nothing to do with the administration. It's the leadership of the team. It's common knowledge that Darren and Les had a bit of a blue a couple of weeks ago. There may be a selection committee of five but it seems that over the years, anyone who had a disagreement with Les or isn't in Les' school of friends doesn't play too many games.'

When contacted by Channel 10 in Melbourne, Hughes repeated his claims, saying his only regret was that he hadn't spoken out two years earlier. Berry kept his counsel throughout the crisis, saying nothing at all and heading to Apollo Bay, in southern Victoria, for a holiday.

Berry did not speak to Hughes at any stage until late in January, well after the initial controversy surrounding his dumping. Hughes and Berry had first crossed paths in 1989–90 when the wicket-keeper was playing for South Australia during his year at the Cricket Academy. The fast bowler was bowling to Joe Scuderi but knew the young non-striker was a Victorian now playing for another State in a bid to establish his career.

Berry never forgot the introduction and quickly became firm friends with Hughes when he returned to Victoria the following summer to play in that Shield-winning side.

'He was bowling to Scuderi and gave him about three bouncers in a row,' Berry remembers. 'He was sharp and was giving him real curry. As he walked back to his mark, he just looked at me and said, "Just wait until I get started on you". I was so terrified.'

While Berry wanted to maintain as low a profile as possible throughout the turmoil, he was greatly indebted to his friend.

'That's something I'll never forget, for him to come out so strongly in my support. It just showed me the strength of Merv Hughes. He got fined for it and copped a lot of abuse but he was prepared to do what he thought was right, no matter the cost.'

Warne, the Victorian vice-captain and the player with the highest profile in Australian cricket, had tried to speak to each selector in the days since Berry had been dropped and was unhappy with the answers he received.

'I was one of the leaders and I felt I should know what was going on. I didn't think it was right the way it all happened,' he says.

The leg-spinner weighed in to the controversy on New Year's Eve in his regular column for the *Sunday Age*, adding considerable fuel to the fire.

'I have found it hard to come to terms with events in Victorian cricket in the past week or so,' Warne wrote.

'Two weeks ago the chairman of the Victorian selectors, John Grant, was publicly praising Berry as one of the best, if not the best, 'keepers in Australia. Now he has been dropped.

'How can this happen? . . . I am really disappointed that Berry had been dropped during his best season because of a personality clash.

'The saddest part of all this is that some friendships have been broken.

Sadly, in 10 years time, when a few of us gather for a barbecue, there will be a few names not on the invitation list.'

Hughes and Warne did not speak to each other about going on the record. Hughes did so after speaking to Dodemaide, while Warne only spoke out after Hughes had made the initial step.

'I had had a gutful of the whole summer of Victorian cricket,' Hughes says. 'There had been discontent in the camp since 1993–94 and I assessed both Dean and Les from a professional point of view. I said they had to accept more responsibility when the team played badly.

'After Adelaide, I was disappointed that, with a young team, the captain would be saying I need a high-order batsman, an all-rounder, and a slow bowler. When you have a young side and you're trying to play good aggressive cricket, you are going to lose some games.

'After that game they held a players' meeting and a number of the guys who spoke up then disappeared from the side. That's why I spoke up.'

Unlikely to play for Victoria again, Hughes did not have a great deal to lose and told Dodemaide it was time someone spoke up — on the record.

'Merv felt he really had to stand up and say something because it was hurting Victorian cricket,' Dodemaide says. 'His stature within the squad was such that he felt he had to use it at that time. It was probably fair enough that he was the only person apart from Deano the press were going to listen to.

'We had lots of chats about it but the best thing for him to do was to do a lot of work, get fit and take wickets for Victoria. I respect him for having the guts and standing up to say what he thought but, at the same time, the squad was the important thing. What he should have done was taken on the challenge and gotten really fit and been taking wickets.'

The one person unfairly caught in the midst of this maelstrom was Roach, who found himself cast as the villain — which he did not deserve.

The VCA moved quickly to try to quell the brewing storm, fining Hughes $1000 for breaching his State contract not to comment publicly on team selection or to bring the game into disrepute. However, the media were now well and truly onto a story about serious conflict and much of the dirty linen was to be aired in public.

Jones maintains the fast bowler should not have spoken out publicly, because he was not at the tumultuous meeting after the Adelaide game.

Just days into the New Year, the season was now spinning out of control and Jones felt the time had come to cross a major bridge and re-open contact with Hughes.

'Merv wasn't at the [players'] meeting and he shouldn't have weighed in,' Jones says. 'I had a go at a few players for not putting in but if everyone was rebuked for saying something, there'd be no coaches left. I find cricketers a funny bunch. In football, you can get yelled at and abused and they just go out and play. In cricket, they hold it really within. We're really thin-skinned compared to other sportsmen. Merv got involved and he shouldn't have. He put an extra rod in the fire and it didn't help at the time.'

*Shane Warne, the new Victorian skipper for 1996–97.*

Victoria were playing an Australian Country XI at Sale in early January when the ice between the pair finally melted. Hughes attended to have a first look at young bowler Nathan King and to offer a bit of moral support to young Footscray team-mate Michael O'Keeffe, who had just been picked for the first time.

While at the game, Hughes was approached by Jones asking if they could talk somewhere. Hughes agreed it was time they spoke, which they did for more than two and a half hours.

'I had realised by then I wasn't going to play and the meeting was just after I had gone in the paper to say Les and Dean should accept more responsibility for the team going badly. I believe that if I hadn't gone out in the press, we still wouldn't be talking.

'I think the only reason he spoke to me was because it was the first time he had seen me since the press reports, and he realised the journos would listen to me and I could cause a lot of damage if I wanted to. He asked what was going on and I reminded him of our conversation at the start of the season that it was business.'

Hughes told Jones the only way Victoria could get back on track would be if Stillman relinquished his job. Jones could not agree with the fast bowler's view, supporting Stillman's role, but the pair acknowledged they had to stop chipping each other, both in the media and in front of the rest of the squad. To have had the State's two most senior players feuding since early October had devastated morale and they agreed no more would be said, unless it was positive.

'I wouldn't say we left on good terms but we sorted out that we would be at least civil to each other,' Hughes says.

Hughes managed to stay out of trouble for the rest of the summer and Victoria eventually claimed the wooden spoon in both the Shield and Mercantile Mutual Cup competitions. Beset by injuries and unhappiness in the early part of the season, his finish with district side Footscray was a struggle for enthusiasm.

Sadly, Jones would have much more trouble to face in what must surely have been the most distressing season of a long career. In late January, days after missing out on the Australian World Cup squad, he would be reported for verbal abuse during a district game and suspended by the VCA for one match. The skipper would also be fined heavily for calling a press conference and launching a diatribe at the State association over the facilities provided for the State squad.

At the conclusion of the season, Stillman resigned just days after Victoria's last game against Queensland while Jones had to wait until early May to hear confirmation that his three-year stint as captain was over. Rumours about his leadership position had been circulating since early February but the news did not come officially until Jones had left the country to take up his position as Derbyshire's import player in the English county competition.

The two biggest profiles in Victorian cricket had gone head-to-head and both had lost out badly. Their friendship had been damaged terribly and the Victorian side had paid heavily for their falling out.

Hughes and Jones had first crossed paths way back in that district second XI game in the late 1970s and had gone all the way to Ashes' victories for Australia together. Hughes feels the loss of the friendship deeply, convinced still it was the hand of Jones that played a major role in the end to his career.

'I don't know how we stand,' he says. 'When he's there, I talk to him and the conversation is civil but it's at the stage where no-one rings the other. We used to play golf once a week and we were tight, but not any more.

'It's not the same as it was five years ago and I think that's sad. I still respect him as a player. There's no doubt he's a very good cricketer but, as a bloke, I don't know where we are. I think that people in positions of authority, be they captains or coaches, shouldn't use that position for self-gain.

'To have known someone for so long and to have played so much cricket with someone, to find out you've been shafted by that person is tough. Life goes on so I try not to dwell on it, but it's disappointing to have been such good friends for so long and then have that disappear over the past two years, because of business.

'I know if I was captain of the Victorian side and Deano came out and said he was fit to play in a game, there would be no question, he would be picked because I would know what he had done over such a long time. Once I couldn't give him anything any more, he seemed to say, "What's the use of the friendship?"'

Both Hughes and Jones have shown a remarkable ability to cope with disappointment throughout their careers. Each was dropped from the Australian side more than once, missing tours, but bounced back to again play for their country. A determination not to be kept down characterised both men, who were each heroes to the average man in the outer.

Jones expects their friendship to eventually be rekindled.

'I think we're good and time heals all wounds. He's got other things in his life now, there's no doubt about that, and I live so far away from him which doesn't help. We don't see each other as much as we would like socially but we've known each other for 20-odd years.

'It would be silly if this thing broke us up, hopefully he can look at things in the light of day now and see why decisions were made.

'I never burnt him at any stage.'

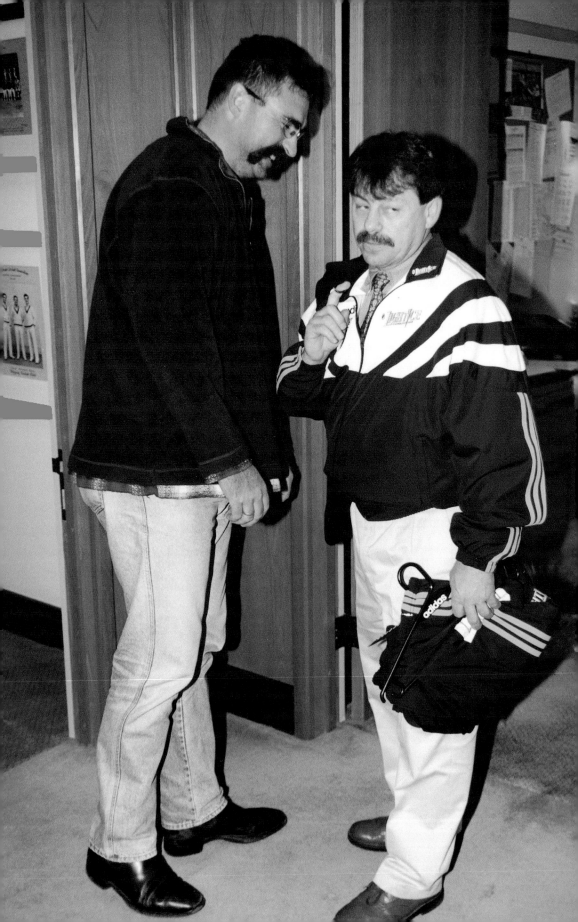

# CHAPTER SEVENTEEN

# THE
# MERV HUGHES WAY

The Victorian Cricket Association confirmed the appointment of John Scholes to the position of Victorian coach, for a two-year term, on May 8, 1996.

The relationship between Scholes and Merv Hughes had now come the full circle since they first crossed paths some 16 years before. Back then, Scholes was Victorian captain when Hughes prepared for his big break into first-class cricket. Now, he would have a pivotal role at the end of Hughes' career. If there was to be one more match for Hughes to play for Victoria, it would be under him. More than likely though, there would not be another game and it would be Scholes' task to guide Hughes out of the first-class arena with as much dignity and as little pain as possible. Scholes decided he would wait until the appointment of the new Victorian captain before discussing the future of Hughes.

As someone who had always been prepared to do his utmost for Victoria, whatever the cost, the events of the 1995–96 season had been difficult for Scholes to watch.

'When I was appointed, the first thing that had to be looked at was the spirit of the team,' Scholes says. 'Two people who had done so many good things together had verbally come out in front of team-mates and friends and had a scathing go at each other.

'That's awfully sad and that cut into team spirit because there would be one group that would support Merv and one group that would support Deano. It goes beyond the playing field then, and cuts into friendships.

*Opposite: Hughes with long-time friend (and 1996–97 Victorian State coach) John Scholes before the September 1996 press conference that was called to announce Hughes' exclusion from the Victorian Shield squad.*

'At the end of the summer, it was on the scoreboard: the team lost, the State lost and the two individuals lost.'

On May 20, the leadership positions for the 1996–97 season were announced, offering one last ray of hope for Hughes. Shane Warne would captain the side and Tony Dodemaide would be his deputy, leading the team for the bulk of the summer while Warne would be away on national duty.

Scholes knew full well Hughes kept talking of how he wanted to play again for Victoria, Warne knew of Hughes' ambition, too. Although Hughes had not appeared for his State since January 1995, and the gap between appearances would have stretched to almost 21 months by the start of the 1996–97 season, neither was prepared to dismiss him out of hand because of his service to the State.

As soon as he was appointed, Warne visited Hughes and told him he would get him a game, provided he would put in a strong pre-season through the 1996 winter.

'I said to Merv, when I was appointed captain, "Get fit and give me a half chance to pick you and I'll push for you", ' Warne says.

'After all he had done for Victoria and Australia, I wanted to see him play a game and be able to say, "This is my last game", and go out with a big finish.'

Scholes knew Hughes had finished the 1995–96 season terribly, struggling with injury for Footscray and devoid of all motivation after his contretemps with officialdom. If any other coach and captain had been appointed, barring probably Dodemaide, it is likely he would have just been summarily dropped from the squad and consigned to history.

Scholes, along with Warne, argued the case to the other selectors that Hughes should be given the winter to do a pre-season; his work ethic over the winter would decide if he would be retained in the squad, come September.

'When I got appointed in May, the way that Merv had finished the previous year it was more than likely he wouldn't be in the State squad,' Scholes says.

'My reasoning to the selectors was that I didn't want to see someone such as Merv, who had the record he did, go out by being left out of the

State squad. I wanted to give him the opportunity to try again because I knew he had the burning desire to do so. In May, I doubted whether he could come up but I wanted to give him that opportunity. I put it to him and said I would support him as long as he did the work and he could show me something in September. By doing it that way, I was going to give Merv a chance to make his own decisions.'

While Hughes may have talked the talk of a return to first-class cricket, he most definitely could not walk the walk and plainly failed to do the work required during the winter of 1996 to be ready for State selection.

A diary forever full of speaking engagements, publicity appearances and promotional work allowed little time for extra training, and the basic work he was supposed to do was invariably compromised by his outside interests.

Between May and August, Hughes would join a 10-day Variety Bash to Darwin, travel to England, and also to New Zealand for a testimonial match. Each trip cost him valuable fitness time and put him further behind in his bid to make a return.

At no stage did Scholes try to stop Hughes from pursuing his outside interests.

'Whether he did the work or not was his call,' Scholes says. 'He went and did other things and not once did I try to stop him from doing those other things. I could see that there was no longer a burning passion there to play cricket. He wouldn't have made those decisions to do that if there still was a burning passion.'

Hughes knew he was doing more than the average club cricketer but certainly less work than a State cricketer needed to do if he hoped to play first-class cricket. For an older cricketer coming back from 12 months on the sidelines, it was obvious he was doing nowhere near enough and would be placing Scholes and Warne in an invidious position.

As always in difficult times, Dodemaide was standing close by his friend.

The newly-appointed vice-captain could see that Hughes was considerably overweight and struggling to keep pace at even the most routine of mid-year sessions. No-one wanted to see him dropped from the State squad, so he sat down with Hughes to ask him whether he would consider retiring.

The pair would talk numerous times between June and September and each time Hughes would declare it was too great a wrench to retire.

'I was looking for the reasons why he wanted to persevere when obviously the motivation wasn't there for training,' Dodemaide says. 'There were a lot of holes in his pre-season when he could and should have been doing some work. I talked to him a lot and asked if he was trying to hang on, why was he hanging on?

'He had had a fantastic career and had achieved 10 times more than most blokes ever dream about. I was asking, as a mate, "What's down the track in five years time and what are your long-term goals?"

'I thought if you go on now you're just trying to hang on and it's certainly not for money because you're costing yourself money. We would go right through all those points and the thing that was frustrating me was that I was worried about his image as well. I would always be his mate and it wouldn't change my relationship with him, but I was worried about his future and the way people would consider him.

'We kept coming back to the same thing, that he didn't want to retire and he wanted to play. He asked why should he stop just because other people think it's a good idea.'

Dodemaide hoped Hughes would retire while he had the opportunity to pursue a successful media career because he felt Hughes was fooling himself if he still wanted to play. If Merv had really wanted to play for Victoria again, he would have done the difficult pre-season work and put himself in contention.

'I reckon I had put forward a better case than Perry Mason and he just looked at me and said, "I defy logic, don't I?"

'At the end of the day, I was looking for the textbook way for him to finish off and go out, the nice way to keep his public image up. That was the logical way of doing it but that's not Merv.

'I have to respect that approach, not because there's any logic involved, but because he's always been that way. He was hoping if other guys fell over, he might be called upon for a Mercantile game.

'I would tell him it's not the safe way and not the smart way, but it's the Merv Hughes way.'

Dodemaide could not talk Hughes into walking away, leaving the task to either Scholes or Warne. No-one in Victorian circles wanted to see Merv summarily dropped from the State squad but the man was steadfast that he would not be retiring to satisfy someone else's view of the right way to do things.

'John started talking to me pretty seriously from about August and said he thought I couldn't catch up and that he wanted me to retire. I said I didn't want to retire,' Hughes says.

'I said I still had dreams and they motivated me to play and it didn't matter whether I honestly thought the selectors would pick me.

'He asked if I would do us all a favour and retire, because it would make things much easier. I didn't want to make it easy for anyone and said I wanted to retire when I was ready.'

Scholes said he did not want to see Hughes limp off a ground somewhere to finish his cricket career but Hughes thought that was the kind of finish he would actually prefer, rather than retiring, playing a full season of grade cricket and never knowing if he could have been picked again.

If he was going to hurt himself, that would be his decision to make. If he was to be dropped, finally, from the Victorian squad, the selectors would have to do it because Hughes was determined not to walk away.

Scholes had seen no improvement whatsoever by the end of August and knew that the fast bowler would be dropped as soon as the cricket season neared. Still, he did not want to see Hughes dropped but he was getting nowhere in his efforts to convince him to retire.

'We had a really strong fitness night at Melbourne Grammar and Merv was going around the circuit and getting further behind and further behind,' Scholes recalls.

'To be honest, it hurt me to see it. I thought he would really hurt himself and we had the Cerebus training camp coming up.

'I knew how hard that would be, but that night in the hall was indicative that his pride wouldn't allow him to give in. If I had had a sledgehammer, I would have hit him over the head that night to put him out of his misery. It was a hard time for me because I knew what was coming.'

Scholes had spoken with Sue Hughes on a number of occasions as well, and felt certain he had at least given his man the chance to decide for himself over the winter. By not doing the work, there could be no option but to drop him from the State squad.

There could not be rules for the squad and a separate set for Merv Hughes so, on September 12, 1996, he was dropped from the Victorian State squad, never to reappear.

The press conference at the VCA was probably the first that has ever been called to announce the dropping of a player from the winter training squad, and it drew a full house. The conference was attended by each of the Melbourne television stations, all three metropolitan newspapers and a decent smattering of radio stations.

Warne and Scholes sat either side of Hughes. Scholes introduced a touch of levity into the proceedings by producing a knife when asked if he had stabbed a friend in the back.

'I have no doubt that trying to keep up with the rest of the squad over the past couple of years is the reason he had injury problems,' Scholes says.

'When we put him out of the squad, I think we did it in the best possible way by having a press conference. Merv had had the opportunity to make his own decisions and he made them.'

Merv Hughes had last played for Victoria in January 1995 and for Australia some eight months before that. It had been three years and one month since he had walked off The Oval in England.

Hughes has no complaints at all with Scholes' treatment of him.

'During one training session, we had to do fifty 50-metre sprints and it was pretty obvious I was in trouble when Shaun Graf [who had retired more than a decade before] was beating me.

'Scholesy was forthright and honest with me. I don't have a problem with that. Getting dropped from the State squad was a business thing and I don't believe it has affected our friendship.'

Scholes and Warne were prepared to offer Hughes the job of fast bowling coach if he retired from district cricket, but the pull of Footscray was far too strong. He continued in grade cricket through the summer of 1996–97 but occasionally worked as an unofficial adviser to the young fast bowlers in the State squad, particularly Brad Williams.

The most important task for Scholes now, was to rebuild morale within the Victorian team. By summer's end, he certainly seemed to have achieved this, even if Victoria would not get near the Shield final and would bow out of the Mercantile Mutual Cup competition at the semi-final stage.

Dean Jones, Matthew Elliott and Darren Berry had all been unhappy figures during the previous summer for various reasons, but each was a pivotal player for Scholes and needed to be playing well and feeling good about his team-mates.

Berry returned to the Victorian side as their first-choice wicket-keeper for the winter Super 8s tournament in northern Queensland and slotted straight back in for the start of the regular season. If he had apparently been dropped for his batting during 1995–96, he would give the selectors no chance of repeating that mistake by pounding a career-best 148 in the first match against New South Wales. As always, his form with the gloves was impeccable.

Matthew Elliott, who had batted superbly in 1995–96 despite the rumblings within the side, continued his giant strides in 1996–97, forcing his way into the Australian side ahead of Michael Slater for the Test series against the West Indies. In his second Test match, at the SCG, Elliott was well on the way to a maiden century, until he ran into batting partner Mark Waugh and severely damaged a knee. However, despite two months on the sidelines, he fought back again and returned to the side that departed for the tour of South Africa in early February, 1997.

As for Jones, back to being purely a player, he started the summer strongly with an unbeaten 93 and unbeaten 100 in the first two Mercantile games, and a knock of 152 in the second Shield game against South Australia. Another century would follow in early December against Tasmania but his season would come to an abrupt halt in mid-January when he succumbed to a lingering ankle complaint, brought on by his heavy commitments with Derbyshire during 1996.

It remains to be seen if he will return to the Victorian side for 1997–98.

Should he not continue, it would be a pity — a disappointment every bit as great as Merv Hughes' unhappy end to his first-class career.

# CHAPTER EIGHTEEN

# ONE OF THE BEST

D uring the course of the 1996–97 Australian season, Merv Hughes dropped a position on the all-time Australian Test wicket-takers list. The fast bowler fell from seventh to eighth spot in November 1996 when Shane Warne accepted a return catch from the West Indies' Shiv Chanderpaul during the second Test, at the SCG, giving Warne his 213th wicket for Australia and taking him past Hughes' tally of 212.

At the rate Glenn McGrath has taken wickets for Australia over the past 18 months, Hughes will probably fall to ninth spot sometime in 1998, provided the lanky New South Welshman can remain injury-free throughout the national side's hectic program.

Hughes finished his Test career with a strike-rate of exactly four wickets per Test, but exactly where he stands among bowlers who have played for Australia is a major point of contention.

In many experts' opinion, Dennis Lillee is the greatest bowler to have been produced by Australia. Undoubtedly, Lillee is the most-admired bowler of those who played both with and against him from the start of the 1970s onwards. His strike-rate of five wickets per Test and a wicket every 52 balls ranks with any bowler from any country. He also scores points on the grounds of longevity, with an international career stretching over 14 seasons from 1970–71 to 1983–84.

Lillee took wickets in all conditions and had that rare, intangible quality of being able to impose his will on a match, securing a breakthrough when

*Opposite: Hughes at Lord's, second Ashes Test, 1993.*

no other bowler would be able to make something happen. His record is all the more impressive when you consider the 18 months he lost, because of a back injury, when he was at his fastest between February 1973 and November 1974, and the further two years he lost to World Series Cricket in 1977–78 and 1978–79. His absences from the Test team in those two periods cost him 11 Test matches in the first instance and a massive 29 in the second (including the five Tests in England in 1977, which Lillee missed because of a back injury). On his career average, Lillee supposedly would have taken 200 wickets in those 40 Tests and at least 160 if we are unkind and only award him four wickets per Test. Adding those wickets to his official career Test record, he rockets past 500 Test wickets and well beyond the reach of current record-holder Kapil Dev.

Merv Hughes is among those jockeying for position on the second rank of Australian bowlers — rivalling everyone from Craig McDermott, whose 291 wickets places him in second position, behind Lillee on the all-time wicket-taking list, onwards.

In trying to underline Merv Hughes' standing as an Australian Test cricketer, I have cut off Australia's bowlers at the point of 75 wickets. A tally of 75 wickets represents what I believe to be a significant career, in light of the limited number of Test matches that could be played at the turn of the century. An Australian player up to the Second World War could go two years without playing a Test match and an outstanding career of five or six years may only net 20 matches in total.

Even a modern-day bowler, averaging an impressive five wickets per game, needs to play at least 18 months of Test cricket to get up to 75 wickets, as well as maintaining his form all through that period. In Australia's history, 40 bowlers have reached the 75-wicket plateau and 27 of those have taken more than 100 wickets. A modern-day bowler with an average of less than 25 runs per wicket is considered to be a champion, but averages do not pose a fair reflection of cricket over the decades.

In Test cricket played between 1877 and 1914, bowlers very much dominated the sport and an average of 16–17, rather than 22–23, was a measure of a great bowler. Similarly, in the period from the 1920s up to the Second World War, it was very much the era of high-scoring batsmen and the better bowlers did well to average in the high 20s.

*England's Kim Barnett, caught at short leg by David Boon off the bowling of Hughes at Lord's in 1989.*

Averages also pay no attention to changes in fielding standards, sizes of grounds and rules. A much more accurate measure of a bowler's worth can be gathered from strike rates. How many balls did it take each Test bowler to secure a wicket? Under this system, the contention that Lillee is the greatest still stands up exceptionally well, as he averaged a wicket every eight and a half overs, or 52.02 balls.

Of all the bowlers to have taken more than 75 wickets for Australia, only Fred 'The Demon' Spofforth, Charles 'The Terror' Turner and Jack Saunders have a better strike-rate than Lillee's. Spofforth (44.52), Turner (51.28) and Saunders (45.13) were all retired from Test cricket by 1907 (Spofforth and Turner by 1894), when wickets were nowhere near as well-prepared and, consequently, bowlers dominated Test cricket.

In terms of strike-rates, Merv Hughes' record stacks up superbly against Australia's other bowlers. Of those to have taken more than 100 Test wickets, Hughes sits comfortably in eighth place, requiring 57.95 balls per wicket. Ahead of him is Turner, Lillee, Jeff Thomson (52.68),

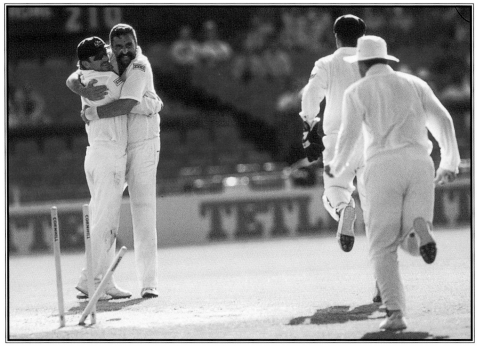

*Hughes and his captain celebrate the demise of Mike Gatting in England's second innings at Old Trafford in 1993.*

Bruce Reid (55.26), the rapidly-advancing McGrath (55.70), McDermott (57.00) and Hugh Trumble (57.44).

The table below is arranged in order of Australia's highest Test wicket-takers, up to April 1997. After each bowler's strike-rate per wicket, a rating is given of his position among those who have taken more than 75 wickets and those who have taken more than 100 wickets.

| Bowler | Wkts | Strike-rate | Rating 75+ | Rating 100+ |
|--------|------|-------------|------------|-------------|
| D.K. Lillee | 355 | 52.02 | 4 | 2 |
| C.J. McDermott | 291 | 57.00 | 9 | 6 |
| R. Benaud | 248 | 77.05 | 35 | 26 |
| G.D. McKenzie | 246 | 71.87 | 30 | 22 |
| S.K. Warne | 240 | 63.40 | 23 | 17 |
| R.R. Lindwall | 228 | 59.87 | 15 | 10 |
| C.V. Grimmett | 216 | 67.19 | 25 | 18 |

| Bowler | Wkts | Strike-rate | Rating 75+ | Rating 100+ |
|--------|------|-------------|------------|-------------|
| M.G. Hughes | 212 | 57.95 | 13 | 8 |
| J.R. Thomson | 200 | 52.68 | 6 | 3 |
| A.K. Davidson | 186 | 62.30 | 22 | 16 |
| G.F. Lawson | 180 | 61.77 | 18 | 13 |
| K.R. Miller | 170 | 61.54 | 17 | 12 |
| T.M. Alderman | 170 | 59.89 | 16 | 11 |
| W.A. Johnston | 160 | 69.05 | 26 | 19 |
| W.J. O'Reilly | 144 | 69.61 | 27 | 20 |
| H. Trumble | 141 | 57.44 | 10 | 7 |
| M.H.N. Walker | 138 | 73.14 | 31 | 23 |
| A.A. Mallett | 132 | 75.68 | 32 | 24 |
| B. Yardley | 126 | 70.71 | 28 | 21 |
| R.M. Hogg | 123 | 62.06 | 21 | 15 |
| M.A. Noble | 121 | 59.17 | 14 | 9 |
| G.D. McGrath | 119 | 55.70 | 8 | 5 |
| B.A. Reid | 113 | 55.26 | 7 | 4 |
| I.W. Johnson | 109 | 80.55 | 37 | 27 |
| G. Giffen | 103 | 62.05 | 20 | 14 |
| A.N. Connolly | 102 | 76.65 | 34 | 25 |
| C.T.B. Turner | 101 | 51.28 | 3 | 1 |
| A.A. Mailey | 99 | 61.81 | 19 | |
| F.R. Spofforth | 94 | 44.52 | 1 | |
| J.W. Gleeson | 93 | 95.24 | 40 | |
| N.J.N. Hawke | 91 | 76.64 | 33 | |
| A. Cotter | 89 | 52.06 | 5 | |
| W.W. Armstrong | 87 | 92.21 | 39 | |
| J.M. Gregory | 85 | 65.67 | 24 | |
| P.R. Reiffel | 80 | 57.80 | 11 | |
| S.R. Waugh | 80 | 79.90 | 36 | |
| J.V. Saunders | 79 | 45.13 | 2 | |
| G. Dymock | 78 | 71.09 | 29 | |
| G.E. Palmer | 78 | 57.91 | 12 | |
| T.B.A. May | 75 | 87.69 | 38 | |

When looking at these figures, Hughes sits ahead of fast or fast–medium bowlers acknowledged as legends such as Ray Lindwall, Keith Miller, Alan Davidson, Bill Johnston, Terry Alderman and Graham McKenzie. As these figures clearly illustrate, his value was as a strike bowler, someone who could make something happen out of nowhere.

He could be expensive at times — as his average in the high 20s attests — but he broke through more frequently for Australia than most of the great bowlers of the past.

Former Australian coach Bob Simpson has always maintained that the Test side lost a truly outstanding bowler when Bruce Reid was unable to survive the injuries that plagued his Test career. Strike-rate figures support Simpson's contention on Reid and also support Lillee's view that McGrath could be a bowler every bit as good as anyone who has gone before him. McGrath lowered his strike-rate from 62 to 55 in the 12 months before the 1997 Ashes series and will inevitably continue to do so if he can stay fit.

Simpson has played alongside, reported on or coached every Australian bowler since the late 1950s and says Hughes deserves to be rated on the level immediately below Lillee, alongside the likes of Lindwall, Davidson, Miller, McKenzie, Thomson and McDermott.

'Merv deserves every bit of credit as a great Australian bowler because his strike-rate was just so good,' Simpson says. 'He was a wicket-taker and he must be remembered as such.

'He got wickets for Australia in the hardest of conditions and he got the big wickets — either breaking a partnership or knocking over the key batsman in the opposition line-up.'

Hughes played a large part of his Test career against the West Indies — 14 of his 53 Tests — and he certainly earned a reputation for taking the important wicket. In those 14 Tests, he dismissed Richie Richardson on nine occasions and Desmond Haynes six times. Richardson and Haynes were the two form batsmen of the West Indies side in the Test series of 1988–89 and 1991.

Between them, Richardson and Haynes scored seven centuries in the nine Tests of those series. And Hughes was the man dismissing them the most frequently.

In Hughes' 20 Tests against England, Graham Gooch, Mike Atherton and Mike Gatting were each claimed on four separate occasions, as was Martin Crowe in the space of five Tests against New Zealand.

Greg Chappell, who played alongside Lillee and was a selector when Hughes made his debut in 1985, said *who* Hughes dismissed was the most important factor in rating him as a Test cricketer.

'I look at who bowlers got out, when they got them out and how they got them out,' Chappell says.

'Dennis Lillee stands out head and shoulders above everyone else while Thommo, until the day he ran into Alan Turner at Adelaide, was just the most lethal thing that has ever been.

'Merv's record puts him up there as one of the best who has ever played Test cricket. By dint of the way he looks, he's very easily under-estimated. I think that's probably happened to him throughout his life and certainly it has happened throughout his cricket career. Batsmen hovered mentally on the borderline of recognising a good fast bowler and someone they thought they could score a few runs from, which was to their peril.'

Greg's elder brother Ian Chappell, who was such a stern critic of Hughes in the early part of his career, goes even further than Greg in his praise of Hughes.

'When nothing was happening for Australia, that's when you called on Merv Hughes and he made something happen,' Ian Chappell says.

'He did that as much with the strength of his personality and his determination as he did with his ability.

'I don't think it's putting Merv in the wrong company to say that's the kind of impact Dennis Lillee had for Australia during his career. When nothing was happening, Dennis was able to impose himself on the opposition and impose himself into the game. Most of the time it was his ability, but a lot of times it was purely his strength of will and determination. Merv could do that as well, and very few bowlers are in that category.'

Those who have watched and played a lot of cricket over three or four decades rank Hughes, without hesitation, as someone who has not received the credit he deserves. In the eyes of those who have been out there in the middle during a Test match, too much attention was paid to Hughes' size and demeanour and not enough paid to his results.

**Above:** *The Australians in party mode after retaining the Ashes at Leeds in 1993. Left to right: Bob Simpson, Merv Hughes, Ian Healy, Michael Slater (obscured), Brendon Julian (obscured) and Allan Border.*

**Below:** *Later that same evening, in the dressing-rooms, Hughes, as usual, had become the centre of attention.*

Former chairman of selectors Lawrie Sawle feels Hughes will become a legend in time.

'I'm not sure if the general public acknowledges him enough and they are wrong if they don't. He might not have looked like the great bowlers from the past but forget about that and look at his results,' Sawle says.

Great fast bowlers have always hunted in packs and few probably realise that the partnership of McDermott and Hughes, over 26 Tests, had a better combined strike-rate than the famous pairing of Lillee and Thomson in the 1970s.

The final immeasurable quantity when judging Merv Hughes is the effect he had on his team-mates in terms of morale within the dressing-rooms. When Merv Hughes played for Australia, he was the team's resident gee-up man, lifting his team-mates when they were struggling.

He was the man who could find a laugh in the most difficult of situations and could relax even in the most tense moments. In the pressured atmosphere of Test cricket, such a quality is highly-valued.

'Merv gets equal credits off the field to on the field, whereas a lot of blokes don't get any credits off the field because their energy goes into themselves and into their own performance,' Ian Healy says.

'Those guys need blokes like Mervyn to get them going and keep the team going. He gets huge credits for that above and beyond whatever he did for Australia. It's a great frustration to me, the way he's perceived by Australia.

'Merv is my most respected and most under-rated team-mate. His presence, his demeanour and his actions were so overriding that people talked about them and forgot about what he was actually achieving.'

Aside from the joking, the clowning, the exercises, the sledging, the bluster and the bravado, so many seem to have forgotten that Merv Hughes was a fast bowler who could move the ball off the seam and swing it every now and then when the conditions were right for him.

Hughes worked in spells far longer than the average quick bowler and, above all, was part of an Australian side that got better as he got better. His improvement was one reason, along with the improvement of some of his team-mates, that an Australian side, which had been at its nadir in 1985, was challenging to become the best in the world at the end of his international career.

Richard Watson
Acting Chief Executive Officer
Australian Cricket Board

*April 23, 1997*

Dear Richard,

It is with great regret and overwhelming disappointment that I write these words.

Since my last appearance for Australia in 1994, I have been working extremely hard (and hoping for several other rival fast bowlers to retire gracefully, injure themselves or burn out) in my aim of securing a third Ashes tour in 1997.

However, after being consistently overlooked by the Victorian selectors, it dismays me greatly to have been similarly overlooked by the national selectors.

It is obvious that with the departure of Lawrie Sawle (chairman) and Bob Simpson (coach) from the selection panel, two of my greatest supporters, that my time is up.

This decision by the national selectors to overlook me has hurt and embarrassed me deeply.

I had felt that the new panel's decision to name Mark Taylor as captain offered me some hope but the recent demise of another fat boy in David Boon has indicated there are limited positions available for overweight cricketers.

With great regret (and overwhelming relief), I must announce that I have now officially retired from international cricket, unless you need me in the next month.

Yours sincerely

**Merv Hughes**

# POSTSCRIPT

There would be no miracle comebacks to the Victorian team for Merv Hughes in the summer of 1996–97. Now playing only for Footscray in the Melbourne district competition, the 53-Test veteran would set his sights on the goal of a second first-grade premiership.

Hughes' outstanding form before Christmas (he had tallied up 38 wickets by the New Year break), saw him mentioned in some areas for one last recall to his State's team but, with his inability to complete a four-day game, the speculation was never that close to the mark. His form did, however, lift Footscray to the top of the ladder going into the last quarter of the season.

However, Footscray would stumble in their last three matches and only just scraped into the top four, where they would lose to eventual premiers Northcote in the semi-finals. As Footscray struggled in the New Year, so did Hughes. The effort of playing a match would leave him unable to train for several days afterwards and a Saturday–Sunday game would dramatically affect his ability to play the following week.

Still, he would finish third in the Ryder Medal, which is awarded to each season's outstanding player in district cricket.

Hughes played for Footscray every week simply because he enjoyed the camaraderie of his team-mates and the thrill of having a game. As their highest-profile cricketer, Hughes worked as hard as anyone to ensure Footscray did well off the field, as well as on the field, during the 1996–97 season.

From arranging raffles, to coaching young bowlers from the thirds in the nets, Hughes would give much to his district club over the summer.

One of the best ways to sum-up Merv Hughes and the way he has touched so many groups of people would be to take a look at the scene

*Opposite:* To comply with the requirements of the Australian Cricket Board's provident fund, all retiring Australian cricketers are required to notify the ACB of their intention to call it quits. This is how Hughes let the Board know.

The team that represented Footscray in the last game of district cricket played at the Western Oval (now EJ Whitten Oval). **Back** (left to right): James Barnard, David Wolfe, Steve Cashin, Merv Hughes, Grant Burns, Tony Dodemaide, Sean Williams, Raynor Reber, Daryll Clemson, Gary Anderton (Coach); **Front:** Chris Burton and Michael O'Keeffe.

at his and wife Sue's house in the northern suburbs of Melbourne on the Sunday before Christmas, 1996.

The Hughes hosted a Christmas party to which they invited everyone they knew, including all the different groups Merv had crossed paths with through his life. Among those present were Australian cricket team-mates, Victorian cricket team-mates, Footscray cricket team-mates, Werribee football team-mates, Werribee basketball team-mates, high school friends from Werribee, high school friends from Myrtleford and his oldest primary school friends.

Few of the eight or nine different groups would have had much in common, other than the fact that they all knew him, yet more than

60 of his friends turned up at his house, including a veritable tribe of small children.

It still amazes Sue just how well Merv keeps in touch with so many different groups of people and remains so loyal to them all. It does mean, though, that she hardly ever gets to use the phone in their house.

In retirement from the Australian team, Merv Hughes can resume the role he always liked to play before he became a national hero with his sporting deeds, a person who enjoyed surrounding himself with as many friends as possible.

To have never lost touch with any of the groups he has shared his time with, through such a busy and transient life, is a mark of his character.

Merv Hughes was an outstanding Test cricketer for his country but is also a deeply loyal person. Once you have earned his friendship, you have it for life.

It is that second achievement of his life on which he prides himself.

*Merv Hughes at The Oval in 1993 ... one of the true champions of Australia's cricket history.*

# THE BEST
# OF THE BEST

Every serious sports fan dreams of an ultimate match-up of their favourite players. A chance to compare performers from different eras to settle an argument once and for all as to who is the best. Merv Hughes is no different.

His dream was to construct an opposition side and be part of an Australian team that would win a hard-fought Test match. Merv Hughes played the bulk of his Test career with a solid core of team-mates — Mark Taylor, David Boon, Allan Border, Steve Waugh, Mark Waugh, Ian Healy, Craig McDermott and Shane Warne — so, as such, there was little point in nominating his all-time Australian team because it virtually picks itself.

In the 53 Tests Hughes played for Australia, he played against England (20 times), West Indies (14), India (six), New Zealand (five), Sri Lanka (three), Pakistan (three) and South Africa (two).

In those Tests between December 1985 and March 1994, the seven opposition countries chose a total of 155 players — a little more than 14 full teams.

I asked Hughes to nominate his 'dream' team — made up of the best of the cricketers he has faced during his career. My parameters were this: pick a side that includes six batsmen, a wicket-keeper and five bowlers, with the choice of 12th man to be made on the day.

This was his response . . . [1]

---

1. Note: the records shown are for Test matches against Australia in which Merv Hughes played.

# O P E N E R S

**GORDON GREENIDGE (WEST INDIES) AND DESMOND HAYNES (WEST INDIES)**

## GORDON GREENIDGE

Played nine Tests against Merv Hughes, five in 1988–89 and four in 1991, scoring 667 runs at 41.69. Greenidge posted 104 at Adelaide Oval in January 1989, and his 226 at Bridgetown in April 1991 was the decisive innings that led to the West Indies winning that Fourth Test match and retaining the Frank Worrell trophy.

## DESMOND HAYNES

Played 14 Tests in the 1988–89, 1991 and 1992–93 series, scoring 1002 runs at 41.75. Haynes was at his peak in the first two series against Merv Hughes and averaged almost 55 in those first nine Tests, including centuries at Perth in December 1988, Sydney in January 1989 and Georgetown in March 1991. His 111 at Georgetown was part of a 297-run stand with Richie Richardson that set up the West Indies' 1–0 lead in that series.

### THE REASONS WHY

'I have to name Greenidge and Haynes as an opening combination because I played against them so many times,' Hughes says.

'I thought they were just fantastic as two cricketers. I think you have to pick openers as a pair because of reasons such as running together and the ability to play off each other, as well as what they did themselves. If I didn't name them as a pair, I would have picked Sunil Gavaskar [India] and Mike Atherton [England].'

### THOSE WHO JUST MISSED OUT

*Sunil Gavaskar (India): One Test, 166 not out.*
*Mike Atherton (England): 12 Tests, 797 runs at 33.20. No hundreds, seven fifties.*

'I would sincerely apologise to Sunil Gavaskar for leaving him out of this side. I only played one Test against him and he was an unbelievable player. He was right at the end of his career but he made 166 not out in my debut Test and we didn't look like getting him out.

'As for Atherton, I like the way he plays cricket. He comes across as a soft, unconvincing player, and not all that determined, but that's completely wrong. I thought that about him, but you have to watch him play to really understand him. The way he's played against Australia, coupled with the tradition tied up in Ashes Test matches, makes him a fantastic player.

'Atherton's performances against Australia have been very good. To make 500 runs in a Test series in England when his side got smacked was a great effort. He came in as a kid in 1989 and you could tell he had something. I think he's a very special player.'

# No. 3
# BATSMAN

## RICHIE RICHARDSON (WEST INDIES)

Richie Richardson played 14 Tests in the same period as Desmond Haynes, covering the 1988–89 series, 1991 in the Caribbean and as captain in 1992–93. He scored 1295 runs in those matches at 56.30, scoring five centuries. His highlights were 122 on a green pitch in Melbourne in December 1988, 104 not out at Kingston in February 1991 to force a draw, and a peerless 182 at Georgetown in March 1991 in just five hours. Richardson's innings at Georgetown swung the series to give the West Indies a 1–0 lead in the rubber.

### THE REASONS WHY

'This was one of the easiest positions to pick. Richie was completely unflappable as a batsman and nothing you ever did would ever seem to worry him. My weapon is obviously the short ball but he loved that and would take you on and take you down. Richie scored at a good pace and when he got going, he was just about impossible to put the brakes on. He could also play a really big innings, and a person who can win you a series is an automatic selection.'

*Brian Lara (West Indies): Five Tests, 466 runs at 58.25. One century.*

'I only played against Brian Lara at the start of his career but I'm sure he would have been in my side if I had played a few more Tests against him. His 277 in Sydney was sensational but he wasn't as dangerous for the rest of that series. He always gave you a chance in the early stages of his innings but he's obviously tightened up so much since then. As a bowler, you worry about a batsman who has shown he can make a really huge score.'

# MIDDLE-ORDER BATSMEN

## GRAHAM GOOCH (ENGLAND), VIV RICHARDS (WEST INDIES) AND ROBIN SMITH (ENGLAND)

## GRAHAM GOOCH

Played 14 Tests against Merv Hughes, in 1989, 1990–91 and 1993, scoring 1169 runs at 43.30. The Essex right-hander had a miserable series in 1989 but led from the front in Australia in 1990–91 and scored two hundreds in 1993 — 133 at Manchester and 120 at Nottingham. His scalp at Manchester was the key wicket for Australia to go on and set up a 1–0 lead in the 1993 Ashes series.

### THE REASONS WHY

'Graham Gooch is probably more of an opening batsman but he did start his career for England in the middle-order and he played there against us in 1993. Because he was so good, he has to be fitted into the team. In 1990 and 1993 he was fantastic. The trauma his side went through was enormous, but he still made a lot of runs. As long as he was at the crease in 1993, England were always in the contest.'

## VIV RICHARDS

Played nine Tests against Australia, in the 1988–89 and 1991 series, scoring 552 runs at 39.43. He made 146 at Perth in December 1988 in Merv's first Test against the West Indies, setting up his side's 2–0 lead in the series. He went from 93 to 146 in just over 40 minutes on the second morning of that Test match and treated the Australian attack with contempt.

### THE REASONS WHY

'Viv Richards was awesome. His power-hitting was intimidating and he is probably the hardest hitter of a ball that I've ever bowled to. I was lucky, or unlucky enough, to come into Test cricket as he was starting to go out. In the Barbados Test match in 1991, he was batting to set up a declaration and he flat-batted me down the ground and nearly killed me. It was going at a million miles an hour. I really did find him intimidating the first few times I played against him because you felt he didn't have a weakness. He was the master.'

## ROBIN SMITH

Played 14 Tests through the 1989, 1990–91 and 1993 series, scoring 1046 runs at 40.23. Smith's best performances in Australia came in 1989, with 143 at Manchester and 101 at Nottingham. He struggled against the spin of Warne and May in 1993 but was always a dangerous player of fast bowling.

### THE REASONS WHY

'Robin Smith was very good in a side that got badly beaten in 1989, which is always a very difficult thing to do. He could hit the ball as hard as anyone and his batting wasn't changed by the situation his team were in. On the field, he and Mark Greatbatch [New Zealand] were the two blokes I had the most passionate hate for, but I got on really well with both of them off the ground. I've always thought that's the way we should play, so I also admire him for that.'

## THOSE WHO JUST MISSED OUT

*Sachin Tendulkar (India): Five Tests, 368 runs at 46.00. Two centuries.*
*Martin Crowe (New Zealand): Five Tests, 368 runs at 36.80. No hundreds, three fifties.*
*Mohammad Azharuddin (India): Six Tests, 209 runs at 20.90.*

'As with Brian Lara, I haven't really played enough against Sachin Tendulkar to get him in there but I thought the way he played in 1991–92 was fantastic.

'Martin Crowe was a very, very good player and technique-wise, he was fantastic. He made a lot of runs against us and the Australia–New Zealand rivalry was very good. They probably go harder at us than we do at them and I thought we under-estimated the New Zealanders a lot of the time. It was their big thing to play well against Australia.

'Mohammad Azharuddin could play some outstanding innings but struggled a bit in Australian conditions.

'I could probably put Ian Botham and Imran Khan at six but I didn't play a whole lot of cricket against them. I certainly rate them though.'


# W I C K E T - K E E P E R

## JEFF DUJON (WEST INDIES)

Dujon played nine Tests against Australia in 1988–89 and 1991, scoring 377 runs at 26.93. In those two series, he kept to Malcolm Marshall, Curtly Ambrose, Courtney Walsh and Patrick Patterson.

### THE REASONS WHY

'I thought he was sensational behind the stumps and very handy with the bat. He was very athletic and very determined, although the facade he put across was very casual. I respected him a lot.'

### THOSE WHO JUST MISSED OUT

*Dave Richardson (South Africa): Kept throughout the 1994 series in South Africa, taking six catches in the two Tests Hughes played in.*

'I didn't play a lot against Dave Richardson but I rate him enormously. I thought he was a very good wicket-keeper who did his stuff with a minimum of fuss. His batting has also gotten better the longer he's been in Test cricket, which is the sign of a good player.'

# N E W - B A L L   B O W L E R S

### MALCOLM MARSHALL (WEST INDIES)

Marshall played nine Tests in 1988–89 and 1991, taking 32 wickets at 24.81. His best performance was in Sydney in January 1989, where he took 5–29 in a match dominated by the spin of Allan Border. Even though the rest of his team-mates struggled with the wicket, Marshall cut his pace and contained the Australians, as well as taking wickets.

### WASIM AKRAM (PAKISTAN)

Wasim played three Tests in the 1989–90 series, taking 17 wickets at 18.71. The left-arm all-rounder started with consecutive hauls of 6–62 and 5–98 at Melbourne and 5–100 in the first innings at Adelaide before a groin injury slowed his progress in that series. He also belted his maiden Test century, 123, in the second Test, at Adelaide.

#### THE REASONS WHY

'Malcolm Marshall was just the king of fast bowlers in my opinion. On the 1988–89 tour, whenever Viv Richards wanted something done, he would bring Marshall back. He had Ambrose and Walsh, who are two pretty fantastic bowlers, but Marshall was a different level again. He was the man when they needed something special.

'As for Wasim Akram, I can't believe how he does some of the things he does. He could bowl over or around the wicket and still swing the ball both ways. That takes a bowler of exceptional skill. Off a short run-up, he was as fast as anyone and his batting could be really dangerous when he decided to work at it. Pretty close to the complete cricketer.'

# OTHER
# PACEMEN

## CURTLY AMBROSE (WEST INDIES)

Ambrose played 14 Tests against Australia in the 1988–89, 1991 and 1992–93 series, taking 74 wickets at just 19.93 apiece. He took five wickets in an innings four times and took 10 wickets in the West Indies' 1-run victory at Adelaide Oval in 1992–93. After setting up the win that brought the West Indies level at 1–1 in the series, he then took 7–25 in the next Test in Perth to ensure the West Indies would win the series.

## WAQAR YOUNIS (PAKISTAN)

Waqar Younis played only three Tests against Merv Hughes, in 1989–90, taking four wickets at 56.00 on his first full tour overseas.

### THE REASONS WHY

'Curtly Ambrose is a fantastic bowler and there doesn't really need to be an explanation given for his inclusion. You only have to look at his figures. He would have been Marshall's new ball partner except for the fact that Akram gives great value by testing batsmen with a right-arm/left-arm combination. Ambrose gives you absolutely nothing and his pace is as good as anyone's.

'I picked Waqar Younis on the strength of his One-day performances against Australia, rather than when he was out here in 1989 and just starting out.

'He is very, very fast when he's got his rhythm and I always like a bowler who is flat-out quick. I watched him in Sharjah in about 1992 and he was tremendous. His inswinger yorkers can take out a batsman at any stage of his innings and he can really slide a good bouncer on to a batsman.'

## THOSE WHO JUST MISSED OUT

*Devon Malcolm (England): Six Tests, 17 wickets at 50.23.*
*Imran Khan (Pakistan): Three Tests, 4 wickets at 41.75.*
*Ian Botham (England): Six Tests, 11 wickets at 41.09.*
*Kapil Dev (India): Six Tests, 33 wickets at 22.84.*
*Sir Richard Hadlee (New Zealand): One Test, three wickets at 36.33.*

'Devon Malcolm was very good on his day but not in the class of the other four. He could be terrifying at times, such as at The Oval in 1993 and the Adelaide Test match in 1995, but he could also be wayward. When he does fire, it's hard to put a lid on him.

'Imran Khan, Ian Botham and Kapil Dev were obviously all outstanding but I only played against them at the end of their careers and not when they were bowling at their absolute best.

'That also applies to Sir Richard Hadlee. I only played one Test against him, in 1987–88, but he was another bowler in a class of his own with his control and the way he could move a ball both ways and swing it both ways.'

# SPINNER

## ABDUL QADIR (PAKISTAN)

Abdul Qadir only played One-day cricket against Merv Hughes, not being included in the side that toured Australia in 1989–90.

### THE REASONS WHY

'Abdul Qadir would have to be the spinner because I didn't have a clue in which direction the ball was going when he was bowling. He had me in huge problems but he also did that against batsmen a lot better than me.

'It must be said that I didn't play against many great spinners. The West Indies would always pick four fast bowlers while England rarely settled on a spinner. Phil Tufnell played in 1990–91 and a bit in 1993 but other countries shuffled through their spinners a lot.'

# MERV HUGHES'
# TEST OPPONENTS

## ENGLAND 20 TESTS, 49 PLAYERS

| | |
|---|---|
| 14 | David Gower, Graham Gooch, Robin Smith |
| 12 | Michael Atherton |
| 10 | Alec Stewart |
| 8 | Allan Lamb, John Emburey, Jack Russell, Phil DeFreitas |
| 7 | Mike Gatting, Angus Fraser |
| 6 | Chris Broad, Gladstone Small, Ian Botham, Devon Malcolm |
| 5 | Graham Dilley, Phil Tufnell, Peter Such |
| 4 | Bill Athey, Jack Richards, Andy Caddick, Phil Edmonds, Neil Foster, Nasser Hussain |
| 3 | Kim Barnett, Tim Curtis, Graeme Hick, Nick Cook, Chris Lewis, Graham Thorpe, Mark Illott |
| 2 | Derek Pringle, Phil Newport, Paul Jarvis, Mark Lathwell, Wayne Larkins, Martin McCague, Martin Bicknell, Matthew Maynard |
| 1 | Mark Ramprakash, Steve Watkin, James Whitaker, Chris Tavare, Martyn Moxon, Eddie Hemmings, John Stephenson, David Capel, Alan Igglesden, Tim Robinson |

## WEST INDIES 14 TESTS, 21 PLAYERS

| | |
|---|---|
| 14 | Desmond Haynes, Richie Richardson, Curtly Ambrose, Courtney Walsh |
| 13 | Carl Hooper |
| 9 | Gordon Greenidge, Viv Richards, Gus Logie, Jeff Dujon, Patrick Patterson, Malcolm Marshall |
| 5 | Phil Simmons, Brian Lara, Keith Arthurton, Ian Bishop |
| 3 | Jimmy Adams, Junior Murray |
| 2 | David Williams |
| 1 | Roger Harper, Kenneth Benjamin, Anderson Cummins |

## INDIA 6 TESTS, 20 PLAYERS

6    Dilip Vengsarkar, Mohammad Azharuddin, Kapil Dev

5    Kris Srikkanth, Sanjay Manjrekar, Sachin Tendulkar, Manoj Prabhakar, Javagal Srinath

4    Ravi Shastri, Venkatapathy Raju

3    Kiran More, Navjot Sidhu

2    Chandra Pandit

1    Sunil Gavaskar, Chetan Sharma, Roger Binny, Syed Kirmani, Shivlal Yadav, Mohinder Armanath, Subroto Banerjee

## NEW ZEALAND 5 TESTS, 21 PLAYERS

5    John Wright, Dipak Patel, Martin Crowe, Danny Morrison

4    Ken Rutherford, Andrew Jones, Mark Greatbatch

3    Chris Cairns, Wille Watson

2    Jeff Crowe, Ian Smith, Michael Owens, Murphy Su'a, Tony Blain

1    Richard Hadlee, John Bracewell, Ewen Chatfield, Robert Vance, Martin Snedden, Adam Parore, Chris Harris

## SRI LANKA 3 TESTS, 18 PLAYERS

3    Roshan Mahanama, Aravinda De Silva, Arjuna Ranatunga, Ravi Ratnayeke, Champaka Ramanayake, Graeme Labrooy

2    Dhammika Ranatunga, Asanka Gurusinha, Asoka De Silva

1    Sanath Kaluperuma, Brendon Kuruppu, Ranjan Madugalle, Roy De Alwis, Kaushnik Amalean, Athula Samarasekera, Gamini Wickremasinge, Hashan Tillekeratne, Rumesh Ratnayake

## PAKISTAN 3 TESTS, 15 PLAYERS

3    Shoaib Mohammed, Javed Miandad, Ijaz Ahmed, Imran Khan, Salim Yousuf, Wasim Akram, Tauseef Ahmed, Waqar Younis

2    Aamir Malik, Rameez Raja

1    Manzoor Akhtar, Aaqib Javed, Salim Malik, Mushtaq Ahmed, Nadeem Ghouri

## SOUTH AFRICA 2 TESTS, 11 PLAYERS

2    Andrew Hudson, Gary Kirsten, Hansie Cronje, Kepler Wessels, Peter Kirsten, Jonty Rhodes, Brian McMillan, Dave Richardson, Craig Matthews, Fanie DeVilliers, Allan Donald

# MERV HUGHES'
# TEST TEAM MATES

## 53 TESTS, 42 PLAYERS

| | |
|---|---|
| 53 | Allan Border (all as captain) |
| 51 | David Boon |
| 46 | Ian Healy |
| 42 | Steve Waugh, Mark Taylor |
| 35 | Dean Jones |
| 32 | Geoff Marsh |
| 29 | Craig McDermott |
| 26 | Mark Waugh |
| 17 | Terry Alderman, Shane Warne |
| 14 | Bruce Reid |
| 12 | Greg Matthews |
| 9 | Geoff Lawson, Peter Taylor, Tim May |
| 8 | Michael Slater |
| 7 | Trevor Hohns, Mike Whitney, Paul Reiffel |
| 6 | Peter Sleep |
| 5 | Carl Rackemann, Tom Moody, Damien Martyn, Justin Langer |
| 4 | Greg Ritchie, Mike Veletta |
| 3 | Tim Zoehrer, Greg Dyer, Greg Campbell |
| 2 | Graeme Wood, Tony Dodemaide, Brendon Julian |
| 1 | Wayne Phillips (SA), David Hookes, Dirk Wellham, Matthew Hayden, Ray Bright, Chris Matthews, Wayne Phillips (Vic), Jo Angel, Glenn McGrath |

# MERV: THE STATISTICS

Note: all statistics are correct as at June 1, 1997

## I. INTRODUCTION

**Mervyn Gregory HUGHES**

Born Euroa, Victoria, 23 November 1961
Right-hand fast bowler
Right-hand batsman

### FIRST-CLASS CRICKET

*Debut:* 1981–82, Victoria v South Australia (Geelong), capturing 3/53 and 0/52; scoring 1 not out; taking one catch).
*Best bowling in an innings:* 8/87, Australia v West Indies (Perth), 1988–89
*Best bowling in a match:* 13/217, Australia v West Indies (Perth), 1988–89
*Best bowling in an innings for Victoria:* 7/81 v Queensland (St Kilda), 1988–89.
*Best bowling in a match for Victoria:* 10/121 v Queensland (St Kilda), 1988–89.
*Highest score:* 72 not out, Australia v West Indies (Adelaide Oval), 1988–89.
*Highest score for Victoria:* 64 not out v England XI (Eastern Oval, Ballarat), 1990–91.

### TEST CRICKET

*Debut:* 1985–86 (December 13–17, 1985) v India (Adelaide Oval), capturing 1/123; scoring 0; taking one catch.
*Best bowling and highest score:* as above.

### TOURS

*Australians to:* England 1989; India 1989; New Zealand 1990; Sharjah 1990; West Indies 1991; New Zealand 1993; England 1993; South Africa 1994.
*Victorians to:* England 1991.
*Hughes was also a member of the Australian squad in the 1992 World Cup, which played matches in Australia and New Zealand (Hughes, though, only played in one match, in Brisbane).*

### INTERNATIONAL ONE-DAY CRICKET

*Debut:* 1988–89 v Pakistan (Adelaide Oval), capturing 3/30, did not bat.
*Best Bowling:* 4/44 v West Indies (Sydney), 1988–89.
*Highest Score:* 20 v England (Manchester), 1993.

### DOMESTIC ONE-DAY CRICKET

*Debut:* 1981–82 v South Australia (Adelaide Oval), capturing 2/59, did not bat.
*Best Bowling:* 4/34 v South Australia (Adelaide Oval) 1986–87.
*Highest Score:* 17 v New South Wales (North Sydney Oval) 1991–92.

## MERV HUGHES CRICKET CAREER – SUMMARY
### Bowling

| Competition | Debut | M | Runs | Wkts | Avge | 5W | 10W | Best |
|---|---|---|---|---|---|---|---|---|
| First-class | 1981–82 | 165 | 17249 | 593 | 29.08 | 21 | 3 | 8/87 |
| Sheffield Shield | 1981–82 | 76 | 8169 | 267 | 30.59 | 10 | 2 | 7/81 |
| Tests | 1985–86 | 53 | 6017 | 212 | 28.38 | 7 | 1 | 8/87 |
| Dom. one-day | 1981–82 | 30 | 1147 | 33 | 34.76 | 0 | – | 4/34 |
| One-day Int. | 1988–89 | 33 | 1134 | 39 | 29.07 | 0 | – | 4/44 |

### Batting

| Competition | Debut | M | Inn | NO | Runs | HS | Avge | 50s | Ct |
|---|---|---|---|---|---|---|---|---|---|
| First-class | 1981–82 | 165 | 196 | 45 | 2649 | 72* | 17.54 | 7 | 56 |
| Sheffield Shield | 1981–82 | 76 | 87 | 25 | 896 | 60* | 14.45 | 1 | 21 |
| Tests | 1985–86 | 53 | 70 | 8 | 1032 | 72* | 16.64 | 2 | 23 |
| Dom. one-day | 1981–82 | 30 | 16 | 4 | 94 | 17 | 7.83 | 0 | 10 |
| One-day Int. | 1988–89 | 33 | 17 | 8 | 100 | 20 | 11.11 | 0 | 6 |

*Denotes not out*

### MISCELLANEOUS

Hughes is the only player to take a Test hat-trick spread over three separate overs (first wicket with last ball of an over; second wicket with first ball of next over to complete first innings; third wicket with first ball of second innings). His 8/87 are the best bowling figures achieved in a Test innings at Perth. His 13/217 are the best bowling figures achieved in an Australia–West Indies Test match and the best Test-match figures achieved at Perth.

Hughes 165 first-class matches can be broken down as follows:

| | | | |
|---|---|---|---|
| *For Australia in Tests:* | 53 | *Victoria in Sheffield Shield:* | 76 |
| *For Australians on tour:* | 26 | *Victoria against overseas teams:* | 7 |
| *For Australian XI in Australia:* | 2 | *For Essex:* | 1 |

In Hughes' 53 Tests, Australia won 25, drew 17, lost 11.

### AUSTRALIAN BOWLERS WITH 200 OR MORE TEST WICKETS

| Bowler | Tests | Balls | Runs | Wkts | Avge | 5W | 10W | Best |
|---|---|---|---|---|---|---|---|---|
| D.K. Lillee | 70 | 18467 | 8493 | 355 | 23.92 | 23 | 7 | 7/83 |
| C.J. McDermott | 71 | 16586 | 8332 | 291 | 28.63 | 14 | 2 | 8/97 |
| R. Benaud | 63 | 19108 | 6704 | 248 | 27.03 | 16 | 1 | 7/72 |
| G.D. McKenzie | 60 | 17681 | 7328 | 246 | 29.78 | 16 | 3 | 8/71 |
| S.K. Warne | 52 | 15219 | 5746 | 240 | 23.94 | 10 | 3 | 8/71 |
| R.R. Lindwall | 61 | 13650 | 5251 | 228 | 23.03 | 12 | 0 | 7/38 |
| C.V. Grimmett | 37 | 14513 | 5231 | 216 | 24.21 | 21 | 7 | 7/40 |
| **M.G. Hughes** | **53** | **12285** | **6017** | **212** | **28.38** | **7** | **1** | **8/87** |
| J.R. Thomson | 51 | 10535 | 5601 | 200 | 28.00 | 8 | 0 | 6/46 |

### LEADING AUSTRALIAN BOWLERS IN TESTS IN ENGLAND

| Bowler | M | Balls | Mdns | Runs | Wkts | Avge | 5W | 10W | Best |
|---|---|---|---|---|---|---|---|---|---|
| D.K. Lillee | 16 | 4815 | 245 | 1974 | 96 | 20.56 | 6 | 2 | 7/89 |
| T.M. Alderman | 12 | 3566 | 144 | 1605 | 83 | 19.33 | 10 | 1 | 6/128 |
| C.V. Grimmett | 13 | 5641 | 285 | 2007 | 67 | 29.95 | 7 | 1 | 6/167 |
| H. Trumble | 16 | 3487 | 229 | 1364 | 67 | 20.35 | 5 | 3 | 8/65 |
| G.F. Lawson | 15 | 3776 | 136 | 1906 | 63 | 30.25 | 3 | 0 | 7/81 |
| R.R. Lindwall | 14 | 3382 | 148 | 1258 | 60 | 20.96 | 5 | 0 | 6/20 |

. . . continued

## LEADING AUSTRALIAN BOWLERS IN TESTS IN ENGLAND (continued)

| Bowler | M | Balls | Mdns | Runs | Wkts | Avge | 5W | 10W | Best |
|---|---|---|---|---|---|---|---|---|---|
| G.D. McKenzie | 13 | 3894 | 174 | 1572 | 53 | 29.66 | 3 | 0 | 7/153 |
| **M.G. Hughes** | **12** | **2914** | **119** | **1460** | **50** | **29.20** | **1** | **0** | **5/92** |
| W.J. O'Reilly | 9 | 3580 | 206 | 1308 | 50 | 26.16 | 4 | 2 | 7/54 |
| K.R. Miller | 15 | 3176 | 159 | 1071 | 44 | 24.34 | 2 | 1 | 5/72 |
| J.R. Thomson | 11 | 2592 | 104 | 1315 | 42 | 31.31 | 1 | 0 | 5/38 |
| W.W. Armstrong | 15 | 3551 | 206 | 1166 | 40 | 29.15 | 3 | 0 | 6/35 |
| F.R. Spofforth | 7 | 1703 | 185 | 604 | 38 | 15.89 | 2 | 1 | 7/44 |
| C.T.B. Turner | 8 | 2067 | 184 | 735 | 38 | 19.34 | 5 | 1 | 6/67 |

## BOWLERS WITH 200 OR MORE FIRST-CLASS WICKETS FOR VICTORIA

| Bowler | M | Runs | Wkts | Avge | 5W | 10W | Best |
|---|---|---|---|---|---|---|---|
| A.N. Connolly | 83 | 8925 | 330 | 27.05 | 12 | 4 | 9/67 |
| H. Ironmonger | 61 | 6964 | 313 | 22.25 | 26 | 8 | 8/31 |
| A.I.C. Dodemaide | 102 | 9528 | 305 | 31.23 | 12 | 0 | 6/67 |
| L.O. Fleetwood-Smith | 51 | 7194 | 295 | 24.39 | 31 | 10 | 9/36 |
| **M.G. Hughes** | **83** | **8809** | **283** | **31.13** | **10** | **2** | **7/81** |
| R.J. Bright | 114 | 9902 | 279 | 35.49 | 11 | 0 | 6/61 |
| I.W. Johnson | 77 | 6560 | 270 | 24.30 | 14 | 3 | 6/27 |
| J.V. Saunders | 51 | 6475 | 264 | 24.53 | 24 | 4 | 8/106 |
| J.D. Higgs | 83 | 8091 | 264 | 30.65 | 13 | 2 | 8/66 |
| M.H.N. Walker | 70 | 6999 | 248 | 28.22 | 11 | 0 | 6/49 |
| W.W. Armstrong | 83 | 5586 | 248 | 22.52 | 7 | 0 | 6/66 |
| D.T. Ring | 67 | 7362 | 236 | 31.19 | 8 | 2 | 6/41 |
| H. Trumble | 47 | 4831 | 229 | 22.10 | 15 | 6 | 8/39 |
| P.R. Reiffel | 57 | 6012 | 203 | 29.61 | 6 | 2 | 6/57 |

## BOWLERS WITH 200 OR MORE SHEFFIELD SHIELD WICKETS FOR VICTORIA

| Bowler | M | Runs | Wkts | Avge | 5W | 10W | Best |
|---|---|---|---|---|---|---|---|
| A.N. Connolly | 71 | 7745 | 297 | 26.08 | 12 | 4 | 9/67 |
| A.I.C. Dodemaide | 92 | 8704 | 278 | 31.30 | 12 | 0 | 6/67 |
| **M.G. Hughes** | **76** | **8169** | **267** | **30.60** | **10** | **2** | **7/81** |
| R.J. Bright | 101 | 8821 | 252 | 35.00 | 10 | 0 | 6/61 |
| L.O. Fleetwood-Smith | 41 | 6034 | 246 | 24.53 | 25 | 8 | 9/135 |
| J.D. Higgs | 75 | 7202 | 240 | 30.01 | 12 | 2 | 8/66 |
| M.H.N. Walker | 62 | 6476 | 220 | 29.44 | 11 | 0 | 6/49 |
| H. Ironmonger | 44 | 5290 | 215 | 24.60 | 16 | 4 | 7/13 |

## 2. FIRST-CLASS CRICKET

### BOWLING – SEASON BY SEASON

| Season (Venue) | M | Balls | Mdns | Runs | Wkts | Avge | 5W | Best |
|---|---|---|---|---|---|---|---|---|
| 1981–82 (A) | 5 | 1156 | 37 | 567 | 18 | 31.50 | 0 | 4/69 |
| 1982–83 (A) | 4 | 955 | 20 | 603 | 11 | 54.81 | 0 | 2/68 |
| 1983 (Essex) | 1 | 188 | 2 | 162 | 6 | 27.00 | 0 | 4/71 |
| 1983–84 (A) | 4 | 654 | 22 | 407 | 5 | 81.40 | 0 | 2/77 |
| 1984–85 (A) | 5 | 986 | 38 | 466 | 11 | 42.36 | 0 | 3/63 |
| 1985–86 (A) | 11 | 2340 | 77 | 1125 | 37 | 30.40 | 0 | 5/53 |
| 1986–87 (A) | 15 | 3427 | 113 | 1623 | 57 | 28.47 | 3 | 5/61 |

## BOWLING – SEASON BY SEASON (continued)

| Season (Venue) | M | Balls | Mdns | Runs | Wkts | Avge | 5W | Best |
|---|---|---|---|---|---|---|---|---|
| 1987–88 (A) | 9 | 1919 | 74 | 930 | 32 | 29.06 | 1 | 5/67 |
| 1988–89 (A) | 13 | 2655 | 97 | 1330 | 41 | 32.43 | 4 | 8/87 |
| 1989 (Eng) | 15 | 2394 | 102 | 1242 | 47 | 26.42 | 3 | 5/37 |
| 1989–90 (A) | 10 | 2570 | 126 | 1129 | 42 | 26.88 | 2 | 5/88 |
| 1990–91 (A) | 10 | 2375 | 87 | 1055 | 48 | 21.97 | 1 | 6/54 |
| 1991 (WI) | 10 | 1829 | 54 | 1052 | 37 | 28.43 | 1 | 5/36 |
| 1991 (Eng) | 1 | 183 | 7 | 85 | 1 | 85.00 | 0 | 1/85 |
| 1991–92 (A) | 12 | 2971 | 120 | 1339 | 53 | 25.26 | 0 | 4/32 |
| 1992–93 (A) | 10 | 2084 | 77 | 954 | 43 | 22.18 | 2 | 6/83 |
| 1993 (NZ) | 4 | 1028 | 55 | 405 | 19 | 21.31 | 0 | 4/21 |
| 1993 (Eng) | 14 | 2822 | 113 | 1420 | 48 | 29.58 | 1 | 5/92 |
| 1993–94 (A) | 2 | 460 | 15 | 319 | 7 | 45.57 | 1 | 5/70 |
| 1994 (SAf) | 5 | 966 | 27 | 563 | 17 | 33.11 | 0 | 4/127 |
| 1994–95 (A) | 5 | 919 | 32 | 473 | 13 | 36.38 | 0 | 4/51 |
| **TOTAL** | **165** | **34881** | **1295** | **17249** | **593** | **29.08** | **21** | **8/87** |

## BOWLING – RECORD IN EACH INNINGS

| Innings | Balls | Mdns | Runs | Wkts | Avge | 5W | Best |
|---|---|---|---|---|---|---|---|
| First | 22241 | 812 | 11028 | 380 | 29.02 | 12 | 7/81 |
| Second | 12640 | 483 | 6221 | 213 | 29.20 | 9 | 8/87 |

## BOWLING – RECORD AGAINST EACH OPPONENT

| Opponent | M | Balls | Mdns | Runs | Wkts | Avge | 5W | Best |
|---|---|---|---|---|---|---|---|---|
| Board XI (WICBC) | 1 | 144 | 0 | 105 | 2 | 52.50 | 0 | 2/70 |
| Boland | 1 | 120 | 5 | 50 | 2 | 25.00 | 0 | 2/21 |
| England | 20 | 4586 | 183 | 2269 | 75 | 30.25 | 1 | 5/92 |
| England XI | 3 | 585 | 22 | 298 | 11 | 27.09 | 0 | 4/51 |
| Essex | 3 | 523 | 18 | 305 | 8 | 38.12 | 1 | 5/64 |
| Glamorgan | 2 | 210 | 8 | 132 | 3 | 44.00 | 0 | 2/67 |
| Gloucestershire | 2 | 186 | 7 | 86 | 5 | 17.20 | 0 | 4/27 |
| Hampshire | 1 | 192 | 5 | 107 | 5 | 21.40 | 0 | 3/60 |
| India | 6 | 1425 | 52 | 634 | 23 | 27.56 | 0 | 4/50 |
| Indians | 1 | 156 | 12 | 42 | 3 | 14.00 | 0 | 3/42 |
| Jamaica | 1 | 135 | 5 | 70 | 2 | 35.00 | 0 | 2/47 |
| Lancashire | 1 | 114 | 6 | 52 | 2 | 26.00 | 0 | 2/32 |
| Leicestershire | 2 | 240 | 8 | 106 | 1 | 106.00 | 0 | 1/18 |
| New South Wales | 16 | 3536 | 131 | 1697 | 58 | 29.25 | 3 | 6/36 |
| New Zealand | 5 | 1340 | 65 | 589 | 25 | 23.56 | 0 | 4/51 |
| New Zealand Board XI | 1 | 234 | 17 | 56 | 6 | 9.33 | 0 | 4/21 |
| New Zealanders | 1 | 188 | 2 | 162 | 6 | 27.00 | 0 | 4/71 |
| Northamptonshire | 1 | 114 | 4 | 60 | 6 | 10.00 | 1 | 5/37 |
| Northern Transvaal | 1 | 168 | 2 | 102 | 5 | 20.40 | 0 | 3/72 |
| Nottinghamshire | 1 | 174 | 12 | 73 | 6 | 12.16 | 1 | 5/38 |
| Orange Free State | 1 | 258 | 7 | 174 | 6 | 29.00 | 0 | 4/127 |
| Pakistan | 3 | 840 | 51 | 357 | 16 | 22.31 | 1 | 5/111 |
| President's XI (WICBC) | 1 | 191 | 3 | 116 | 9 | 12.88 | 1 | 5/36 |
| Queensland | 14 | 2833 | 75 | 1623 | 59 | 27.50 | 2 | 7/81 |
| Somerset | 2 | 342 | 16 | 165 | 5 | 33.00 | 0 | 2/26 |
| South Africa | 2 | 420 | 13 | 237 | 4 | 59.25 | 0 | 3/59 |
| South Australia | 17 | 3848 | 117 | 1972 | 47 | 41.95 | 0 | 4/32 |
| Sri Lanka | 3 | 788 | 31 | 407 | 16 | 25.43 | 2 | 5/67 |

. . . continued

## BOWLING – RECORD AGAINST EACH OPPONENT (continued)

| Opponent | M | Balls | Mdns | Runs | Wkts | Avge | 5W | Best |
|---|---|---|---|---|---|---|---|---|
| Sri Lankans | 1 | 276 | 6 | 139 | 2 | 69.50 | 0 | 1/56 |
| Sussex | 1 | 156 | 6 | 77 | 2 | 38.50 | 0 | 2/58 |
| Tasmania | 12 | 2738 | 112 | 1098 | 51 | 21.52 | 4 | 5/61 |
| Trinidad | 1 | 72 | 2 | 50 | 2 | 25.00 | 0 | 2/50 |
| Under 23 XI (WI) | 1 | 252 | 11 | 122 | 3 | 40.66 | 0 | 2/90 |
| Warwickshire | 1 | 144 | 8 | 70 | 2 | 35.00 | 0 | 2/62 |
| West Indians | 3 | 570 | 17 | 290 | 9 | 32.22 | 0 | 3/44 |
| West Indies | 14 | 2886 | 104 | 1524 | 53 | 28.75 | 3 | 8/87 |
| Western Australia | 17 | 3807 | 147 | 1779 | 52 | 34.21 | 1 | 6/54 |
| Worcestershire | 1 | 90 | 5 | 54 | 1 | 54.00 | 0 | 1/31 |
| **TOTAL** | **165** | **34881** | **1295** | **17249** | **593** | **29.08** | **21** | **8/87** |

## BOWLING – RECORD IN EACH COUNTRY

| Country | M | Balls | Mdns | Runs | Wkts | Avge | 5W | Best |
|---|---|---|---|---|---|---|---|---|
| Australia | 115 | 25471 | 935 | 12320 | 418 | 29.47 | 16 | 8/87 |
| England | 31 | 5587 | 224 | 2909 | 102 | 28.52 | 4 | 5/37 |
| New Zealand | 4 | 1028 | 55 | 405 | 19 | 21.31 | 0 | 4/21 |
| South Africa | 5 | 966 | 27 | 563 | 17 | 33.11 | 0 | 4/127 |
| West Indies | 10 | 1829 | 54 | 1052 | 37 | 28.43 | 1 | 5/36 |

## BOWLING – RECORD ON EACH GROUND

| Venue | M | Balls | Mdns | Runs | Wkts | Avge | 5W | Best |
|---|---|---|---|---|---|---|---|---|
| Adelaide | 16 | 3683 | 115 | 1945 | 49 | 39.69 | 2 | 5/64 |
| Ballarat | 1 | 263 | 10 | 104 | 4 | 26.00 | 0 | 2/42 |
| Brisbane | 14 | 2729 | 87 | 1516 | 55 | 27.56 | 0 | 5/70 |
| Carlton | 1 | 192 | 6 | 84 | 3 | 28.00 | 0 | 3/84 |
| Devonport | 2 | 480 | 21 | 169 | 16 | 10.56 | 2 | 5/53 |
| Geelong | 2 | 504 | 17 | 247 | 9 | 27.44 | 0 | 4/69 |
| Hobart | 5 | 1354 | 58 | 577 | 30 | 19.23 | 1 | 5/88 |
| Launceston | 2 | 301 | 11 | 145 | 2 | 72.50 | 0 | 1/47 |
| Melbourne | 33 | 7362 | 290 | 3478 | 95 | 36.61 | 3 | 6/36 |
| Newcastle | 1 | 294 | 8 | 164 | 6 | 27.33 | 1 | 5/74 |
| Perth | 15 | 3661 | 143 | 1710 | 70 | 24.42 | 4 | 8/87 |
| St Kilda | 11 | 2518 | 79 | 1162 | 49 | 23.71 | 1 | 7/81 |
| Sydney | 11 | 1956 | 87 | 913 | 28 | 32.60 | 1 | 6/83 |
| Wangaratta | 1 | 174 | 3 | 106 | 2 | 53.00 | 0 | 2/106 |
| Birmingham | 3 | 498 | 23 | 215 | 4 | 53.75 | 0 | 2/62 |
| Bristol | 2 | 186 | 7 | 86 | 5 | 17.20 | 0 | 4/27 |
| Chelmsford | 4 | 711 | 20 | 467 | 14 | 33.35 | 1 | 5/64 |
| Hove | 1 | 156 | 6 | 77 | 2 | 38.50 | 0 | 2/58 |
| Leeds | 2 | 499 | 22 | 254 | 10 | 25.40 | 0 | 3/36 |
| Leicester | 2 | 240 | 8 | 106 | 1 | 106.00 | 0 | 1/18 |
| Lord's | 2 | 588 | 28 | 242 | 10 | 24.20 | 0 | 4/52 |
| Manchester | 3 | 593 | 23 | 303 | 12 | 25.25 | 0 | 4/59 |
| Neath | 2 | 210 | 8 | 132 | 3 | 44.00 | 0 | 2/67 |
| Northampton | 1 | 114 | 4 | 60 | 6 | 10.00 | 1 | 5/37 |
| Nottingham | 3 | 614 | 28 | 292 | 17 | 17.17 | 2 | 5/38 |
| Southampton | 1 | 192 | 5 | 107 | 5 | 21.40 | 0 | 3/60 |
| Taunton | 2 | 342 | 16 | 165 | 5 | 33.00 | 0 | 2/26 |
| The Oval | 2 | 554 | 21 | 349 | 7 | 49.85 | 0 | 3/110 |
| Worcester | 1 | 90 | 5 | 54 | 1 | 54.00 | 0 | 1/31 |

## BOWLING – RECORD ON EACH GROUND (continued)

| Venue | M | Balls | Mdns | Runs | Wkts | Avge | 5W | Best |
|---|---|---|---|---|---|---|---|---|
| Auckland | 1 | 243 | 8 | 121 | 4 | 30.25 | 0 | 3/67 |
| Christchurch | 1 | 275 | 16 | 106 | 6 | 17.66 | 0 | 4/62 |
| New Plymouth | 1 | 234 | 17 | 56 | 6 | 9.33 | 0 | 4/21 |
| Wellington | 1 | 276 | 14 | 122 | 3 | 40.66 | 0 | 3/100 |
| Bloemfontein | 1 | 258 | 7 | 174 | 6 | 29.00 | 0 | 4/127 |
| Cape Town | 1 | 150 | 2 | 92 | 0 | – | 0 | 0/12 |
| Johannesburg | 1 | 270 | 11 | 145 | 4 | 36.25 | 0 | 3/59 |
| Stellenbosch | 1 | 120 | 5 | 50 | 2 | 25.00 | 0 | 2/21 |
| Verwoerdburg | 1 | 168 | 2 | 102 | 5 | 20.40 | 0 | 3/72 |
| Basseterre | 1 | 191 | 3 | 116 | 9 | 12.88 | 1 | 5/36 |
| Bridgetown | 2 | 457 | 8 | 274 | 7 | 39.14 | 0 | 4/44 |
| Georgetown | 1 | 143 | 4 | 112 | 0 | – | 0 | 0/19 |
| Kingston | 2 | 396 | 14 | 216 | 6 | 36.00 | 0 | 4/67 |
| Kingstown | 1 | 252 | 11 | 122 | 3 | 40.66 | 0 | 2/90 |
| Pointe-a-Pierre | 1 | 72 | 2 | 50 | 2 | 25.00 | 0 | 2/50 |
| Port-of-Spain | 1 | 102 | 5 | 48 | 4 | 12.00 | 0 | 4/48 |
| St John's | 1 | 216 | 7 | 114 | 6 | 19.00 | 0 | 4/65 |

## HUGHES DISMISSED THE FOLLOWING BATSMEN MOST OFTEN

| No. | Batsman |
|---|---|
| 11 | R.B. Richardson (WI). |
| 7 | A.M.J. Hilditch (S Aust), D.L. Haynes (WI), T.M. Moody (WA), D.B. Vengsarkar (Ind). |
| 6 | M.A. Atherton (Eng), D.C. Boon (Tas), C.L. Hooper (WI), D.M. Wellham (NSW/Tas/Qld), M.R.J. Veletta (WA). |
| 5 | G.A. Bishop (S Aust), A.R. Caddick (Eng), J. Cox (Tas), M.D. Crowe (NZ), P.J.L. Dujon (WI), G.A. Gooch (Eng/Essex), D.I. Gower (Eng/Hamp), S.V. Manjrekar (Ind), B.P. Patterson (WI), G.M. Ritchie (Qld), R.A. Smith (Eng/Hamp), M.A. Taylor (NSW), C.A. Walsh (WI), M.E. Waugh (NSW/Essex), G.M. Wood (WA). |
| 4 | C.E.L. Ambrose (WI), C.W.J. Athey (Eng), T.J. Barsby (Qld), A.R. Border (Qld), M.W. Gatting (Eng), M.J. Greatbatch (NZ), G.A. Hick (Qld/Eng), A.L. Logie (WI), C.J. McDermott (Qld), G.R. Marsh (WA), G.R.J. Matthews (NSW), S.M. Small (NSW), R.D. Woolley(Tas). |
| 3 | W.S. Andrews (WA), M.P. Bicknell (Eng), I.R. Bishop (WI), B.C. Broad (Eng), D.J. Buckingham (Tas), P.E. Cantrell (Qld), S.C. Clements (WA), B.A. Courtice (Qld), W.M. Darling (S Aust), P.A. Emery (NSW), C.G. Greendige (WI), I.A. Healy (Qld), Ijaz Ahmed (Pak), Kapil Dev (Ind), M.S. Kasprowicz (Qld), G.F. Labrooy (SL), M.N. Lathwell (Eng/Somerset), S.G. Law (Qld), M.J. McCague (Eng), K.H. MacLeay (WA), D.E. Malcolm (Eng), M.D. Marshall (WI), C.R. Miller (S Aust), D.N. Patel (NZ), W.B. Phillips (S Aust), A.Ranatunga (SL), J.R. Ratnayeke (SL), R.C.Russell (Eng), G. Shipperd (WA/Tas), Shoaib Mohammed (Pak), N.S. Sidhu (Ind), P.R. Sleep (S Aust), G.C. Small (Eng), A.J. Stewart (Eng), G.S. Trimble (Qld), P.C.R. Tufnell (Eng), S.R. Waugh (NSW), K.C. Wessels (Qld/SAf), T.J. Zoehrer (WA). |

## HOW HUGHES TOOK HIS WICKETS

| Mode of Dismissal | No. | Percentage |
|---|---|---|
| Caught | 262 | 44.18% |
| Bowled | 138 | 23.27% |
| Caught by wicket-keeper | 109 | 18.38% |
| Leg before wicket | 74 | 12.48% |
| Caught and bowled | 8 | 1.35% |
| Hit wicket | 2 | 0.34% |

## FIVE WICKETS IN AN INNINGS

| Bowling | For | Opponent | Venue | Season |
|---|---|---|---|---|
| 5/74 | Victoria | New South Wales | Newcastle | 1985–86 |
| 5/53 | Victoria | Tasmania | Devonport | 1985–86 |
| 5/73 | Victoria | Tasmania | Devonport | 1986–87 |
| 5/61 | Victoria | Tasmania | Melbourne | 1986–87 |
| 5/73 | Victoria | Tasmania | Melbourne | 1986–87 |
| 5/67 | AUSTRALIA | SRI LANKA | Perth | 1987–88 |
| 7/81 | Victoria | Queensland | St Kilda | 1988–89 |
| 5/130 | AUSTRALIA | WEST INDIES | Perth | 1988–89 |
| 8/87 | AUSTRALIA | WEST INDIES | Perth | 1988–89 |
| 6/36 | Victoria | New South Wales | Melbourne | 1988–89 |
| 5/37 | Australians | Northamptonshire | Northampton | 1989 |
| 5/38 | Australians | Nottinghamshire | Nottingham | 1989 |
| 5/64 | Australians | Essex | Chelmsford | 1989 |
| 5/88 | AUSTRALIA | SRI LANKA | Hobart | 1989–90 |
| 5/111 | AUSTRALIA | PAKISTAN | Adelaide | 1989–90 |
| 5/64 | Victoria | Western Australia | Perth | 1990–91 |
| 5/36 | Australians | President's XI | St Kitts | 1991 |
| 6/83 | Victoria | New South Wales | Sydney | 1992–93 |
| 5/64 | AUSTRALIA | WEST INDIES | Adelaide | 1992–93 |
| 5/92 | AUSTRALIA | ENGLAND | Nottingham | 1993 |
| 5/70 | Victoria | Queensland | Brisbane | 1993–94 |

## TEN WICKETS IN A MATCH

| Bowling | For | Opponent | Venue | Season |
|---|---|---|---|---|
| 10/134 | Victoria | Tasmania | Melbourne | 1986–87 |
| 10/121 | Victoria | Queensland | St Kilda | 1988–89 |
| 13/217 | AUSTRALIA | WEST INDIES | Perth | 1988–89 |

## BATTING AND FIELDING – SEASON BY SEASON

| Season (Venue) | M | Inn | NO | Runs | HS | Avge | 50s | 0s | Ct |
|---|---|---|---|---|---|---|---|---|---|
| 1981–82 (A) | 5 | 6 | 2 | 24 | 17 | 6.00 | 0 | 1 | 1 |
| 1982–83 (A) | 4 | 4 | 3 | 14 | 14* | 14.00 | 0 | 1 | 1 |
| 1983 (Essex) | 1 | 2 | 0 | 10 | 10 | 5.00 | 0 | 1 | 0 |
| 1983–84 (A) | 4 | 3 | 0 | 28 | 15 | 9.33 | 0 | 0 | 2 |
| 1984–85 | 5 | 4 | 2 | 33 | 13 | 16.50 | 0 | 0 | 1 |
| 1985–86 (A) | 11 | 11 | 1 | 120 | 47 | 12.00 | 0 | 3 | 1 |
| 1986–87 (A) | 15 | 18 | 3 | 170 | 33* | 11.33 | 0 | 4 | 8 |
| 1987–88 (A) | 9 | 10 | 0 | 95 | 24 | 9.50 | 0 | 2 | 2 |
| 1988–89 (A) | 13 | 17 | 5 | 272 | 72* | 22.66 | 1 | 1 | 7 |
| 1989 (Eng) | 15 | 16 | 4 | 246 | 71 | 20.50 | 1 | 1 | 1 |
| 1989–90 (A) | 10 | 14 | 6 | 291 | 60* | 36.37 | 1 | 0 | 3 |
| 1990–91 (A) | 10 | 14 | 3 | 213 | 64* | 19.36 | 1 | 2 | 5 |
| 1991 (WI) | 10 | 13 | 1 | 77 | 21 | 6.41 | 0 | 3 | 5 |
| 1991 (Eng) | 1 | 2 | 2 | 72 | 60* | – | 1 | 0 | 0 |
| 1991–92 (A) | 12 | 15 | 1 | 231 | 36 | 16.50 | 0 | 2 | 5 |
| 1992–93 (A) | 10 | 15 | 4 | 166 | 43 | 15.09 | 0 | 1 | 6 |
| 1993 (NZ) | 4 | 5 | 1 | 127 | 45 | 31.75 | 0 | 0 | 1 |
| 1993 (Eng) | 14 | 12 | 3 | 299 | 71 | 33.22 | 2 | 1 | 3 |
| 1993–94 (A) | 2 | 3 | 0 | 10 | 8 | 3.33 | 0 | 1 | 0 |
| 1994 (SAf) | 5 | 5 | 1 | 71 | 30 | 17.75 | 0 | 1 | 1 |
| 1994–95 (A) | 5 | 7 | 3 | 80 | 38* | 20.00 | 0 | 1 | 3 |
| **TOTAL** | **165** | **196** | **45** | **2649** | **72*** | **17.54** | **7** | **26** | **56** |

## BATTING AND FIELDING – RECORD IN EACH INNINGS

| Innings | Inn | NO | Runs | HS | Avge | 50s | 0s | Ct |
|---|---|---|---|---|---|---|---|---|
| First | 134 | 21 | 1807 | 72* | 15.99 | 4 | 18 | 32 |
| Second | 62 | 24 | 842 | 71 | 22.15 | 3 | 8 | 24 |

## BATTING AND FIELDING – RECORD AGAINST EACH OPPONENT

| Opponent | M | Inn | NO | Runs | HS | Avge | 50s | 0s | Ct |
|---|---|---|---|---|---|---|---|---|---|
| Board XI (WICBC) | 1 | 1 | 0 | 8 | 8 | 8.00 | 0 | 0 | 2 |
| Boland | 1 | – | – | – | – | – | 0 | 0 | 0 |
| England | 20 | 21 | 0 | 278 | 71 | 13.23 | 1 | 3 | 5 |
| England XI | 3 | 4 | 2 | 137 | 64* | 68.50 | 1 | 0 | 2 |
| Essex | 3 | 4 | 2 | 78 | 60* | 39.00 | 1 | 1 | 1 |
| Glamorgan | 2 | 1 | 0 | 71 | 71 | 71.00 | 1 | 0 | 0 |
| Gloucestershire | 2 | 2 | 1 | 60 | 46* | 60.00 | 0 | 0 | 0 |
| Hampshire | 1 | 1 | 1 | 61 | 61* | – | 1 | 0 | 1 |
| India | 6 | 9 | 0 | 154 | 36 | 17.11 | 0 | 1 | 5 |
| Indians | 1 | 1 | 0 | 23 | 23 | 23.00 | 0 | 0 | 0 |
| Jamaica | 1 | 1 | 0 | 3 | 3 | 3.00 | 0 | 0 | 0 |
| Lancashire | 1 | 1 | 0 | 4 | 4 | 4.00 | 0 | 0 | 0 |
| Leicestershire | 2 | 2 | 1 | 12 | 7 | 12.00 | 0 | 0 | 0 |
| New South Wales | 16 | 18 | 2 | 141 | 23 | 8.81 | 0 | 2 | 6 |
| New Zealand | 5 | 6 | 1 | 138 | 45 | 27.60 | 0 | 0 | 0 |
| New Zealand Board XI | 1 | 1 | 0 | 10 | 10 | 10.00 | 0 | 0 | 1 |
| New Zealanders | 1 | 2 | 0 | 10 | 10 | 5.00 | 0 | 1 | 0 |
| Northamptonshire | 1 | 2 | 1 | 24 | 12* | 24.00 | 0 | 0 | 1 |
| Northern Transvaal | 1 | 1 | 0 | 30 | 30 | 30.00 | 0 | 0 | 0 |
| Nottinghamshire | 1 | 1 | 0 | 0 | 0 | 0.00 | 0 | 1 | 0 |
| Orange Free State | 1 | 1 | 0 | 8 | 8 | 8.00 | 0 | 0 | 0 |
| Pakistan | 3 | 4 | 2 | 48 | 32 | 24.00 | 0 | 0 | 1 |
| President's XI (WICBC) | 1 | 2 | 1 | 16 | 10* | 16.00 | 0 | 0 | 0 |
| Queensland | 14 | 21 | 9 | 158 | 38* | 13.16 | 0 | 1 | 5 |
| Somerset | 2 | 3 | 2 | 72 | 36 | 72.00 | 0 | 0 | 1 |
| South Africa | 2 | 3 | 1 | 33 | 26* | 16.50 | 0 | 1 | 1 |
| South Australia | 17 | 22 | 7 | 311 | 60* | 20.73 | 1 | 4 | 4 |
| Sri Lanka | 3 | 5 | 1 | 113 | 30 | 28.25 | 0 | 0 | 1 |
| Sri Lankans | 1 | 2 | 0 | 15 | 15 | 7.50 | 0 | 1 | 0 |
| Sussex | 1 | – | – | – | – | – | 0 | 0 | 0 |
| Tasmania | 12 | 8 | 1 | 146 | 47 | 20.85 | 0 | 1 | 3 |
| Trinidad | 1 | – | – | – | – | – | 0 | 0 | 0 |
| Under 23 XI (WI) | 1 | 1 | 0 | 9 | 9 | 9.00 | 0 | 0 | 1 |
| Warwickshire | 1 | 1 | 1 | 27 | 27* | – | 0 | 0 | 0 |
| West Indians | 3 | 2 | 0 | 38 | 24 | 19.00 | 0 | 0 | 2 |
| West Indies | 14 | 22 | 3 | 268 | 72* | 14.10 | 1 | 5 | 10 |
| Western Australia | 17 | 18 | 6 | 140 | 33* | 11.66 | 0 | 4 | 3 |
| Worcestershire | 1 | 2 | 0 | 5 | 3 | 2.50 | 0 | 0 | 0 |

## BATTING AND FIELDING – RECORD IN EACH COUNTRY

| Country | M | Inn | NO | Runs | HS | Avge | 50s | 0s | Ct |
|---|---|---|---|---|---|---|---|---|---|
| Australia | 115 | 141 | 33 | 1747 | 72* | 16.17 | 3 | 19 | 45 |
| England | 31 | 32 | 9 | 627 | 71 | 27.26 | 4 | 3 | 4 |
| New Zealand | 4 | 5 | 1 | 127 | 45 | 31.75 | 0 | 0 | 1 |
| South Africa | 5 | 5 | 1 | 71 | 30 | 17.75 | 0 | 1 | 1 |
| West Indies | 10 | 13 | 1 | 77 | 21 | 6.41 | 0 | 3 | 5 |

## BATTING AND FIELDING – RECORD ON EACH GROUND

| Venue | M | Inn | NO | Runs | HS | Avge | 50s | 0s | Ct |
|---|---|---|---|---|---|---|---|---|---|
| Adelaide | 16 | 22 | 6 | 434 | 72* | 27.12 | 2 | 2 | 7 |
| Ballarat | 1 | 2 | 2 | 100 | 64* | – | 1 | 0 | 1 |
| Brisbane | 14 | 21 | 6 | 183 | 38* | 12.20 | 0 | 2 | 8 |
| Carlton | 1 | 1 | 0 | 13 | 13 | 13.00 | 0 | 0 | 0 |
| Devonport | 2 | – | – | – | – | – | 0 | 0 | 1 |
| Geelong | 2 | 1 | 1 | 1 | 1* | – | 0 | 0 | 1 |
| Hobart | 5 | 5 | 0 | 118 | 47 | 23.60 | 0 | 1 | 1 |
| Launceston | 2 | 2 | 0 | 25 | 24 | 12.50 | 0 | 0 | 0 |
| Melbourne | 33 | 37 | 4 | 425 | 36 | 12.87 | 0 | 5 | 11 |
| Newcastle | 1 | 2 | 0 | 8 | 8 | 4.00 | 0 | 1 | 0 |
| Perth | 15 | 20 | 5 | 171 | 33* | 11.40 | 0 | 6 | 2 |
| St Kilda | 11 | 15 | 7 | 133 | 22* | 16.62 | 0 | 1 | 6 |
| Sydney | 11 | 11 | 1 | 99 | 21 | 9.90 | 0 | 1 | 7 |
| Wangaratta | 1 | 2 | 1 | 37 | 25 | 37.00 | 0 | 0 | 0 |
| Birmingham | 3 | 3 | 1 | 67 | 38 | 33.50 | 0 | 0 | 0 |
| Bristol | 2 | 2 | 1 | 60 | 46* | 60.00 | 0 | 0 | 0 |
| Chelmsford | 4 | 6 | 2 | 88 | 60* | 22.00 | 1 | 2 | 1 |
| Hove | 1 | – | – | – | – | – | 0 | 0 | 0 |
| Leeds | 2 | 1 | 0 | 71 | 71 | 71.00 | 1 | 0 | 0 |
| Leicester | 2 | 2 | 1 | 12 | 7 | 12.00 | 0 | 0 | 0 |
| Lord's | 2 | 1 | 0 | 30 | 30 | 30.00 | 0 | 0 | 0 |
| Manchester | 3 | 3 | 0 | 9 | 4 | 3.00 | 0 | 0 | 0 |
| Neath | 2 | 1 | 0 | 71 | 71 | 71.00 | 1 | 0 | 0 |
| Northampton | 1 | 2 | 1 | 24 | 12* | 24.00 | 0 | 0 | 1 |
| Nottingham | 3 | 2 | 0 | 17 | 17 | 8.50 | 0 | 1 | 0 |
| Southampton | 1 | 1 | 1 | 61 | 61* | – | 1 | 0 | 1 |
| Taunton | 2 | 3 | 2 | 72 | 36 | 72.00 | 0 | 0 | 1 |
| The Oval | 2 | 3 | 0 | 40 | 21 | 13.33 | 0 | 0 | 0 |
| Worcester | 1 | 2 | 0 | 5 | 3 | 2.50 | 0 | 0 | 0 |
| Auckland | 1 | 2 | 1 | 64 | 33 | 64.00 | 0 | 0 | 0 |
| Christchurch | 1 | 1 | 0 | 45 | 45 | 45.00 | 0 | 0 | 0 |
| New Plymouth | 1 | 1 | 0 | 10 | 10 | 10.00 | 0 | 0 | 1 |
| Wellington | 1 | 1 | 0 | 8 | 8 | 8.00 | 0 | 0 | 0 |
| Bloemfontein | 1 | 1 | 0 | 8 | 8 | 8.00 | 0 | 0 | 0 |
| Cape Town | 1 | 1 | 0 | 0 | 0 | 0.00 | 0 | 1 | 0 |
| Johannesburg | 1 | 2 | 1 | 33 | 26* | 33.00 | 0 | 0 | 1 |
| Stellenbosch | 1 | – | – | – | – | – | 0 | 0 | 0 |
| Verwoerdburg | 1 | 1 | 0 | 30 | 30 | 30.00 | 0 | 0 | 0 |
| Basseterre | 1 | 2 | 1 | 16 | 10* | 16.00 | 0 | 0 | 0 |
| Bridgetown | 2 | 3 | 0 | 14 | 8 | 4.66 | 0 | 0 | 3 |
| Georgetown | 1 | 2 | 0 | 21 | 21 | 10.50 | 0 | 1 | 0 |
| Kingston | 2 | 2 | 0 | 3 | 3 | 1.50 | 0 | 1 | 1 |
| Kingstown | 1 | 1 | 0 | 9 | 9 | 9.00 | 0 | 0 | 1 |
| Pointe-a-Pierre | 1 | – | – | – | – | – | 0 | 0 | 0 |
| Port-of-Spain | 1 | 1 | 0 | 0 | 0 | 0.00 | 0 | 1 | 0 |
| St John's | 1 | 2 | 0 | 14 | 13 | 7.00 | 0 | 0 | 0 |

## THE FOLLOWING BOWLERS CAPTURED HUGHES' WICKET MOST OFTEN

| No. | Bowler |
|---|---|
| 8 | C.E.L. Ambrose (WI). |
| 4 | Kapil Dev (Ind), G.F. Lawson (NSW), T.B.A. May (S Aust), B.P. Patterson (WI), C.A. Walsh (WI), A.K. Zesers (S Aust). |
| 3 | N.A. Foster (Eng), A.R.C. Fraser (Eng), C.D.Matthews (WA), J. Srinath (Ind). |

## THE FOLLOWING BOWLERS CAPTURED HUGHES' WICKET MOST OFTEN (cont.)

| No. | Bowler |
|---|---|
| 2 | I.T. Botham (Eng), N.G.B. Cook (Eng/Nort), E.A.R. de Silva (SL), P.H. Edmonds (Eng), W.J. Holdsworth (NSW), R.G. Holland (NSW), C.L. Hooper (WI), C.J. McDermott (Qld), J.N. Maguire (Qld), T.M. Moody (WA), D.K. Morrison (NZ), D.N. Patel (NZ), D.R. Pringle (Eng/Essex), N.V. Radford (Worc), D. Tazelaar (Qld), Wasim Akram (Pak), M.R. Whitney (NSW). |

## HOW HUGHES WAS DISMISSED

| Mode of Dismissal | No. | Percentage |
|---|---|---|
| Caught | 67 | 44.37% |
| Bowled | 36 | 23.84% |
| Caught by wicket-keeper | 24 | 15.90% |
| Leg before wicket | 13 | 8.61% |
| Caught and bowled | 5 | 3.31% |
| Run Out | 5 | 3.31% |
| Stumped | 1 | 0.66% |

## 3. TEST CRICKET

### BOWLING — SERIES BY SERIES

| Series (Opponent) | M | Balls | Mdns | Runs | Wkts | Avge | 5W | Best |
|---|---|---|---|---|---|---|---|---|
| 1985–86 (Ind) | 1 | 228 | 6 | 123 | 1 | 123.00 | 0 | 1/123 |
| 1986–87 (Eng) | 4 | 819 | 26 | 444 | 10 | 44.40 | 0 | 3/134 |
| 1987–88 (NZ) | 1 | 210 | 12 | 97 | 5 | 19.40 | 0 | 3/40 |
| 1987–88 (SL) | 1 | 234 | 9 | 128 | 5 | 25.60 | 1 | 5/67 |
| 1988–89 (WI) | 4 | 979 | 41 | 503 | 14 | 35.92 | 2 | 8/87 |
| 1989 (Eng) | 6 | 1136 | 41 | 615 | 19 | 32.36 | 0 | 4/71 |
| 1989–90 (NZ) | 1 | 336 | 15 | 143 | 7 | 20.42 | 0 | 4/51 |
| 1989–90 (SL) | 2 | 554 | 22 | 279 | 11 | 25.36 | 1 | 5/88 |
| 1989–90 (Pak) | 3 | 840 | 51 | 357 | 16 | 22.31 | 1 | 5/111 |
| 1990–91 (Eng) | 4 | 853 | 38 | 365 | 15 | 24.33 | 0 | 4/37 |
| 1991 (WI) | 5 | 1035 | 33 | 589 | 19 | 31.00 | 0 | 4/44 |
| 1991–92 (Ind) | 5 | 1197 | 46 | 511 | 22 | 23.22 | 0 | 4/50 |
| 1992–93 (WI) | 5 | 872 | 30 | 432 | 20 | 21.60 | 1 | 5/64 |
| 1993 (NZ) | 3 | 794 | 38 | 349 | 13 | 26.84 | 0 | 4/62 |
| 1993 (Eng) | 6 | 1778 | 78 | 845 | 31 | 27.25 | 1 | 5/92 |
| 1994 (SA) | 2 | 420 | 13 | 237 | 4 | 59.25 | 0 | 3/59 |
| **TOTAL** | **53** | **12285** | **499** | **6017** | **212** | **28.38** | **7** | **8/87** |

### BOWLING — RECORD IN EACH INNINGS

| Innings | Balls | Mdns | Runs | Wkts | Avge | 5W | Best |
|---|---|---|---|---|---|---|---|
| First | 7174 | 268 | 3678 | 130 | 28.29 | 3 | 5/64 |
| Second | 5111 | 231 | 2339 | 82 | 28.52 | 4 | 8/87 |

## BOWLING – RECORD AGAINST EACH COUNTRY

| Country | M | Balls | Mdns | Runs | Wkts | Avge | 5W | Best |
|---|---|---|---|---|---|---|---|---|
| England | 20 | 4586 | 183 | 2269 | 75 | 30.25 | 1 | 5/92 |
| India | 6 | 1425 | 52 | 634 | 23 | 27.56 | 0 | 4/50 |
| New Zealand | 5 | 1340 | 65 | 589 | 25 | 23.56 | 0 | 4/51 |
| Pakistan | 3 | 840 | 51 | 357 | 16 | 22.31 | 1 | 5/111 |
| South Africa | 2 | 420 | 13 | 237 | 4 | 59.25 | 0 | 3/59 |
| Sri Lanka | 3 | 788 | 31 | 407 | 16 | 25.43 | 2 | 5/67 |
| West Indies | 14 | 2886 | 104 | 1524 | 53 | 28.75 | 3 | 8/87 |
| **v England** | | | | | | | | |
| In England | 12 | 2914 | 119 | 1460 | 50 | 29.20 | 1 | 5/92 |
| In Australia | 8 | 1672 | 64 | 809 | 25 | 32.36 | 0 | 4/37 |
| **v New Zealand** | | | | | | | | |
| In New Zealand | 3 | 794 | 38 | 349 | 13 | 26.84 | 0 | 4/62 |
| In Australia | 2 | 546 | 27 | 240 | 12 | 20.00 | 0 | 4/51 |
| **v West Indies** | | | | | | | | |
| In West Indies | 5 | 1035 | 33 | 589 | 19 | 31.00 | 0 | 4/44 |
| In Australia | 9 | 1851 | 71 | 935 | 34 | 27.50 | 3 | 8/87 |

## BOWLING – RECORD IN EACH COUNTRY

| Country | M | Balls | Mdns | Runs | Wkts | Avge | 5W | Best |
|---|---|---|---|---|---|---|---|---|
| Australia | 31 | 7122 | 296 | 3382 | 126 | 26.84 | 6 | 8/87 |
| England | 12 | 2914 | 119 | 1460 | 50 | 29.20 | 1 | 5/92 |
| New Zealand | 3 | 794 | 38 | 349 | 13 | 26.84 | 0 | 4/62 |
| South Africa | 2 | 420 | 13 | 237 | 4 | 59.25 | 0 | 3/59 |
| West Indies | 5 | 1035 | 33 | 589 | 19 | 31.00 | 0 | 4/44 |

## BOWLING – RECORD ON EACH GROUND

| Venue | M | Balls | Mdns | Runs | Wkts | Avge | 5W | Best |
|---|---|---|---|---|---|---|---|---|
| Adelaide | 7 | 1563 | 56 | 843 | 24 | 35.12 | 2 | 5/64 |
| Brisbane | 6 | 1285 | 53 | 608 | 28 | 21.71 | 0 | 4/50 |
| Hobart | 1 | 320 | 14 | 156 | 8 | 19.50 | 1 | 5/88 |
| Melbourne | 6 | 1464 | 70 | 626 | 15 | 41.73 | 0 | 3/34 |
| Perth | 6 | 1618 | 63 | 752 | 39 | 19.28 | 3 | 8/87 |
| Sydney | 5 | 872 | 40 | 397 | 12 | 33.08 | 0 | 3/70 |
| Birmingham | 2 | 354 | 15 | 145 | 2 | 72.50 | 0 | 2/68 |
| Leeds | 2 | 499 | 22 | 254 | 10 | 25.40 | 0 | 3/36 |
| Lord's | 2 | 588 | 28 | 242 | 10 | 24.20 | 0 | 4/52 |
| Manchester | 2 | 479 | 17 | 251 | 10 | 25.10 | 0 | 4/59 |
| Nottingham | 2 | 440 | 16 | 219 | 11 | 19.90 | 1 | 5/92 |
| The Oval | 2 | 554 | 21 | 349 | 7 | 49.85 | 0 | 3/110 |
| Auckland | 1 | 243 | 8 | 121 | 4 | 30.25 | 0 | 3/67 |
| Christchurch | 1 | 275 | 16 | 106 | 6 | 17.66 | 0 | 4/62 |
| Wellington | 1 | 276 | 14 | 122 | 3 | 40.66 | 0 | 3/100 |
| Cape Town | 1 | 150 | 2 | 92 | 0 | – | 0 | 0/12 |
| Johannesburg | 1 | 270 | 11 | 145 | 4 | 36.25 | 0 | 3/59 |
| Bridgetown | 1 | 313 | 8 | 169 | 5 | 33.80 | 0 | 4/44 |
| Georgetown | 1 | 143 | 4 | 112 | 0 | – | 0 | 0/19 |
| Kingston | 1 | 261 | 9 | 146 | 4 | 36.50 | 0 | 4/67 |
| Port-of-Spain | 1 | 102 | 5 | 48 | 4 | 12.00 | 0 | 4/48 |
| St John's | 1 | 216 | 7 | 114 | 6 | 19.00 | 0 | 4/65 |

## HUGHES DISMISSED THE FOLLOWING BATSMEN:

| No. | Batsman |
|---|---|
| 9 | R.B. Richardson (WI) |
| 6 | D.L. Haynes (WI), C.L. Hooper (WI), D.B. Vengsarkar (Ind) |
| 5 | A.R. Caddick (Eng), S.V. Manjrekar (Ind), C.A. Walsh (WI) |
| 4 | C.E.L. Ambrose (WI), M.A. Atherton (Eng), M.D. Crowe (NZ), P.J.L. Dujon (WI), M.W. Gatting (Eng), G.A. Gooch (Eng), M.J. Greatbatch (NZ), B.P. Patterson (WI), R.A. Smith (Eng) |
| 3 | C.W.J. Athey (Eng), B.C. Broad (Eng), D.I. Gower (Eng), C.G. Greenidge (WI), G.A. Hick (Eng), Ijaz Ahmed (Pak), Kapil Dev (Ind), G.F. Labrooy (SL), D.E. Malcolm (Eng), D.N. Patel (NZ), Shoaib Mohammed (Pak), N.S. Sidhu (Ind), G.C. Small (Eng), A.J. Stewart (Eng), P.C.R. Tufnell (Eng) |
| 2 | M.P. Bicknell (Eng), C.L. Cairns (NZ), Javed Miandad (Pak), A.J. Lamb (Eng), M.N. Lathwell (Eng), C.C. Lewis (Eng), A.L. Logie (WI), M.J. McCague (Eng), M.D. Marshall (WI), K.S. More (Ind), Rameez Raja (Pak), M.R. Ramprakash (Eng), A.Ranatunga (SL), R.J. Ratnayake (SL), J.R. Ratnayeke (SL), I.V.A. Richards (WI), R.C. Russell (Eng), Saleem Yousuf (Pak), I.D.S. Smith (NZ), P.M. Such (Eng), J.G. Wright (NZ) |
| 1 | Aamer Malik (Pak), J.C. Adams (WI), M. Azharuddin (Ind), K.J. Barnett (Eng), I.R. Bishop (WI), T.E. Blain (NZ), I.T. Botham (Eng), N.G.B. Cook (Eng), W.J. Cronje (SA), J.J. Crowe (NZ), A.C. Cummins (WI), T.S. Curtis (Eng), R.G. de Alwis (SL), P.A.J. DeFreitas (Eng), G.R. Dilley (Eng), J.E. Emburey (Eng), N.A. Foster (Eng), A.P. Gurusinha (SL), R.J. Hadlee (NZ), E.E. Hemmings (Eng), N. Hussain (Eng), P.W. Jarvis (Eng), A.H. Jones (NZ), S.M.S. Kaluperuma (SL), G Kirsten (SA), B.C. Lara (WI), W. Larkins (Eng), R.S. Madugalle (SL), C.R. Matthews (SA), M.P. Maynard (Eng), D.K. Morrison (NZ), J.R. Murray (WI), M. Prabhakar (Ind), C.P.H. Ramanayake (SL), D. Ranatunga (SL), K.R. Rutherford (NZ), Salim Malik (Pak), P.V. Simmons (WI), K. Srikkanth (Ind), M.L. Su'a (NZ), G.P. Thorpe (Eng), S.L. Venkatapathy Raju (Ind), Waqar Younis (Pak), Wasim Akram (Pak), W. Watson (NZ), K.C. Wessels (SA), A.D.G. Wickremasinghe (SL) |

## HOW HUGHES TOOK HIS WICKETS

| Mode of Dismissal | No. | Percentage |
|---|---|---|
| Caught in the field | 100 | 47.17% |
| Caught wicket-keeper | 52 | 24.53% |
| Leg Before Wicket | 32 | 14.62% |
| Bowled | 23 | 11.32% |
| Caught and Bowled | 5 | 2.36% |

*The most catches taken off Hughes' bowling were by wicket-keeper I.A. Healy, with 46. The most catches taken off Hughes' bowling by a fieldsman other than Healy were 16 by D.C. Boon (then M.E. Waugh 12, M.A. Taylor 11, S.R. Waugh 11, A.R. Border 10)*

## BATTING AND FIELDING – SERIES BY SERIES

| Series (Opponent) | M | Inn | NO | Runs | HS | Avge | 50s | 0s | Ct |
|---|---|---|---|---|---|---|---|---|---|
| 1985–86 (India) | 1 | 1 | 0 | 0 | 0 | 0.00 | 0 | 1 | 1 |
| 1986–87 (Eng) | 4 | 6 | 0 | 31 | 16 | 5.16 | 0 | 2 | 2 |
| 1987–88 (NZ) | 1 | 1 | 0 | 5 | 5 | 5.00 | 0 | 0 | 0 |
| 1987–88 (SL) | 1 | 1 | 0 | 8 | 8 | 8.00 | 0 | 0 | 1 |
| 1988–89 (WI) | 4 | 5 | 2 | 109 | 72* | 36.33 | 1 | 1 | 3 |
| 1989 (Eng) | 6 | 5 | 0 | 127 | 71 | 25.40 | 1 | 0 | 0 |
| 1989–90 (NZ) | 1 | 1 | 0 | 16 | 16 | 16.00 | 0 | 0 | 0 |
| 1989–90 (SL) | 2 | 4 | 1 | 105 | 30 | 35.00 | 0 | 0 | 0 |
| 1989–90 (Pak) | 3 | 4 | 2 | 48 | 32 | 24.00 | 0 | 0 | 1 |
| 1990–91 (Eng) | 4 | 5 | 0 | 44 | 30 | 8.80 | 0 | 1 | 3 |
| 1991 (WI) | 5 | 8 | 0 | 41 | 21 | 5.12 | 0 | 3 | 2 |

. . . continued

## BATTING AND FIELDING – SERIES BY SERIES (continued)

| Series (Opponent) | M | Inn | NO | Runs | HS | Avge | 50s | 0s | Ct |
|---|---|---|---|---|---|---|---|---|---|
| 1991–92 (Ind) | 5 | 8 | 0 | 154 | 36 | 19.25 | 0 | 0 | 4 |
| 1992–93 (WI) | 5 | 9 | 1 | 118 | 43 | 14.75 | 0 | 1 | 5 |
| 1993 (NZ) | 3 | 4 | 1 | 117 | 45 | 39.00 | 0 | 0 | 0 |
| 1993 (Eng) | 6 | 5 | 0 | 76 | 38 | 15.20 | 0 | 0 | 0 |
| 1994 (SA) | 2 | 3 | 1 | 33 | 26* | 16.50 | 0 | 1 | 1 |
| **TOTAL** | **53** | **70** | **8** | **1032** | **72*** | **16.64** | **2** | **10** | **23** |

## BATTING AND FIELDING – RECORD IN EACH INNINGS

| Innings | Inn | NO | Runs | HS | Avge | 50s | 0s | Ct |
|---|---|---|---|---|---|---|---|---|
| First | 47 | 4 | 698 | 72* | 16.23 | 2 | 8 | 16 |
| Second | 23 | 4 | 334 | 32 | 17.58 | 0 | 2 | 7 |

## BATTING AND FIELDING – RECORD AGAINST EACH COUNTRY

| Opponent | M | Inn | NO | Runs | HS | Avge | 50s | 0s | Ct |
|---|---|---|---|---|---|---|---|---|---|
| England | 20 | 21 | 0 | 278 | 71 | 13.23 | 1 | 3 | 5 |
| India | 6 | 9 | 0 | 154 | 36 | 17.11 | 0 | 1 | 5 |
| New Zealand | 5 | 6 | 1 | 138 | 45 | 27.60 | 0 | 0 | 0 |
| Pakistan | 3 | 4 | 2 | 48 | 32 | 24.00 | 0 | 0 | 1 |
| South Africa | 2 | 3 | 1 | 33 | 26* | 16.50 | 0 | 1 | 1 |
| Sri Lanka | 3 | 5 | 1 | 113 | 30 | 28.25 | 0 | 0 | 1 |
| West Indies | 14 | 22 | 3 | 268 | 72* | 14.10 | 1 | 5 | 10 |

## BATTING AND FIELDING – RECORD IN EACH COUNTRY

| Country | M | Inn | NO | Runs | HS | Avge | 50s | 0s | Ct |
|---|---|---|---|---|---|---|---|---|---|
| Australia | 31 | 45 | 6 | 638 | 72* | 16.35 | 1 | 6 | 20 |
| England | 12 | 10 | 0 | 203 | 71 | 20.30 | 1 | 0 | 0 |
| New Zealand | 3 | 4 | 1 | 117 | 45 | 39.00 | 0 | 0 | 0 |
| South Africa | 2 | 3 | 1 | 33 | 26* | 16.50 | 0 | 1 | 1 |
| West Indies | 5 | 8 | 0 | 41 | 21 | 5.12 | 0 | 3 | 2 |

## BATTING AND FIELDING – RECORD ON EACH GROUND

| Venue | M | Inn | NO | Runs | HS | Avge | 50s | 0s | Ct |
|---|---|---|---|---|---|---|---|---|---|
| Adelaide | 7 | 10 | 3 | 204 | 72* | 29.14 | 1 | 1 | 5 |
| Brisbane | 6 | 9 | 1 | 84 | 25 | 10.50 | 0 | 2 | 6 |
| Hobart | 1 | 2 | 0 | 57 | 30 | 28.50 | 0 | 0 | 0 |
| Melbourne | 6 | 10 | 2 | 139 | 36* | 17.37 | 0 | 0 | 3 |
| Perth | 6 | 8 | 0 | 81 | 24 | 10.12 | 0 | 3 | 2 |
| Sydney | 5 | 6 | 0 | 73 | 21 | 12.16 | 0 | 0 | 4 |
| Birmingham | 2 | 2 | 0 | 40 | 38 | 20.00 | 0 | 0 | 0 |
| Leeds | 2 | 1 | 0 | 71 | 71 | 71.00 | 1 | 0 | 0 |
| Lord's | 2 | 1 | 0 | 30 | 30 | 30.00 | 0 | 0 | 0 |
| Manchester | 2 | 2 | 0 | 5 | 3 | 2.50 | 0 | 0 | 0 |
| Nottingham | 2 | 1 | 0 | 17 | 17 | 17.00 | 0 | 0 | 0 |
| The Oval | 2 | 3 | 0 | 40 | 21 | 13.33 | 0 | 0 | 0 |
| Auckland | 1 | 2 | 1 | 64 | 33 | 64.00 | 0 | 0 | 0 |
| Christchurch | 1 | 1 | 0 | 45 | 45 | 45.00 | 0 | 0 | 0 |
| Wellington | 1 | 1 | 0 | 8 | 8 | 8.00 | 0 | 0 | 0 |
| Cape Town | 1 | 1 | 0 | 0 | 0 | 0.00 | 0 | 1 | 0 |
| Johannesburg | 1 | 2 | 1 | 33 | 26* | 33.00 | 0 | 0 | 1 |

## BATTING AND FIELDING – RECORD ON EACH GROUND (continued)

| Venue | M | Inn | NO | Runs | HS | Avge | 50s | 0s | Ct |
|---|---|---|---|---|---|---|---|---|---|
| Bridgetown | 1 | 2 | 0 | 6 | 3 | 3.00 | 0 | 0 | 1 |
| Georgetown | 1 | 2 | 0 | 21 | 21 | 10.50 | 0 | 1 | 0 |
| Kingston | 1 | 1 | 0 | 0 | 0 | 0.00 | 0 | 1 | 1 |
| Port-of-Spain | 1 | 1 | 0 | 0 | 0 | 0.00 | 0 | 1 | 0 |
| St John's | 1 | 2 | 0 | 14 | 13 | 7.00 | 0 | 0 | 0 |

## THE FOLLOWING BOWLERS CAPTURED HUGHES' WICKET

| No. | Bowler |
|---|---|
| 8 | C.E.L. Ambrose (WI) |
| 4 | Kapil Dev (Ind), C.A. Walsh (WI) |
| 3 | A.R.C. Fraser (Eng), B.P. Patterson (WI), J. Srinath (Ind) |
| 2 | I.T. Botham (Eng), P.H. Edmonds (Eng), N.A. Foster (Eng), C.L. Hooper (WI), D.K.Morrison (NZ), D.N. Patel ( NZ), Wasim Akram (Pak) |
| 1 | K.N. Amalean (SL), M.P. Bicknell (Eng), I.R. Bishop(WI), N.G.B. Cook (Eng), P.A.J. DeFreitas (Eng), E.A.R. de Silva (SL), G.R. Dilley (Eng), J.E. Emburey (Eng), M.C. Ilott (Eng), B.M. McMillan (SA), D.E. Malcolm (Eng), M.D. Marshall (WI), C.R. Matthews (SA), M. Prabhakar (Ind), D.R. Pringle (Eng), R.J. Ratnayake (SL), G.C. Small (Eng), M.C. Snedden (NZ), P.M. Such (Eng), S.R. Tendulkar (Ind), P.C.R. Tufnell (Eng), S.L. Watkin (Eng) |

## HOW HUGHES WAS DISMISSED

| Mode of Dismissal | No. | Percentage |
|---|---|---|
| Caught | 31 | 50.00% |
| Caught by wicket-keeper | 12 | 19.36% |
| Bowled | 11 | 17.74% |
| Leg Before Wicket | 7 | 11.29% |
| Run Out | 1 | 1.61% |

## 4. ONE-DAY INTERNATIONAL CRICKET

### BOWLING – RECORD IN EACH SERIES

| Season (venue) | Comp | M | Balls | Mdns | Runs | Wkts | Avge | Best |
|---|---|---|---|---|---|---|---|---|
| 1988–89 (A) | World Series | 9 | 414 | 4 | 309 | 14 | 22.07 | 4/44 |
| 1989 (Ind) | Nehru Cup | 4 | 186 | 1 | 122 | 4 | 30.50 | 2/27 |
| 1989–90 (A) | World Series | 5 | 266 | 4 | 151 | 5 | 31.00 | 2/41 |
| 1990 (NZ) | Rothmans | 2 | 66 | 0 | 64 | 3 | 21.33 | 3/36 |
| 1990 (Shar) | Australasian | 2 | 120 | 3 | 70 | 1 | 70.00 | 1/15 |
| 1990–91 (A) | World Series | 1 | 48 | 0 | 40 | 0 | – | 0/40 |
| 1991 (WI) | Cable & Wireless | 1 | 59 | 0 | 33 | 3 | 11.00 | 3/33 |
| 1992 (A/NZ) | World Cup | 1 | 54 | 1 | 49 | 1 | 49.00 | 1/49 |
| 1993 (NZ) | BNZ | 5 | 240 | 6 | 145 | 4 | 36.25 | 1/23 |
| 1993 (Eng) | Texaco | 3 | 186 | 3 | 132 | 3 | 44.00 | 2/41 |
| **TOTAL** | | **33** | **1639** | **22** | **1115** | **38** | **29.34** | **4/44** |

### BOWLING – RECORD AGAINST EACH COUNTRY

| Opponent | M | Balls | Mdns | Runs | Wkts | Avge | Best |
|---|---|---|---|---|---|---|---|
| Bangladesh | 1 | 60 | 3 | 15 | 1 | 15.00 | 1/15 |
| England | 3 | 186 | 3 | 132 | 3 | 44.00 | 2/41 |
| India | 3 | 132 | 1 | 112 | 4 | 28.00 | 3/36 |

. . . continued

## BOWLING – RECORD AGAINST EACH COUNTRY (continued)

| Opponent | M | Balls | Mdns | Runs | Wkts | Avge | Best |
|----------|---|-------|------|------|------|------|------|
| New Zealand | 7 | 312 | 6 | 213 | 4 | 53.25 | 1/23 |
| Pakistan | 7 | 360 | 6 | 236 | 7 | 33.71 | 3/30 |
| Sri Lanka | 4 | 224 | 1 | 135 | 5 | 27.00 | 2/41 |
| West Indies | 8 | 365 | 2 | 272 | 14 | 19.42 | 4/44 |

## HOW HUGHES TOOK HIS WICKETS

| Mode of Dismissal | No. | Percentage |
|-------------------|-----|------------|
| Bowled | 13 | 34.21% |
| Caught | 12 | 31.58% |
| Caught by Wicket-keeper | 9 | 23.68% |
| Leg Before Wicket | 3 | 7.90% |
| Caught and Bowled | 1 | 2.63% |

## BATTING AND FIELDING – RECORD IN EACH SERIES

| Season (Venue) | Competition | M | Inn | NO | Runs | HS | Avge | 0s | Ct |
|----------------|-------------|---|-----|-----|------|-----|------|-----|-----|
| 1988–89 (A) | World Series | 9 | 4 | 1 | 25 | 13 | 8.33 | 1 | 1 |
| 1989 (Ind) | Nehru Cup | 4 | 4 | 2 | 12 | 8* | 6.00 | 1 | 0 |
| 1989–90 (A) | World Series | 5 | 1 | 1 | 0 | 0* | – | 0 | 3 |
| 1990 (NZ) | Rothmans | 2 | – | – | – | – | – | 0 | 0 |
| 1990 (Shar) | Australasian | 2 | 2 | 1 | 19 | 10* | 19.00 | 0 | 0 |
| 1990–91 (A) | World Series | 1 | – | – | – | – | – | 0 | 0 |
| 1991 (WI) | Cable & Wireless | 1 | – | – | – | – | – | 0 | 1 |
| 1992 (A/NZ) | World Cup | 1 | 1 | 1 | 0 | 0* | – | 0 | 0 |
| 1993 (NZ) | BNZ | 5 | 4 | 2 | 24 | 12* | 12.00 | 1 | 0 |
| 1993 (Eng) | Texaco | 3 | 1 | 0 | 20 | 20 | 20.00 | 0 | 1 |
| **TOTAL** | | **33** | **17** | **8** | **100** | **20** | **11.11** | **3** | **6** |

## BATTING AND FIELDING – RECORD AGAINST EACH COUNTRY

| Opponent | M | Inn | NO | Runs | HS | Avge | 0s | Ct |
|----------|---|-----|-----|------|-----|------|-----|-----|
| Bangladesh | 1 | 1 | 1 | 10 | 10* | – | 0 | 0 |
| England | 3 | 1 | 0 | 20 | 20 | 20.00 | 0 | 1 |
| India | 3 | 2 | 1 | 1 | 1 | 1.00 | 0 | 0 |
| New Zealand | 7 | 4 | 2 | 24 | 12* | 12.00 | 1 | 0 |
| Pakistan | 7 | 3 | 0 | 17 | 9 | 5.66 | 1 | 1 |
| Sri Lanka | 4 | 2 | 2 | 8 | 8* | – | 0 | 2 |
| West Indies | 8 | 4 | 2 | 20 | 13 | 10.00 | 1 | 2 |

# 5. ONE-DAY DOMESTIC CRICKET

## BOWLING

| M | Balls | Runs | Wkts | Avge | Best |
|---|-------|------|------|------|------|
| 29 | 1499 | 1129 | 33 | 34.21 | 4–34 |

## BATTING

| M | Inn | NO | Runs | HS | Avge | Ct |
|---|-----|-----|------|-----|------|-----|
| 29 | 16 | 4 | 94 | 17 | 7.83 | 10 |

## ᵛ B I B L I O G R A P H Y ᵛ

**Newspapers:** the *Australian,* the *Age,* the *Sun,* the *Herald* (Melbourne), the *Herald-Sun,* the *Daily Telegraph* (London), the *Advertiser* (Adelaide), the *Courier Mail,* the *Sydney Morning Herald*

**Almanacs:** Wisden Cricketers' Almanack, 1970, 1987–95; ABC Cricket Book, 1985–86, 1986–87, 1988–89, 1993–94

**Books:** *Border and Beyond,* Mark Ray, ABC Books, Sydney 1995; *Merv and Me,* Merv Hughes and Ian Cover, Ironbark, Sydney 1993; *Steve Waugh's Ashes Diary,* Steve Waugh, Ironbark, Sydney 1993; *Wisden Book of Test Cricket Volume I,* Bill Frindall, Queen Anne, London 1979; *Wisden Book of Test Cricket Volume II,* Bill Frindall, Queen Anne, London 1990 ;*ABC Guide to Australian Test Cricketers,* Rick Smith, ABC Books, Sydney 1993; *Chappelli: The Cutting Edge,* Ian Chappell, Swan, Nedlands, 1992; *Merv: My Life and Other Funny Stories,* Merv Hughes and David Emerson, Pan Macmillan, Sydney 1990; *The Reasons Why,* Bob Simpson, HarperCollins*Publishers,* Sydney 1996; *The Border Years,* Gideon Haigh, The Text, Melbourne 1994; *The Ian Healy Story,* Ian Healy, Swan, Dalkeith, 1996; *Calypso Cricket,* Roland Fishman, Margaret Gee, Sydney 1991; *Caribbean Odyssey,* Mike Coward, Simon and Schuster, Sydney 1991; *Australia vs the New South Africa,* Mike Coward, Simon and Schuster, Sydney 1994; *Hookesy,* David Hookes, ABC Books, Sydney 1993; *Steve Waugh's South African Tour Diary,* Steve Waugh, Ironbark Press, Sydney 1994

# INDEX

Alcott, Errol 7, 68, 72, 76, 91, 131, 134,
    147, 154, 166, 195, 205, 207, 209,
    221, 225, 254
Alderman, Terry 3, 30, 32, 93, 94, 101,
    102–3, 105, 108–9, 125, 126, 153,
    203, 317
Alexander, Harry 9
Alley, Phil 131
Ambrose, Curtly 79, 81, 83, 86, 97, 119,
    157, 163
Anderton, Gary 21
Andrews, Wayne 115
Angel, Jo 215, 254
Armanath, Mohinder 43
Arthurton, Keith 157, 158
Atherton, Michael 110–11, 115, 121, 140,
    175, 181, 190, 261, 319
Athey, Bill 51
Ayres, Warren 271, 281
Azharuddin, Mohammad 147

Bacher, Ali 217
Bailhache, Robin 5, 101
Bakker, Jason 271
Baldry, Bob 24
Barsby, Trevor 115
Battersby, Dr Cam 229, 234–5, 236, 245
Benaud, Richie 205, 316
Berry, Darren 116, 271, 273, 289, 296,
    298–9, 311
Bevan, Michael 264
Billman, Geoff 26
Binny, Roger 43
Bishop, Glenn 149
Bishop, Ian 157
Blewett, Greg 264
Boon, David 6–7, 42, 47, 54, 62, 65,
    78, 87, 94, 101, 123, 158, 173, 185,
    189, 220, 233
Border, Allan 6, 38, 41, 45, 47, 50–1, 54,
    61–2, 64, 65–6, 72–3, 74–5, 78, 84, 86,

89, 91, 93–4, 94, 101, 103–4, 108, 118,
    119, 125, 131, 142–3, 144, 147–8, 153,
    155, 158, 159, 160, 163, 167, 176–7,
    178, 179–80, 185, 197, 203, 218, 220,
    238, 245, 246, 249
Bosch, Tertius 221
Botham, Ian 48, 49, 50, 101
Brayshaw, James 116–19, 120–1
Bright, Ray 17, 24, 27, 41
Burns, Danny 33, 40
Buzzard, Neil 295

Cairns, Chris 167, 208, 209
Callen, Ian 25
Campbell, Greg 101, 102, 131
Carr, Donald 226, 227, 229, 236
Chanderpaul, Shivnarine 313
Chappell, Greg 248, 264–5, 319
Chappell, Ian 38, 41, 46, 47, 54, 74, 77,
    90–1, 113, 276, 319
Childs, John 149
Conn, Malcolm 298
Cook, Simon 210, 274, 292
Corbett, Troy 271, 274
Corling, Grahame 113–14
Coward, Mike 230–1
Crafter, Tony 150
Craig, Ian 224
Croft, Colin 81
Crompton, Alan 160, 170, 184, 213–14,
    231, 245
Cronje, Hansie 222, 226, 227, 267
Crowe, Martin 37, 62–7, 121–2, 166–7,
    169, 175, 208, 319
Cullinan, Daryll 213

Darling, Joe 224
Davidson, Alan 18, 317
DeFreitas, Phil 181
Denness, Mike 30
De Silva, Aravinda 126, 127, 155

Dev, Kapil 42, 43
De Villiers, Fanie 233
Dimattina, Michael 78, 294
Dodemaide, Tony 30–1, 59, 68–9, 70, 71,
    78, 82–3, 85–6, 149, 155, 156, 210,
    254, 271, 274, 276, 281, 285, 289–90,
    300, 307–8
Donald, Allan 233
Dujon, Jeff 87, 140, 143, 158
Dyer, Greg 64, 78

Eastwood, Ken 17–18, 20, 22
Edmonds, Phil 48
Elizabeth, Queen 107
Elliott, Matthew 271, 273, 293, 311
Elworthy, Steve 221
Emburey, John 48, 54

Fleming, Damien 148, 150, 210, 254,
    258, 259, 264, 274, 285
Fletcher, Keith 30
Foster, Neil 30, 188
Fraser, Angus 110, 200

Garner, Joel 79, 81–2
Gatting, Mike 47–9, 51–3, 54, 101, 110,
    181, 183, 186, 319
Gaunt, Ron 17, 18, 22
Gavaskar, Sunil 43–6
Gilbert, Dave 37, 39, 48
Gomes, Larry 82
Gooch, Graham 30, 103, 107, 110, 140,
    175, 182, 186, 193, 196, 261, 319
Gower, David 48, 49, 101, 107, 108, 191
Graf, Shaun 211, 212
Grant, John 211, 279, 295, 299
Greatbatch, Mark 115, 126, 127, 168–70
Greenidge, Gordon 81, 84, 87–9, 140,
    143, 144–5, 158

Hadlee, Sir Richard 35, 37, 62–4, 167
Halbish, Graham 230, 235, 245
Harvey, Ian 211, 212, 271, 274
Hayden, Matthew 173, 180, 220
Haynes, Desmond 81, 84, 85, 141, 142,
    143, 157, 158, 318
Haysman, Mike 29

Healy, Ian 78, 86, 87, 93, 94, 120, 150,
    200, 239, 247
Hewett, Ian 274
Hibbert, Paul 25
Hick, Graeme 115, 175, 184–5, 190–1,
    200, 201–3, 261
Hodge, Brad 271, 273
Hogg, Rodney 28–9, 30, 32, 248, 317
Holding, Michael 4, 79, 81–2
Holdsworth, Wayne 2, 174, 177, 180
Hookes, David 26
Hooper, Carl 84, 115, 143, 158
Hudson, Andrew 226
Hughes, Freda (MH's mother) 10
Hughes, Gary (MH's brother) 10, 13
Hughes, Ian (MH's father) 10–11, 15
Hughes, Kim 70, 83, 116, 217
Hughes, Madeline (MH's daughter) 257
Hughes, Merv
    early years: born 10; childhood 10–11;
        school life 11–13; plays for Werribee
        14–15; at Footscray 17–25
    1981–82 season: joins Victorian
        Sheffield Shield squad 26–8;
        nominated for Esso scholarship 29–31
    1983 playing in England, for Essex 30
    1985 north with Gavin Whiting 33–5
    1985–86 season: selected for Test
        series 38–40; unjustly accused of
        drunkenness 41–2; plays against
        India 42–6
    1986–87 season: solid start with Victorian
        side 48; plays against England 49–51,
        53–5; returns to Victorian side 55–9
    1987–88 season: Test matches against
        New Zealand 63–9; commitment to
        Victoria questioned 69–71; Test
        against Sri Lanka 72–4; Allan Border's
        public blasting 74–6
    1988–89 season: disappointing form
        jeopardises selection 82; Test series
        against the West Indies 84–91,
        94–101; Gordon Greenidge's snub
        87–9; becomes cult figure 92;
        one-day circuit 92; most feared
        Shield bowler 135–6
    1989 Ashes tour 101–11

1989–90 season 126–7; tours England 125–6; Test series against Pakistan 128–34

1990–91 season: the test for new batsmen 134; Ashes 139–40; tours West Indies 140–7

1991–92 season 149–50; injures Jamie Siddons 138–9; Tests against India 147–9; Test series against India 153; passed over for Sri Lanka 154–6; World Cup tournament 154

1992–93 season: Sheffield Shield 156; Test series against West Indies 156–63; attempts farting record 157; reported 159, 163; New Zealand tour 166–71; spitting incident 169–71

1993 Ashes tour 2–3; concern about form 175–6, 179; form improves 181, 183; in fine form 185–6, 187, 188, 190; lack of rest results in injury 192–3; unsure for fourth Test 196; journos challenge MH with bet 198–9

1993–94 season: trains with Australian side 208–9; not selected for Victorian side 210–12; rejoins Victorian side 214–15; selected for South African tour 215

1994 South African tour: fitness in question 221; misses One-dayers 222; ICC hearing 226; spitting incident 233–5; fined by ACB 236, 242, 244; effect of disciplinary record 239, 246; addicted to movies 243–4; last game for Australia 248–9; dropped for One-day tournament 250; dropped from side 251; ACB fine explained 252–3

1994–95 season: last chance for Test side selection 261; in Australia A squad 264–5; unable to regain fitness 266–7; looks to Victorian selection 268–70

1995–96 season: out of Victorian side 271; not selected for Victorian squad 278–80; plays trial match at Frankston 285; fights with Dean Jones 289–90, 293–5; press write him off 291–2; isolated from Victorian squad 295–6;

criticises State selection criteria 298, 300; meets with Jones 301–2

1996–97 season: abuses Brayshaw 115–19; poor pre-season training 306–7; refuses to retire 308–10; plays for Footscray 323

career analysis 205, 254–5, 270–1, 274–81, 313–15, 317–21

football 13, 14, 22, 26, 32, 35

humour 4–5, 15, 71–2, 223–4, 321

injuries: back 31, 32, 221; calf muscle 251–2; general 91, 193, 266–8; hamstring 29; knee 5–7, 131–4, 162, 166, 174–5, 177–8, 196–8, 203, 209; surgery 171, 205–7

marriage 146

personal life 257–8

sledging 114–23, 130, 175, 184, 227, 279, 286–7

style 3–5, 127, 239, 263

weight 72, 76–7, 82, 134, 147, 148, 154, 166, 195, 209, 221, 275–6

Hughes, Peta (MH's sister) 10

Hughes, Sue (MH's wife, nee Kelly) 146, 241, 250, 257, 324

Hurst, Alan 17, 25

Hussain, Nasser 203

Ijaz Ahmed 130

Jacobs, Ken 25

James, Lindsay 22

Jarvis, Greg 293

Javed Miandad 128

Johnson, Martin 48

Johnston, Bill 317

Jones, Andrew 78

Jones, Dean 21–2, 26, 27, 47, 49, 55, 59, 62, 66, 72–3, 74–6, 78, 93, 94, 97–8, 107, 128, 210, 211, 219–20, 259, 268–9, 270, 271, 273, 278, 283–91, 292–5, 296–7, 300–3, 311

Joslin, Les 17

Julian, Brendon 2, 174, 180, 198, 215

Kendrick, Neil 180

Kerr, Rob 29

King, Nathan 301
Kirsten, Gary 226, 227
Kirsten, Peter 245–6

Lamb, Allan 48, 49
Langer, Justin 163
Lara, Brian 140, 158
Larkin, Rohan 271
Laughlin, Trevor 24
Lawry, Bill 17, 62, 217
Lawson, Geoff 30, 32, 37–9, 49, 77, 84,
    85–7, 94, 101, 102, 105, 108–9, 125,
    126, 317
Lever, John 30
Lillee, Dennis 3, 30, 77, 203, 248,
    313–14, 315, 319
Lindwall, Ray 18, 205, 316
Lloyd, Clive 81–2
Logie, Gus 82, 157

McCooke, Steve 20
McCurdy, Rod 25, 30, 32
McDermott, Craig 2, 31, 32, 37–8, 43, 46,
    48–9, 64, 67, 71, 78–9, 82–3, 92, 126,
    136, 139–40, 140, 142–3, 145, 146,
    147, 153, 154, 155, 158, 163, 171,
    173, 176, 178, 181, 187, 189, 206,
    207, 220, 263, 266, 314, 316, 321
McDonald, Ian 41, 87, 131, 154, 159,
    166, 171
McGrath, Glenn 123, 207, 213, 214,
    220–1, 245, 258, 266, 313, 316, 318
McKenzie, Graham 18, 316
Mackerdhuj, Krish 218
McLean, Ricky 14
McMillan, Brian 245–6
McPhee, Mark 70, 71, 116
Maguire, John 30, 32
Majid Khan 170
Malcolm, Devon 1, 200
Manjrekar, Sanjay 147
Marsh, Geoff 39, 41, 47, 51, 54, 55, 59,
    62, 78, 94, 118, 120, 141, 261, 267, 283
Marsh, Rod 248, 273
Marshall, Malcolm 79, 81, 83, 140, 158
Martyn, Damien 157, 180, 191, 264
Matthews, Chris 48, 82, 83

Matthews, Greg 30, 49, 51, 53, 115,
    160, 271
May, Tim 1–3, 66–7, 78, 86, 94, 117,
    149, 163, 181, 188, 200, 233–4, 243,
    250, 317
Merriman, Bob 253
Meyer, Barrie 1
Miller, Keith 317
Mitchell, Kevin 158
Moody, Tom 59, 70, 264
Moores, Peter 177
Morris, Kevin 14
Morrison, Danny 167
Murphy, Tony 180

Nobes, Paul 118

O'Donnell, Simon 63, 93, 99, 149, 153,
    154, 270
O'Keeffe, Michael 301
O'Reilly, Bill 283

Pascoe, Len 30
Patel, Dipak 167
Patterson, Patrick 83, 93
Phillips, Ray 31
Prisnall, Clint 23–4, 40
Prue, Terry 87, 159

Rackemann, Carl 30, 32, 94, 101
Rameez Raja 130
Ramprakash, Mark 1
Randell, Steve 159, 163
Reed, Ron 291–2
Reid, Bruce 39, 46, 48, 49, 55, 64, 67–8,
    78–9, 82, 92, 126, 139, 140, 143, 153,
    154, 316, 318
Reiffel, Paul 1–3, 148, 150, 154, 171,
    173–4, 191, 199–200, 207, 210, 214,
    220–1, 249, 254, 263, 264, 274, 281,
    285, 293, 317
Rhodes, Jonty 226
Richards, David 101
Richards, Viv 79, 81, 84–5, 89, 122, 140,
    145, 158
Richardson, Richie 81–2, 85, 141–2,
    144–5, 156–7, 158, 318

Roach, Peter 273, 300
Roberts, Andy 81
Robinson, Richie 25
Russell, Jack 107
Rutherford, Ken 171, 208

Saker, David 271, 274, 285
Salim Yousuf 130
Saunders, Jack 315
Sawle, Lawrie 39, 46, 51, 54, 71, 77, 93,
    101, 109, 126, 134, 135, 155, 215,
    255, 267, 321
Scholes, John 25, 27–8, 211, 275, 305–7,
    309, 310
Sharma, Chetan 43
Shastri, Ravi 43, 148
Sheahan, Paul 24
Shepherd, David 227
Shipperd, Greg 70
Shoaib Mohammad 130
Siddons, Jamie 70–1, 78–9, 116, 123,
    136–9, 294
Sidhu, Navjot 147
Simpson, Bob 47, 53, 61–2, 101,
    108, 134, 143–4, 145, 147, 154,
    159, 220, 245, 246–7, 249–50,
    275, 284, 318
Slater, Michael 173, 180, 189, 218, 223
Sleep, Peter 54, 67, 78
Small, Steve 115
Smith, Robin 105, 107, 140, 181, 191
Spofforth, Fred 315
Srikkanth, Kris 43, 45, 147
Stewart, Alec 181, 261
Stillman, Les 211, 268–9, 270–1, 275,
    279, 280–1, 295, 296, 302
Su'a, Murphy 167
Subba Row, Raman 159
Such, Peter 181

Tamblyn, Geoff 295
Taylor, Mark 94, 103, 128, 134–5, 140,
    154, 156, 178, 181, 189, 197–8, 218,
    220, 223, 238–9, 242–3, 245, 250–1,
    262, 271
Taylor, Peter 54, 78
Tendulkar, Sachin 148

Thomson, Jeff 30, 32, 77, 315, 319
Thorpe, Graham 193, 261
Timmins, Col 163
Trott, Albert 283
Trumble, Hugh 316
Tucker, Adrian 213
Tufnell, Phil 181
Turner, Charles 315

Van Noordwyk, Chris 221
Veletta, Michael 59, 78
Vengsarkar, Dilip 43, 147
Venter, Kosie 223

Walker, Max 25, 317
Walsh, Courtney 81, 83, 84, 98, 140,
    157, 162, 163
Walters, Doug 283
Waqar Younis 119–20
Warne, Shane 1–3, 148, 150, 155, 160,
    163, 166, 173, 175, 180, 182–3, 183,
    187, 200, 203, 209, 213, 226, 227,
    242–3, 248, 263, 274, 281, 285, 294,
    299, 310, 313, 316
Wasim Akram 119, 128, 129–31
Watts, Gary 294
Waugh, Mark 68, 140, 156–7, 158, 178,
    189, 198, 213, 219, 271
Waugh, Steve 47, 54, 55, 64, 68,
    73, 74–6, 78, 83, 86, 94, 96, 99,
    103, 122, 155, 156–7, 178, 243,
    248, 271, 317
Wells, Colin 177
Wessels, Kepler 226, 245
Whiting, Gavin 12, 13, 33, 40
Whitney, Mike 30, 68, 94, 96, 98, 101,
    153, 154, 155, 271
Williams, Brad 271, 274, 285
Wood, Graeme 58, 59, 70, 78, 86,
    93, 116
Wrigglesworth, Ian 271
Wright, John 64

Yallop, Graham 25

Zoehrer, Tim 78